SOPHIE GRIGSON'S herbs

SOPHIE GRIGSON'S
herbs

BBC

For Lucy and Emily, with love

Food photography by Jess Koppel

This book is published to accompany the television series *Sophie Grigson's Herbs*, which was produced by BBC Birmingham.

Series Producer: Mary Clyne
Director: Stuart Bateup

Published by BBC Worldwide Ltd,
Woodlands, 80 Wood Lane,
London W12 0TT

First published 1999
Reprinted 1999
© Sophie Grigson 1999
The moral right of the author
has been asserted.

Photography © Jess Koppel 1999

ISBN 0 563 38442 5

Commissioning Editor: Viv Bowler
Project Editor: Sally Potter
Copy Editor: Jane Middleton
Designers: Andrew Barron &
Collis Clements Associates
Art Director: Ellen Wheeler
Home Economist: Lyn Rutherford
Stylist: Roisin Nield

The recipe for Wild Garlic Sauce on page 40 is reprinted with permission of Pavilion Books from *Fruits of the Forest* by Sue Style. Constance Spry's Spiced Plums in Blackcurrant Leaves on page 150 is reprinted with permission of J. M. Dent from *The Constance Spry Cookery Book* by Constance Spry. The recipe for Thyme Sorbet on page 16 is reprinted with permission of Grub Street from *Ices* by Caroline Liddell and Robin Weir.

Set in Swiss 721
Printed and bound by Butler & Tanner Ltd, Frome, Somerset
Colour separations by Radstock Reproductions Ltd, Midsomer Norton
Jacket printed by Lawrence Allen Ltd, Weston-Super-Mare

Photograph, page 2:
An Excellent Mixed Salad (page 165)

contents

cook's notes

Recipes are not written to be followed exactly, with the exception, perhaps, of those for cakes and biscuits. Certainly, recipes that contain generous quantities of herbs must be seen as guidelines rather than rigidly written lists of rules and regulations. Herbs vary enormously in intensity of flavour. Time of year, type of soil they are grown in, climate, location, variety, all these things will have a greater or lesser impact. When I write that you will need two tablespoons of chopped greenery, this is the amount that I liked when I tested the recipe. Since the herbs that you are using will not taste exactly the same as mine, and it is more than likely that your palate will not be the same as mine, you will have to make allowances. In other words, smell and stir and taste and adjust wherever you can. It is for these reasons that herbal quantities are often, deliberately, rather vague – a handful of this, a sprig of that, a bunch of something else. There is no good answer to 'How long is a sprig?' It depends on the herb, it depends on your fancy. Don't let this worry you. The more you cook with fresh herbs, the easier it becomes. Trust your instincts, trust your tastebuds. Relax, so that you can take pleasure in cooking with some of the most sensuous ingredients to be had.

I do adhere to certain conventions, which it may be helpful to know. All herbs used in the recipes are fresh unless otherwise stated. All spoon measurements are rounded, unless otherwise stated. I use a 15 ml tablespoon and a 5 ml teaspoon. All eggs are large (the old size 1 or 2), and, in my kitchen at least, free range. Pepper and nutmeg should always be freshly ground when needed. I use nothing but extra virgin olive oil for cooking and for salads, but if you find the flavour too strong, feel free to replace it with plain olive oil. Of the tasteless, bland oils, I usually use sunflower.

On the whole, you should try to stick with either the metric measurements or the imperial ones, not a mish-mash of both. Treat timings as distinctly approximate. We're back to the guidelines again. Ovens vary, pans vary, hobs vary. All these things will affect the length of time any dish needs to cook. Judge by eye, by smell and by taste. You are the one cooking up these recipes in your own kitchen, with your own equipment, and you must be the final arbiter.

acknowledgements

Right up there at the top of the list comes the team led by Mary Clyne at BBC Birmingham. They spiritually held my hand, and gave encouragement when things were slow-going and uncertain. The support proffered by Mary and Slavka Bradley has been enormously helpful and valuable, not to mention the runproof mascara, paper hankies and courgettes. Claire Walls and Chris Hardman have provided invaluable work. Cheers, girls. New boys on the block, Oliver Clark and Stuart Bateup, have completed the team. For the first time in my life I have been able to banter Latin botanical names and gorgeous pin-ups in almost the same breath. Over at BBC Worldwide, my thanks go to my editor, Viv Bowler, and to Sally Potter, for nursing the book through to fruition. Patience is a virtue, and one they've both got. Barely a batted eyelid at my piecemeal delivery. Jane Middleton has worked tirelessly to iron out the glitches and errors of this herby manuscript. Of course, I also owe a continuing debt of thanks to my friend Jess Koppel, for her fabulous photographs, and to Lyn Rutherford for her delicious interpretations of my recipes. Once again Roisin Nield has tracked down beautiful dishes and pans.

A special thank you, in memoriam, to all those writers of herbals and allied works from centuries past, who have informed, amused and delighted me with wonderful turns of phrase, illuminating the magic that herbs have always encapsulated for humankind. Culpeper, Gerard, Mrs M. Grieve, Parkinson, Turner, Evelyn and the rest ... and naturally to Shakespeare who, though not a herbalist, peppered his works with herbs and fragrant flowers.

Writing a book about herbs in mid-winter is mad, to say the least. If it hadn't been for Peter Turner of the National Herb Centre, who came up trumps with out-of-season herbs and flowers, there would have been far fewer recipes in the book. Thanks again to Slavka and Oli, who scoured the corner shops of Birmingham in quest of rare herbs. Back at home, Wendy Malpass, Sue Elliott and Ros Wilson all slaved over hot stoves, smoothing the edges of roughly hewn recipes, while Michele kept the rising mountains of paperwork at bay, fielded awkward phone calls, typed in recipes, and tasted as often as possible! William, my husband, has kept the household running and washed and the garden kempt while I have been lost to the processor. It is thanks to his green fingers that our herb garden is as lush and beguiling as it is. An enormous debt of gratitude goes to Jennine Bierton, who keeps my children's spirits high when I am flagging. And, of course, the biggest thank you of all, to Florence and Sidney for just being themselves, and occasionally, just occasionally, beginning to believe that green herbs are not toxic but actually rather wonderful.

introduction

When I think of herbs I see and smell a summer garden, with thickets of scented leaves, and long, neat rows of parsley, clumps of chives with their purple pom-poms, stands of trembling, feathery dill and fennel, the architectural stature of lovage and angelica, and that is just the beginning. In fact, it is our garden, with its brick paths and ordered chaos, so different in early morning, at midday in balmy June sunshine, in soft summer rain or thunder-loud pelting storms, or indeed in the snows of winter, when spears of tough rosemary and determined thyme pierce the white blanket here and there.

Herbs are inescapably sensuous and that, perhaps, is one of the reasons the human race is so very attached to these leaves and stems with their sometimes strange, sometimes pungent, oft-times perfumed aromas. Nutritionally we use too little to make any true impact on our health, but their very greenness has an air of vitality that works on our mind to make us feel more alive. First and foremost, though, we use herbs because they have the power to transform other ingredients, magically breathing new depths and discoveries into their flavours, enhancing, delighting but rarely masking or distracting (unless, of course, that is the cook's intention...).

Herbs have been used since time immemorial, right around the world. Of course they have. Why waste some fragrant plant that grows, rather handily, all around and appears to have no unpleasant side effects? Wild herbs have long been man's companions and helpmates, offering not only their flavour to liven up plain foods but often more in the form of remedies for illnesses and ailments both minor and major. Some of their supposed medicinal properties have proved fanciful but many more are now validated by modern science. Old wives' tales are not always foolish.

In this book, however, it is their culinary prowess that leads the way. After centuries of loving and nurturing these little kitchen gods in sweet-scented herb gardens and pots gathered around the kitchen door, we have done them a great disservice in more recent times. After the culinary ravages of the Second World War and the austerity of rationing came supermarkets. And with supermarkets came racks of dried herbs – far more convenient than greenery...for retailers especially. The public was somehow bamboozled into believing that it was worth paying for dried parsley and even, oh how adventurous, dried basil. It is a myth that lingers on, but vastly diminished now that swathes of packs of fresh herbs swing alongside the fresh fruit and vegetables in the brightly lit aisles.

When I started to write about food and cooking, back in 1983, editors always insisted that I give quantities of dried herbs alongside handfuls of fresh. I lived then in a small flat in an area of London with strong Greek and West Indian communities, slap bang opposite a marvellous Italian deli. Supplies of supermarket fresh herbs were erratic but I could lay my hands on heavenly big bunches of fresh coriander, flat-leaved parsley and cool mint with ease, while a yen for tomatoes and fresh basil meant no more than crossing the road. I grew a few more herbs, those that I couldn't find so readily, in windowboxes. I had fresh herbs to hand and I knew that dried are no substitute, though occasionally they can prove a valuable alternative.

Nouvelle cuisine, and then the growing passion for all things foodie in the mid to late eighties, brought the pleasures of fresh herbs back into focus. Now, fifteen years later, no editor ever asks if I'd care to suggest a quantity of dried coriander leaf instead of fresh. In supermarkets, even small ones, there is a considerable variety of fresh herbs to choose from, and the range expands with the customers' knowledge and demands. I've even seen that delicious old English favourite, lovage, with its notes of citrus and spice over a celery base, tucked into little flat-packs for sale in Daventry of all places.

We all know that the use of fresh herbs has burgeoned in the nineties, and the facts back that up. In the UK alone, the value of sales of fresh cut herbs has risen from roughly £250,000 in the late seventies to a staggering £40 million in 1996, and it is still growing. Safeway's says that its sales of fresh and pot-grown herbs have risen by an amazing 500 per cent over the past year. Nothing airy-fairy and romantic about that. There are even, would you believe, several hundred herb sites on the Internet. But then practically everything in creation has a site

these days, so I suppose that's not so surprising.

And yet...I suspect that many people do not get the full value out of their fresh herbs, whether they grow them themselves or buy them in. And I suspect, too, that many stick safely with the ones they know, not quite daring to try the more unusual types, tempting though they may be. In this book I have tried to convey some of my enthusiasm for the vast panoply of fresh herbs, not forgetting the odd few that are actually improved by drying, such as bay and oregano. While writing the chapters I have developed new passions for herbs that I had only brushed past before – the lovely lemon verbena, for instance, and the unexpectedly musky, earthy tones of blackcurrant leaves. Yet I have also rediscovered how thrilling some of our more familiar herbs can be when given the chance to shine. Parsley can be every bit as exciting as exotic coriander – parsley salads, for instance, are delicious – while our natural herbal inheritance deserves just as much attention as more fashionable basil and the like. Lovage, rocket and lavender were once much-loved, well-used British herbs, which suffered at the hands of the Victorians, who liked their food plain and plentiful. Thyme, rosemary and sage are quintessentially European herbs, with echoes of the sunny south and the respectability of British citizenship. From the East come lemon grass and kaffir lime leaves, both of which have enormous value outside Asian cuisine as well as within.

All in all some fifty of the most important culinary herbs are brought together in these pages. It is by no means an exhaustive collection – nature has blessed the human race with a phenomenal number of fragrant, edible leaves – but it does include what I think are the most pleasurable and useful herbs in the kitchen. Many are available from supermarkets, though some will have to be grown at home if they are to be properly sampled and savoured. Plant nurseries and seed merchants (see pp. 212–13) are the places to explore if you really want to begin to discover the breadth and depth of the magic of herbs. There is nothing better than being able to pick them from your own garden or windowbox right at the very moment you need them, in the exact quantities that meet your needs and desires.

thyme
Thymus species

We grow three different kinds of thyme in our garden. When we first came here to our present home we soon tracked down two well-established bushes of lemon thyme, one of them conveniently near the kitchen door, clinging stubbornly to a dry-stone wall. Laziness, immediate need and rain all led me into using it more than I would ever have imagined. I've come to rely on its delicious citrus overtones and warm thyme background. It goes particularly well with fish and white meats and is lovely, if unexpected, in sweet dishes. It also, as I once discovered in adverse circumstances in the middle of the Amazon jungle, makes a brilliant infusion which soothes upset stomachs most efficaciously.

Be that as it may, it cannot fully replace true garden thyme, *Thymus vulgaris*, with its unparalleled soft warmth and accommodating spiciness. Lemon thyme, *Thymus citriodorous*, is too specific; common thyme has that remarkable property given to only a handful of herbs – it has a strong, unforgettable character all of its own and yet it blends tactfully into the background when that is what is required of it, still crucial as part of the backdrop though not immediately identifiable. It will take the leading role without a moment's hesitation but is just as much at home in the chorus.

When we planted up our vegetable garden, with its frequent borders of herbs, we added a couple of bushes of true thyme, without which no herb garden could possibly earn its keep; a variegated thyme, which is pretty, though not as full and pungent – I use it as a finishing touch for dishes, sprinkled on just before serving rather than melded into the very fabric; and a low edging of wild thyme which, to be frank, was something of a disappointment. Wild thyme needs the beating sun of the Mediterranean and its native habitat to come into its own. Up in the hills of Provence, wild thyme, or *serpolet*, is an altogether different, more thrilling creature, with an intensity driven by the rigours of the heat, dryness and arid soil. Back here it is better sown between paving stones as an aromatic garden carpet for feet, only occasionally making its way into the cooking pots as an adjunct to common thyme rather than as an alternative.

Opposite
**Clockwise from top left: thyme, bay leaves, rosemary, sage, purple sage
Centre: winter savory**

The two types of thyme that we don't have, and that I yearn for, are caraway thyme, with its aniseedy overtones, which was once rubbed into great joints of beef before roasting (it was, so it is said, known as herb baronne, as in baron of beef, though this may have more to do with its Latin name, *Thymus herba-barona*); and, even more to my liking, the marvellous, perfumed orange thyme (*Thymus citriodorous* 'Frangrantissimus'), which encompasses wafts of orange blossom, orange zest and thyme all in one heavenly nostrilful. If you can get orange thyme, try using it to flavour ice-cream or syllabubs, cheesecake, fruit salads or even cakes (make a bed of the sprigs on the base of the tin before pouring in the batter) and biscuits.

These few types of thyme are but the tip of the iceberg. The *Thymus* species is a prolific regenerator with hundreds of varieties, each sharing something of the classic thyme character but with its own individual stamp that it hands on to its native cuisine. If you are travelling in the Middle East, you would do well to search out their special form of thyme, *za'atar*, which carries in its leaves a blend of oregano and savory and a slight sweetness offsetting a hint of bitterness. It features strongly in the herb blend of the same name, mixed with sesame seeds and sumac, superb with slow-roast meats or on breads and braised vegetables.

Back here at home, you can make a good case for including thyme in practically any savoury dish you care to mention. It lives for stuffings, is essential in any bouquet garni and in most stews or soups but particularly those that include plenty of red wine, onions and garlic (most notably the French *daubes de boeuf*), sends shivers of delight through cheese dishes, pâtés, sautés and even simple vegetable dishes. Its fame has spread across the New World, making it a great favourite not only in the Caribbean but also in Mexico and throughout Latin America.

Some experts write that the leaves of the thyme plant lose some of their pungency when in flower. This may be, but the flowers are pretty and tasty enough to use in their own right. Try pressing them into slices of goat's cheese before grilling (see p. 184), or scattering them over simple seared meat or fish dishes shortly before serving. You can even candy them, by dipping them first into lightly beaten egg white, then into caster sugar and allowing to dry. They make pretty, scented decorations for creamy or fruity summer puddings.

Storage and Preservation

Woody, fresh-cut sprigs of thyme will keep happily for a week or so, wrapped in a few sheets of damp kitchen paper, stashed in a plastic bag in the vegetable drawer of the fridge. Any more than that and you might as well dry them, tied together in a bunch and strung from the ceiling in a warm, dry, airy place. If you have any choice about the matter, pick branches of thyme just before they come into flower, when they are at their peak.

Seared Chicken with Three Thymes

Since we are lucky enough to have three distinct forms of thyme in our garden, I occasionally bring them together to form a more complex thyme scent. The mixture comes together well in this dish of marinated chicken, though of course you can make a fine version using just one type on its own. I sear the chicken on a griddle or cast-iron pan but when the sun is shining and you are in the mood, try cooking it over the hot charcoal of a barbecue. It is, incidentally, very good sandwiched between two halves of a ciabatta loaf, along with lettuce, tomato and plenty of mayo, though you may well prefer to serve it more conventionally with new potatoes (boiled with a sprig of mint or, better still, roasted with olive oil, rosemary and garlic) and a green vegetable of one sort or another.

Serves 4

4 chicken breasts
3 tablespoons mixed wild, garden and lemon thyme leaves
     (or just garden thyme if that makes life easier)
4 tablespoons olive oil
juice of 1 lemon
3 garlic cloves, crushed
salt and pepper

To serve
½ lemon
½ tablespoon roughly chopped thyme leaves of whichever sort
     you fancy

Put the chicken breasts into a shallow dish or a plastic bag (with no holes in it). Bruise the thyme leaves in a mortar, then mix with the olive oil, lemon juice, garlic, salt and pepper. Pour this marinade over the chicken pieces in their dish or bag, then turn the pieces so that they are evenly coated. Cover the dish or knot the bag. Leave to marinate for at least 4 hours, turning the pieces, or the bag, every now and then.

To sear the chicken, put a griddle or a heavy cast-iron frying pan over a high heat and leave for 5 minutes until ferociously hot. Place the chicken pieces on it in a single layer, skin-side down, then leave for 4–5 minutes before turning. Give them 4–5 minutes (depending on size) on the other side. Reduce the heat and give them another 4–10 minutes or so, until cooked through.

Place the cooked chicken on individual plates or one large serving dish. (For a more elegant presentation, slice each breast, then fan out on individual plates.) Quickly squeeze the juice of the ½ lemon over the chicken breasts and sprinkle with the fresh thyme leaves. Serve immediately.

Beef Stewed with Thyme, Allspice and Coconut

This is an uncommonly good beef stew from the Caribbean, flavoured with thyme, allspice and coconut. The most unusual part is the initial heating of sugar and oil, which speeds up the browning of the meat very pleasingly. The finished stew is sweetish – from the sugar, of course, but also from the onions, which will have melted down to thicken the sauce. All in all, it's relatively light on meat but big on flavour.

I used pieces of top rump, which is a tender cut, when I made the stew, but if you use a cheaper piece of braising steak you may find that you have to extend the cooking time a little and add a touch more coconut milk. The recipe is adapted from one given by Cristine MacKie in her book *Trade Winds*. Serve it with plain boiled rice.

Serves 4

90 ml (3 fl oz) coconut or sunflower oil
2 tablespoons caster sugar
750 g (1 lb 10 oz) good stewing beef, cut into 3 cm (1¼ inch) chunks, trimmed
1 large onion, very finely chopped
3 generous sprigs of thyme
2 garlic cloves, crushed
1 teaspoon allspice berries, bruised
200–300 ml (7–10 fl oz) coconut milk (see opposite)
salt and pepper

Put the oil and sugar in a heavy flameproof casserole. Heat over a moderate heat, stirring occasionally, until the sugar is golden brown and molten. Have faith. At first it clumps mercilessly and shows no inclination to soften. It will, and eventually forms pools of molten brown within the oil. Dry the pieces of beef. Add them to the pan and stir with a wooden spoon until the meat is a rich brown colour. Now add the onion and stir. Reduce the heat right down low, season generously with salt and cover the pan. Leave to sweat for 15 minutes, by which time the meat will have thrown off a surprising amount of liquid and the onion should have more or less dissolved into the juices, thickening them slightly.

Uncover and add all the remaining ingredients, using the lower quantity of coconut milk. Stir, then simmer, covered, for an hour or until the beef is very tender. Check occasionally and if it seems to be getting a little dry, add more coconut milk. In fact, you should end up with a fairly generous amount of sauce. Once the beef is fully tender and the sauce reduced to a good consistency, taste and adjust the seasoning.

Coconut Milk

The best coconut milk is made from a fresh coconut (the semi-transparent liquid that sloshes around inside is coconut juice, a refreshing drink but not the same as coconut milk). The second-best option is to use desiccated coconut. Tinned coconut milk is a useful standby but it does have an odd, slimy feel when boiled down which I don't care for a great deal.

To make milk from a fresh coconut, you need to crack it open. Clamp the coconut in a vice, or get some brave soul to hold it for you. Pierce a hole through two of the eyes, and drain out the juice. Tap the coconut all over with a hammer to loosen the flesh inside, then bash your hammer down repeatedly at the centre of the 'ribs' that run from top to bottom of the coconut, until it cracks open. Prise the flesh from the shell and don't worry about the brown inner skin. Break up the bits and process them in a food processor until finely chopped.

Now add 600 ml (1 pint) hot water. When cool enough to handle, knead the flesh with your hands, then strain off the milk, squeezing it out with your hands. This is thick coconut milk. If you repeat this last process with the squeezed coconut and a new batch of water you will get thin coconut milk. Mix thick and thin and you have medium coconut milk (which is usually just referred to as coconut milk).

To make coconut milk from desiccated coconut, put 250 g (9 oz) unsweetened desiccated coconut into the processor with 300 ml (½ pint) hot water. Process and strain, squeezing out the milk. This is thick coconut milk. Repeat for thin coconut milk. Mix the two, as above, for medium milk.

Whether you start with fresh coconut or desiccated, the milk will keep in the fridge for 48 hours. The thick coconut cream will rise to the top, setting in a dense waxy layer. Once it warms up to room temperature it mixes back in easily. You can also freeze coconut milk.

Glazed Carrots with Cinnamon and Lemon Thyme

Lemon thyme and cinnamon together bring out the best in carrots. A sprig of thyme cooked with the carrots imparts a hint of its scent right into their core, while a final dressing of lemon thyme leaves brings a second fresh dose. Serve the carrots with grilled or roast lamb, or a juicy steak.

Serves 4

600 g (1 lb 5 oz) carrots, thickly sliced
45 g (1½ oz) butter
45 g (1½ oz) granulated or caster sugar
1 cinnamon stick
1 sprig of lemon thyme
¾–1 teaspoon fresh lemon thyme leaves
salt

Put all the ingredients except the lemon thyme leaves into a pan with almost, but not quite, enough water to cover the carrots. Bring up to the boil, then leave to simmer, uncovered, for about 12 minutes, stirring occasionally, by which time the carrots should be tender (and I mean tender, not *al dente*). Scoop them out and reserve. Boil the liquid down hard until it is reduced to a thin layer of syrup on the bottom of the pan (if you are short of time, transfer the liquid to a wide frying pan to speed the process up, but take care that it doesn't burn). Return the carrots to the pan and turn them in the syrup, coating them well, until piping hot. Remove the thyme sprig and cinnamon stick, then stir in the reserved lemon thyme leaves. Taste and adjust the seasoning, then serve.

Previous page
Glazed Carrots with Cinnamon and Lemon Thyme

Thyme Sorbet

Scenting a white wine sorbet with thyme may seem a weird idea but the end result is amazingly good, with an exotically pure kind of taste. Serve it as part of a selection of sorbets and ice-creams, or scooped into small melon halves to refresh on a hot summer's day.

The recipe comes from the very best guide to ice-cream making, *Ices* by Caroline Liddell and Robin Weir.

To make the sugar syrup stir 500 g (1 lb 2 oz) sugar with 500 ml (16 fl oz) water over a moderate heat until the sugar has dissolved to make a clear syrup. Draw off the heat and leave to cool. You will end up with more than you need, but leftover syrup can be stored, almost indefinitely, in a sealed jar in the fridge.

Serves 6–8

10 g (¼ oz) or 4 x 5 cm (2 inch) sprigs of thyme
500 ml (16 fl oz) sugar syrup
250 ml (8 fl oz) water
250 ml (8 fl oz) dry white wine
2 tablespoons lemon juice

Put the thyme into a pan with the sugar syrup and water. Bring slowly up to the boil. Draw off the heat and add the wine. Cover and leave to cool. Chill overnight in the fridge, then add the lemon juice and strain.

If you have an ice-cream machine, freeze the sorbet in that. If not, pour the mixture into a shallow freezer container and pop into the freezer, turned to its coldest setting. Leave until the edges are solid but the centre still liquid. Break up the edges and push them into the centre. Return to the freezer and repeat once. Now leave until the sorbet is set right through but not yet rock hard. Scrape the contents of the container into a food processor and quickly process to smooth out jagged ice crystals. Scrape the mush back into the container and return post-haste to the freezer. If you don't have a food processor you'll have to beat the sorbet with all your might to break down the crystals. Now leave until fully set. Transfer from the freezer to the fridge to 'ripen' – or in other words, soften – about 20–25 minutes before serving.

rosemary
Rosmarinus officinalis

Long, long ago, up on the barren, heat-scarred heights of Mount Etna, an evil sorceress looked down jealously on the bounty and happiness of the people who lived below her in the fertile plains of Sicily. Unable to bear it any longer, she cast a spell over the island, annihilating love and peace and killing all plants, bar a mere handful of poisonous leaves. The people despaired and the sea grew angry. So great was the Woman of Etna's power that she managed to still the ocean's rage, but as the last wave crashed on to the cliffs it swept away a young girl. She cried out to her family to remember her, and where her fingers slithered in vain over the drenched rocks, the rosemary plant sprang up.

And that, my friends, is how rosemary came into being. A myth it may be, but it tells us much of the power of one of the most beautiful and romantic of all herbs. Rosemary is indeed native to the Mediterranean, and it does thrive on rocky shores swept by the salt winds from the sea. Its very name, from the Latin *ros marin*, means dew of the sea. In Sicily and throughout Italy it is employed exuberantly in cooking, married with tender young lamb, of course, but also with other meats, with seafood and often, spectacularly well, with vegetables.

It is likely that the Romans brought it to our shores, and for that we must thank them heartily, for it has become an important herb to us here as well, even if we don't use it with quite such wanton abandon. In the southern parts of the British Isles it grows with remarkable gusto for a heat-loving plant, and even further north it will survive harsher winters with a little loving protection. Excessive rain, rather than cold, is its greatest enemy. It is evergreen, so can be enjoyed all year round. There's something immensely cheering about the sight of a rosemary bush, thrusting its way through a light blanket of snow on an icy winter's day.

Smell rosemary carefully before buying for planting – some varieties are heavy on camphor, making them quite unsuitable for culinary purposes unless you have a fetish for things medicinal.

'There's rosemary, that's for remembrance,' says Hamlet to the ever more demented Ophelia, echoing again the Sicilian story of the plant's creation. In the past its symbolism made it as integral to wedding ceremonies – in the bride's bouquet, or strewn before her as she made her way to the altar – as to funerals, where it was cast over the coffin in its earthen hole.

And we still love it, this herb of happiness and memories, solemn moments and reflection. In the middle of winter it conjures up the scent of summer and the sound of summer bees buzzing around its blue flowers (the Virgin Mary, on the flight to Palestine, is said to have laid her cloak down over a rosemary bush, turning its white flowers blue). The flowers themselves make pretty points of blue dotted over savoury and sweet dishes but, of course, it is the narrow, pointed leaves that matter above all. They are tailor made for pushing into small slits in a leg of lamb, along with thin shards of garlic, before roasting, to send their aromatic scent deep into the meat, but try them too with pork – the camphor element balances the fattiness of good free-range pork – or even with goose. This is a mere beginning. One brilliant combination is rosemary with gamy red mullet, again in tandem with generous helpings of garlic and good olive oil. I'm very partial to a sprinkling of rosemary with juicy, fat, sweet scallops, too. With other, more subtle fish, it needs a lighter hand, but will still sit well. I love rosemary added to roast vegetables and in particular roast red onions – just pop a sprig or two into the pan with all the other raw ingredients, then let the flavour waft in over long cooking. Sautéed potatoes are superb with a scattering of roughly chopped rosemary leaves, added towards the end of the cooking time so that they don't burn to smithereens.

If you have a big, lusty bushful of rosemary, then you may well have to prune it back in the summer. Left with a heap of rosemary cuttings, don't just bin them. Organize a barbecue and select the sturdiest rosemary stems to act as skewers, gently imparting their flavour from the inside out. Try loading them up with cubes of pork or lamb and vegetables, chunks of monkfish or, for a real luxury, a mixture of monkfish and scallops, brushed well with oil and seasoned before they go over the embers. My friend Sue can never resist laying a spare sprig of rosemary on the hotplate of our Aga or her Raeburn, which sends whiffs of charring rosemary round the house like incense. If your barbecue is up and running, throw handfuls of rosemary cuttings on the coals to put your guests in a convivial state of mind.

Some years ago I came up with the idea of infusing a syrup with rosemary to pour over blood oranges. It makes a superb, refreshing early-spring dessert. All of a sudden, over the past year or so, the notion of using rosemary in sweet dishes seems to have caught on. Rosemary syrup can be poured over sturdy plain cakes to turn them sweet and sticky, or whipped into cream to make a syllabub (see Lemon Grass and Ginger Syllabub on p. 137 for the basic method, substituting a few sprigs of rosemary for the lemon grass and ginger). It seems a downright peculiar idea at first but give it a try and you will soon be won over.

Storage and Preservation

Rosemary is made of stern, tough stuff and in the short term it will keep fresh with relatively little loss of flavour. If it is only a question of a day or two, then it won't come to much harm just left out in the kitchen. Wrapped in a damp tea towel or kitchen paper and stashed in the vegetable drawer of the fridge it should survive happily for a week and more.

There is absolutely no point in drying rosemary, unless you just like the look of a bundle of dried twigs strung on the wall or from the ceiling. Even then, think twice – the leaves shed even more readily than Christmas tree needles. The flavour of dried rosemary is acceptable but not a patch on fresh and, after all, it is a year-round herb, so why go for second best? Besides, the dried needles of rosemary are irksome and unpleasant in the mouth. If you are landed with an excess, far better to stuff a few sprigs into bottles of olive oil or good wine vinegar for rosemary salad dressings, into a jar of sugar to make rosemary sugar for cakes or fruit salads, or to make an infusion to use as a hair rinse – I'm told it leaves hair gleaming and shiny.

Everyone loves sautéed potatoes, so if you are feeling loving and generous take the time to stand over a frying pan for quarter of an hour or so to make them. You can leave them plain, seasoning with no more than a shake of salt, but for a change try them with rosemary and the salty virtue of olives. They are especially good with fish.

Serves 3

550 g (1 lb 4 oz) maincrop potatoes (slightly waxy varieties such as Cara or Picasso are particularly good for this, though King Edward and Maris Piper are perfectly acceptable)
3 tablespoons olive oil
2 teaspoons finely chopped rosemary leaves
60 g/2 oz black or green olives, pitted and chopped
salt

Peel the potatoes and cut into 1–2 cm (½–¾ inch) dice. Heat the olive oil over a moderately high heat in a wide frying pan. Add the potatoes in a single layer (if you have more than you can fit in, use a second pan) and sauté, keeping them moving more or less continuously, until crusty, brown and tender. This should take around 12–15 minutes. About 5 minutes before they are done, sprinkle over the rosemary, and continue cooking. When more or less done, stir in the olives, then turn the mixture out on to a plate lined with a double layer of kitchen paper. Drain briefly, then sprinkle lightly with salt and serve.

Opposite
Rosemary-wrapped Fillet of Lamb with Tomato and Olive Relish
(page 20)

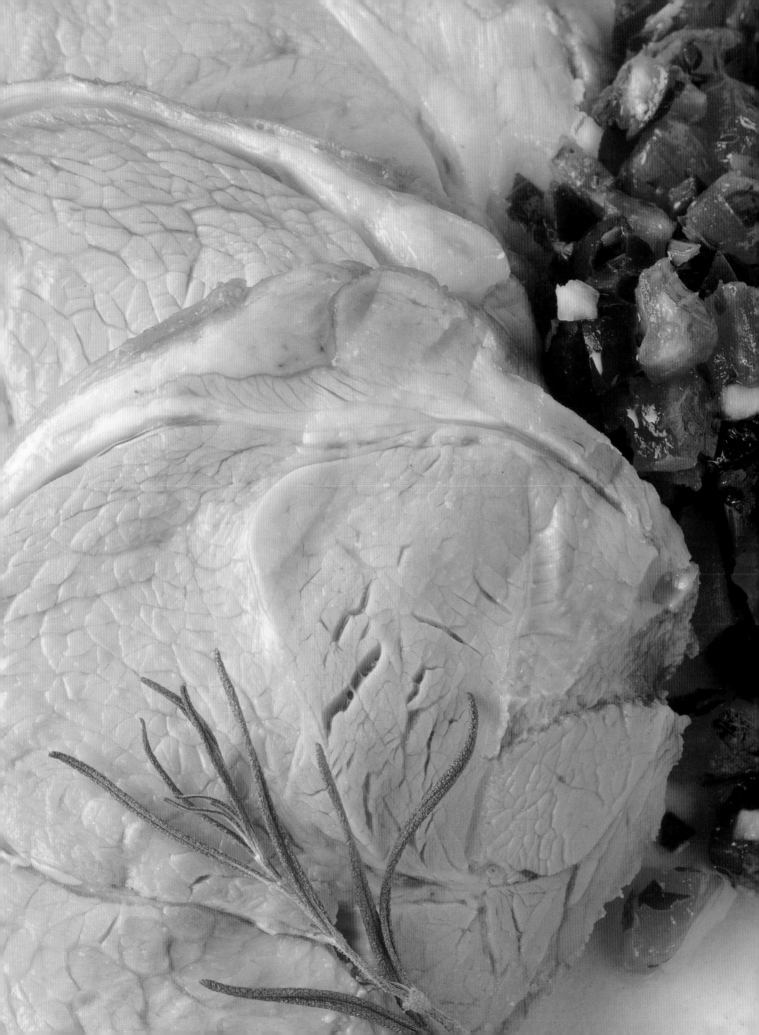

Rosemary-wrapped Fillet of Lamb with Tomato and Olive Relish

A recipe for the gardener who has a lusty rosemary bush in need of a good cutting-back session. The tenderest of all cuts of tender lamb is baked in a jacket of rosemary sprigs, cushioning it from harm and gently perfuming the lamb as it imbibes the heat. The smell as it cooks is sheer heaven. Serve sliced juicily, with this olive, tomato, parsley and lemon relish.

Serves 6

a little olive oil
2 garlic cloves, sliced
1 piece of lamb leg fillet, weighing about 850–900 g
   1 lb 14 oz–2 lb) (or 2 loin fillets or a boned rolled shoulder)
masses of long rosemary sprigs

For the relish
2 tomatoes, skinned, deseeded and diced very small
60 g (2 oz) black olives, pitted and finely chopped
finely grated zest of 1 lemon
3 tablespoons finely chopped parsley
2 garlic cloves, very finely chopped
½ teaspoon caster sugar
1 tablespoon lemon juice
4 tablespoons olive oil
salt and pepper

Pre-heat the oven to 200°C/400°F/Gas Mark 6.

Heat enough oil to cover the bottom of a frying pan large enough to take the fillet. Add the sliced garlic and fry until beginning to brown. Scoop out and reserve. Raise the heat under the pan. Add the fillet and brown quickly on all sides.

Find a loaf tin, or something similar, into which the lamb will just fit – and don't worry if it is a bit on the snug side or pokes up above the rim. Make a thick bed of rosemary sprigs in the bottom. Lay the fillet in it, scatter over the fried garlic, then pack in more rosemary, tucking it down the sides and ends and stashing it thickly over the top of the fillet. Press it down firmly, then cover the dish tightly with foil to keep the rosemary in place. Roast for 30 minutes for rare lamb and up to 45 minutes if you prefer it cooked through.

Meanwhile, make the relish by mixing all the ingredients together. Adjust the seasoning, adding salt and pepper to taste, then cover and set aside.

Take the lamb out of the oven, uncover and leave to rest for 15–20 minutes. Unpack, discarding all the rosemary. Pour off the juices (strain if there are too many needles of rosemary floating about in them). Slice the meat about 5 mm (¼ inch) thick and serve with the tomato and olive relish and the pan juices.

Gigot de Lotte
(Monkfish with Garlic and Rosemary)

A skinned and beheaded tail of monkfish bears a passing resemblance to a leg of lamb and is sometimes known, therefore, as a *gigot*. The piscine *gigot* can, as it happens, be cooked in a similar fashion to the meaty one, studded with slivers of garlic and needles of rosemary, then roasted in a hot oven.

Serves 4–6

900 g–1.5 kg (2–3 lb) monkfish tail
2 garlic cloves, cut into fine shards
the leaves of a small sprig of rosemary
1 red onion, thinly sliced
1 glass of dry white wine
110 ml (4 fl oz) extra virgin olive oil
salt and loads of freshly ground pepper

Pre-heat the oven to 190°C/375°F/Gas Mark 5.

Make slits all over the monkfish tail and push in slivers of garlic and rosemary leaves, using the handle of a teaspoon or some other thin, blunt instrument.

Place the onion slices in an ovenproof dish and sit the monkfish on top. Pour over the wine and oil, then season with salt and pepper. Roast for 25–30 minutes, until just cooked through, basting occasionally with the pan juices.

The Peat Inn's Rosemary and Chocolate Pots

This extraordinary recipe came to me in a roundabout way from David Wilson, who runs The Peat Inn restaurant in Fife. Rosemary and chocolate sounds an odd sort of mixture but I can assure you that it tastes superb and, believe me, the odd-sounding method really does work. The result is dark and wildly rich, with a softly grainy texture – it's rather like eating soft, ultra-superb chocolate fudge. The flavour of rosemary is noticeable but hard to identify if you don't know what it is.

Use the best plain chocolate (at least 60 per cent cocoa solids, preferably more) for this pudding – anything less is unworthy.

Serves 8–10

250 g (9 oz) granulated sugar
250 ml (8 fl oz) dry white wine
juice of ½ lemon
600 ml (1 pint) double cream
1 sprig of rosemary
165 g (5½ oz) plain chocolate, grated

To serve
8–10 small sprigs of rosemary
a few slivered or chopped almonds

Mix the sugar, white wine and lemon juice in a heavy-based pan. Stir over a medium heat until the sugar has completely dissolved. Stir in the double cream. Let the mixture bubble quietly, stirring frequently, until thickened a little – allow about 20 minutes.

Add the rosemary sprig, then the chocolate, stirring until completely dissolved. Bring back to the boil and simmer very gently for about 15–20 minutes, until the mixture is dark and thick. Strain into a jug, then cool until tepid, stirring frequently to prevent the mixture separating and becoming oily. Pour into 8–10 small ramekins or glasses and chill until softly set. Decorate each pot with a sprig of rosemary and a sprinkling of almonds.

sage
Salvia officinalis

Sage is a strong herb which strides in without hesitation or dissembling. Some might even call it aggressive, verging on belligerent, but that is really only true of dried sage which, in my opinion, should be tipped straight down the drain before its musty, all-pervasive, camphorous soul can out again. Fresh sage, on the other hand, is something I would not be without. I love the lively, slightly bitter, pleasingly resinous, warm spiciness that makes it quite unique amongst herbs. I love the look of the leaves, too, soft to the touch yet substantial, subtle grey-green or bruised purple, followed by glorious purple-pink flowers. There are other combinations to admire as well: golden sage, with its gold-green leaves, white sage with its white flowers, and other variations on *Salvia officinalis*, the common garden sage.

For centuries, sage has been held in the highest esteem, grown in the past principally for its astonishing medicinal value. It is native to the Mediterranean and still grows wild there on limestone rock and sun-drenched slopes. The ancient Greeks and Romans considered it most efficacious as an antidote to snake bites, amongst other things, and its power lived on through the Middle Ages. At some time or other it has been supposed to be a cure for practically any ailment you care to mention, from barrenness in women to fevers, spots and even the dreaded plague. Sage tea, when made with fresh leaves, is really rather pleasant and soothing as long as it is not too strong. I've seen it described as a 'grateful tea', an apt description for a remedy for nausea and a tonic for nerves. Those of you who are studying may well have reason to be grateful for a cup of gentle sage tea, as it is, apparently, a surefire bet for relieving exam stress.

One thing that certainly does seem to be true is that sage aids digestion and soothes the stomach, and this is part of the reason it is so often used with fatty meats. The other part is that it tastes so good with them, its notes of camphor balancing the richness of the flesh. Here in Britain we use it primarily with pork, in a sage and onion stuffing which, when properly made with fresh sage, is a thing of great joy. The same stuffing goes well, too, with goose, and sage is also surprisingly good with duck.

In Germany they choose sage to partner oily eel, a lovely combination which surfaces again in Italy, where sage is used with considerable verve and skill. Fresh, it may simply be infused in butter with garlic, to sauce gnocchi (see p. 108) or polenta (I like to layer freshly made polenta with sage-scented melted butter and gorgonzola or pecorino, then whip it into the oven for a short while until sizzling and bubbling). Italian mammas and chefs may also employ it with veal and discreetly with fish.

Like the Italians, the British love sage with cheese. This is a fine combination, not only in the famous Sage Derby cheese but also in home-cooked dishes. Try adding a few shredded sage leaves to Welsh rarebit, or scattering them under the cheese for cheese on toast, or stirring them into the base for a cheese soufflé.

Strolling out into our herb garden one day, I was mightily pleased to see our sage bush thriving, strong and vigorous, elbowing a nearby thyme plant out of the way. I felt sorry for the thyme but a flourishing sage plant is a sign of a prosperous household, so that's one thing less to worry about. It is also supposed to indicate that there is a strong woman ruling the home. Well, maybe, but I'm not quite sure what my husband would say about that ...

Storage and Preservation
The fresh leaves are fairly tough, so will keep in the vegetable drawer of the fridge, in a plastic bag, for a week without detriment, as long as they are not wet. Sage is an evergreen, in leaf all year round, so I can't see any point at all in preserving it for winter use. Dried sage is vile and dangerous, the ruination of many a good stuffing or British sausage. Avoid the temptation to dry your sage – it really isn't worth it.

Two Real Sage and Onion Stuffings

Sage and onion stuffing is a part of our culinary heritage that we ought to be proud of, and yet it is hard to get excited about what is so often dished up under this name. Packet sage and onion is a travesty of the real thing, musty with dried sage and reeking all too often of cheap fats. Real sage and onion stuffing, made with fresh sage, fresh onions and dripping, lard or butter, is quite different and deserves a renaissance. It is very easy to make and doesn't even take that long. The sage makes it the perfect stuffing for fatty meats, such as pork, duck and goose, and it is even rather good with oily fish like mackerel and herring.

In fact, when I was looking at recipes for sage and onion stuffing, some of them in old cookery books as well as new, I found a couple made not with breadcrumbs but with potato as a base, occasionally mixed with apple for an extra note of sweetness. Both the standard version and the potato-based one are delicious, so I give both here for you to take your pick.

Bathing the sage in boiling water for a couple of minutes makes a noticeable difference to the stuffing, enhancing and brightening the flavour of the sage while reducing its underlying note of bitterness. Remember, too, that stuffings of all sorts should be emphatically flavoured and seasoned. What tastes about right when it is first made and still in the bowl will seem bland and insipid when it has been roasted in a joint of meat (and that is equally true of stuffings for vegetables, as it happens). Quite how much sage you use depends on your taste and what the stuffing is for – the fattier the meat the more sage it can take.

Standard Sage and Onion Stuffing

1½ large onions (around 500 g/1 lb 2 oz in total), chopped
60 g (2 oz) butter, lard or pork dripping
2½–3 tablespoons chopped sage
125 g (4 oz) fresh white breadcrumbs
salt and pepper

Fry the onions in the fat until very tender, then draw off the heat. While they are cooking, pour boiling water over the sage, leave for 1 minute, then drain. Mix the sage with the onions and their cooking fat, the breadcrumbs and salt and pepper.

Sage, Onion, Potato and Apple Stuffing

2 onions, chopped
60 g (2 oz) butter, lard or pork dripping
2 eating apples or 1 large cooking apple, peeled, cored and diced
2½–3 tablespoons chopped sage
250 g (9 oz) mashed cooked potatoes
salt and pepper

Fry the onions in the fat until very tender. Add the apple and fry until it has collapsed to a mush if it is a cooking apple or until softened if you are using eating apples. Meanwhile, pour boiling water over the sage, leave for 1 minute, then drain. Mix the apple and onion with the sage, potatoes and salt and pepper.

Roast Loin of Pork with
Sage and Onion Stuffing

A real, old-fashioned Sunday roast for the family, with lovely crisp crackling, tender meat and the perfect stuffing for it (see p. 23). If you can buy free-range pork from a traditional breed of pig (a good butcher should be able to get it for you without too much trouble if you order in advance), so much the better, for it will have all the rich savouriness of meat as some of us remember it from our childhood, before intensive farming and an obsession with leanness sent flavour into obscurity.

For really crisp crackling, particularly on a relatively small joint like this, I find that roasting the skin separately at a high heat is the most successful solution. When ordering the meat, ask the butcher to score the skin for crackling and then lift it off with about half the fat layer in tow, leaving just enough on the meat itself to baste it as it cooks. Ask the butcher, too, to bone the meat and cut a generous flap or pocket for stuffing.

Serves about 6

1 loin of pork, weighing around 1.3–1.5 kg (2½–3 lb) with
    bone, boned, skin scored and cut off (see above)
sage and onion stuffing or sage, onion, potato and apple
    stuffing (see previous page)
salt

Pre-heat the oven to 230°C/450°F/Gas Mark 8.

Take the skin from the pork and dry assiduously with a paper towel. Lay it in a shallow baking dish or tray, scored-side up, and rub generously with salt. Roast all on its own for about 20 minutes, until very crisp. Remove from the oven and drain off the fat (which could be used to make the stuffing, if you haven't already done it, for cooking stuffing balls (see below) or for sautéing potatoes).

Unless you are intending to make the stuffing with the pork fat from the crackling, make the stuffing while the crackling is cooking. Open out your boned loin of pork and spread the stuffing thickly over the inside or if the butcher has cut a pocket, stuff the stuffing into that. Either way, you won't need it all. Rope in a helper and together carefully tie the loin up with the stuffing inside, using several lengths of string so that it forms a nice roundish joint. Don't worry if some of the stuffing oozes out. Pat back in what will fit easily and return the rest to the bowl.

Weigh the joint and calculate the cooking time as follows: allow 33 minutes per 500 g (30 minutes per lb), plus 30 minutes extra. Sit the joint on a rack over a roasting tin. Place it in the oven, then reduce the heat to 180°C/350°F/Gas Mark 4 and roast at this lower heat for the remainder of the cooking time.

Roll any remaining stuffing into balls about 3 cm (1¼ inches) in diameter. About 25 minutes before the pork is done, place them in a baking dish with a little oil or pork fat and roast in the oven with the pork, turning occasionally so that they brown evenly.

Once it is cooked, let the joint rest for 20–30 minutes before serving. Pop the crackling back in the oven for 10 minutes to heat through. Serve the pork, crackling and stuffing balls with apple sauce.

Spiedini di Maiale

A few years ago, I was lucky enough to be tutoring an Italian cookery holiday high up in the Tuscan hills. One afternoon we were making these skewers of pork to grill over the embers of the fire, when Antonella, who did the washing-up, grabbed my hand and dragged me out to the meadow. 'Here,' she said firmly, 'we always slip a little wild fennel in with the liver.' We picked a huge bunch of wild fennel, took it back to the kitchen and added it to the little faggots of liver tied up in caul fat. The combination of both fennel and sage gives the mixed meats strung together on the skewers a remarkable flavour.

Ask your butcher to supply the caul fat. It serves two important functions: to stop the sausage falling off the skewers and to baste the liver as it cooks, keeping it moist. It is cheap to buy, and any that you don't use straight away will freeze beautifully.

Serves 6

caul fat
250 g (9 oz) pork fillet or other tender cut
250 g (9 oz) pig's liver
250 g (9 oz) luganega sausage, or other meaty pork sausage
200 g (7 oz) pancetta
a few generous sprigs of fennel, wild if available
2 yellow or red peppers, deseeded and cut into squares
plenty of sage leaves
olive oil
salt and pepper

Put the caul fat in a shallow dish and cover with warm water. Leave to soak and soften for 10 minutes, then drain. Cut the various meats into pieces about 3–4 cm (1–1½ inches) square and, where relevant, 1 cm (½ inch) thick. Cut the caul fat into squares and wrap neatly around the pieces of liver, tucking a small piece of fennel inside, and around the pieces of sausage. Thread up the skewers, making sure that some of each meat gets on to each skewer, along with squares of pepper and 3 or 4 sage leaves. Keep covered until ready to cook.

Brush the *spiedini* with olive oil, season with salt and pepper and cook over a barbecue or under the grill, turning freqently and brushing with oil, until cooked through. Serve hot.

Sage, Anchovy and Tomato Fritters

This recipe, with its deep-fried morsels cherished in a crisp batter, is delightfully dual-purpose. You can make it pure and simple – just the fritters themselves in their batter, sprinkled with a little salt, and a squeeze of lemon juice, then they're ready to be popped into the eager mouths of friends and family. Just the ticket for a warm pre-prandial bite with drinks before you get down to the main business of the meal. Or if you really want to turn these fritters into something outstanding, serve them with the Agro Dolce Vinaigrette (see p. 26), sweet and sour with its pine nuts and currants. This pair make plates, or at least ample napkins, fairly essential but the combination is totally sensational (ours disappeared in no time at all, with children and grown-ups clamouring for more). To make a more obvious first course, lay the hot fritters on individual beds of salad leaves, tossed with some of the dressing, then drizzle the rest over them.

There's far more batter than you will need but it is such a lovely, light, crisp one that I was loath to change the balance of ingredients to reduce quantities. I'm afraid that it won't keep, but if you are prepared to carry on frying, and have extra stocks of sage, tomato and anchovies, you might make your way through a fair amount of it.

Serves 6 with drinks, 4–6 as a first course

olive oil and/or sunflower oil for deep-frying
12 tinned anchovy fillets
18 sage leaves
2 plum tomatoes, skinned, deseeded and cut into long strips
salt
Agro Dolce Vinaigrette (see page 26) or lemon wedges, to
    serve
about 100 g (3½ oz) mixed small lettuce leaves, or lamb's
    lettuce or rocket (if serving as a first course)

For the batter
225 g (8 oz) plain flour, sifted
½ teaspoon salt
1 egg, separated
1 tablespoon sunflower oil
300 ml (½ pint) lager
125 ml (4 fl oz) cold water

Agro Dolce Vinaigrette

To prepare the batter, sift the flour with the salt. Make a well in the centre and add the egg yolk, oil and half the lager. Mix, gradually drawing in the flour to make a smooth batter and adding more lager as you go until it is all incorporated. Whisk in the water. Let the batter stand for half an hour if you have time. Immediately before using, whisk the egg white until it forms soft peaks and then fold it into the batter.

Either use a proper deep-fryer, or fill a deep frying pan with a 2 cm (¾ inch) depth of oil, or use a wok, which is what I prefer to fry in. For something like this I usually use a half and half mixture of olive and sunflower oil. Heat it up until there is a gentle heat haze – about 180°C/360°F, or until a cube of bread fizzles instantly and excitedly as soon as it enters the oil and begins to brown within 20 seconds. Dry the anchovies, wiping off the oil with kitchen paper (otherwise the batter tends to float off them). One by one, dip the sage leaves, anchovies and strips of tomato into the batter, coating completely, then slide them into the hot oil. Deep-fry until puffed and golden brown, turning once. Drain quickly on kitchen paper and sprinkle the sage and tomato fritters with a little salt. Serve immediately, with the vinaigrette or with lemon wedges.

If serving as a first course, toss the salad leaves with about two-thirds of the dressing and arrange on individual plates. Keep the fritters hot as they are fried, then arrange them on the leaves and drizzle over the last of the dressing. Serve immediately.

This is a delicious sweet and sour dressing, based on southern Italian sweet and sour combinations, though I like to make it with aromatic sherry vinegar rather than ordinary red wine vinegar, or even the more heat-sensitive balsamic vinegar. It is marvellous with the sage fritters on p. 25, but lovely, too, with sturdy salads – try dressing a mixture of watercress and orange with it.

Makes enough for about 6 servings

2 tablespoons pine nuts
3 tablespoons currants
2 tablespoons sherry vinegar
5 tablespoons olive oil
3 tablespoons water
2 tablespoons caster sugar
a little salt and lots of freshly ground black pepper

Put all the ingredients into a saucepan and stir over a low heat until the sugar has dissolved. Bring up to the boil and simmer gently for 3 minutes. Draw off the heat and leave to cool. Taste. It should seem fairly strong but if it is overwhelming, let it down a little with a touch more water or oil.

Opposite
**Sage,
Anchovy
and Tomato
Fritters**
(page 25)

winter and summer savory

Satureia montana and *Satureia hortensis*

Just opposite the door of our house, clinging to the dry stone wall, are two big spherical clumps of savory. They were there when we moved in, scenting the air if one brushed past them, as we did the first day we ever saw the house, with the sun blazing down. I'd come across savory occasionally in the past but this was the first time that I'd had such a prolific, beautiful source of the herb literally right at hand. I've grown to love the scent of it, combining, as it does, elements of all the warm, spicy herbs – sage, thyme, hyssop, marjoram – jostling prettily together.

There are two distinct forms of savory: winter savory (*Satureia montana*) is a perennial evergreen, with narrow, spiky leaves and lilac-pink flowers that lure the bees to gossip around it (the leaves alleviate the pain of bee or wasp stings if rubbed quickly over them); and then there is summer savory (*Satureia hortensis*), with its red-purple stems, white or pale-mauve flowers and long, more curvaceous leaves, with much the same sort of flavour but a little lighter, with perhaps even a hint of mint creeping into the cocktail. This second savory is an annual, which needs to be replaced each year, and grows easily from seed.

The two plants share the Latin name *Satureia*, which takes us back to a time when the herb was thought to be a favourite of the satyrs, since it was believed to have aphrodisiac powers. It was even used in love potions, though the uncharitable might think that its greatest contribution to passion is its ability to calm flatulence. *Montana* indicates that winter savory grows in the mountains, and indeed it does thrive in poor, rocky soil, while *hortensis* denotes a garden-loving plant. Its anti-flatulence properties may also explain why savory is so strongly recommended as a flavouring for beans of all kinds, so much so that it is sometimes called the bean herb. It also happens to complement the flavour of both fresh beans (particularly broad beans) and dried pulses, from lentils through to kidney beans and further. A few sprigs thrown in with the beans as they cook leave a gentle waft of spiciness in their wake.

But don't restrict savory to beans. It goes very well with vegetables, such as artichokes, courgettes and particularly root vegetables. The lighter summer savory is delicious chopped and mixed with cream cheese or young goat's cheese, along with a sprinkling of chives and maybe a little crushed garlic, or can be used to season fish – tuck a sprig or two inside sardines or red mullet and marinate them with more savory, plus garlic, lemon and olive oil, for grilling over the barbecue, or slip it inside trout to soften the muddy taste of so many farmed trout. Both types of savory sit well with fatty meat; like so many of the other hardy herbs they are excellent in stews of pork, or in stuffings for goose, duck or even leaner veal. I often include a sprig in a bouquet garni for hearty soups, or let a few inches slip into a tomato sauce as it simmers down. I also love olive oil flavoured with sprigs of savory – superb for scenting tomato sauces, in marinades, brushed over chicken, fish or lamb before grilling or barbecuing, or drizzled lightly over them after they have been cooked. Simply tuck a small handful of savory sprigs into a bottle and fill up with extra virgin olive oil.

Storage and Preservation

The leaves of both winter and summer savory can be kept for several days, in a plastic bag, in the vegetable drawer of the fridge. Both forms of savory dry well, losing relatively little of their flavour. Harvest the leaves in the morning of a dry day, shortly before flowering, then tie them in bunches and hang from a nail in a dry, airy, dark place. Strip the leaves from the stalks when dry and store in airtight containers out of the light.

Grilled Red Mullet with Savory, Orange and Anchovy Sauce

Red mullet is a big fish in terms of flavour – it's not known as the gamecock of the sea for nothing – and it can take big, lusty partners without the blink of a fin. It is notoriously good with rosemary but maybe even better with the spicy warmth of savory. Salty anchovies, gutsy garlic and sweet oranges breathe in a taste of the south, in a sauce that takes literally only a few minutes to make.

Serves 4

4 red mullet, weighing around 175–200 g (6–7 oz) each, cleaned and scaled, livers retained for the sauce
4 sprigs of savory
olive oil
salt and pepper
lemon wedges, to serve

For the sauce
2 oranges
4 tablespoons olive oil
2 garlic cloves, chopped
6 tinned anchovy fillets, roughly chopped
the livers from the red mullet, if available
½ tablespoon chopped savory
1 tablespoon lemon juice

Make two diagonal slashes across the thickest part of the body of each red mullet on both sides. Season well, inside and out, with salt and pepper. Tuck a sprig of savory in the stomach cavity of each fish. Set aside until needed. Peel the oranges for the sauce, cutting down to the flesh, then slice. Reserve the slices and the juice that seeps out.

Pre-heat the grill (or barbecue) thoroughly. Brush the red mullet generously with olive oil and lay, head to tail, on the grill rack. Cook for about 4 minutes on each side, until just cooked through. Transfer to a warm serving dish.

The sauce can be made as the fish are cooking. Heat the oil in a medium frying pan and add the garlic, anchovies and livers, if using. Cook over a moderate heat (but not too hot, mind, or you'll burn the garlic), crushing down the anchovy fillets and livers until they have dissolved into the oil. Now add the savory and plenty of pepper. Stir, then add the orange slices, their juice and the lemon juice. Simmer very gently for 1–2 minutes to heat through. Spoon the sauce over the red mullet and serve immediately, with lemon wedges.

Grilled Quail with Savory and Lemon Aïoli

A finger-lickin' good dish to launch a meal in a substantial sort of a way. It's a sticky business eating the quail and there's no point attempting it with a knife and fork. Tear them apart with your fingers and teeth and enjoy yourself. Don't forget to provide napkins and, if you are feeling very nice, finger bowls with slices of lemon bobbing in them.

Serves 4 as a starter, 2 as a main course

4 quail, spatchcocked (see p. 77)
2 tablespoons chopped savory
1 tablespoon honey
juice of ½ lemon
4 tablespoons olive oil
salt and pepper

For the lemon aïoli
2 garlic cloves, peeled
1 egg yolk
finely grated zest of ½ lemon
1–2 tablespoons lemon juice
110 ml (4 fl oz) sunflower oil
60 ml (2 fl oz) lemon olive oil (see p.134)

Put the quails breast-side up in a shallow dish. Mix together all the remaining ingredients (except for those for the aïoli) and pour over. Turn the quails a couple of times to coat in the marinade, then cover and leave for at least 2 hours, or better still overnight, to absorb the flavours.

To make the aïoli, first of all ensure that all the ingredients are at room temperature. Put the garlic and a good pinch of salt in a mortar or sturdy bowl. Pound to a paste with the pestle or the end of a rolling pin. Work in the yolk, zest and juice. Mix the oils together in a jug. Whisking constantly, start adding the oil, drop by drop at first. When about a third of it has been incorporated increase the flow slightly, to a slow trickle. Continue adding the oil until it is all whisked in and a glossy cushion of golden mayonnaise reclines in the bowl. Taste and adjust the seasoning, adding more salt or lemon juice as needed. Cover and keep cool until the quails are cooked.

To cook the quails, pre-heat the grill or barbecue thoroughly. Grill the quails, breast-side to heat first, for about 7–10 minutes, turning once or twice, until cooked through. Serve piping hot, with the aïoli.

Borlotti Beans with Savory and Deep-fried Celery

Ancient wisdom has it that savory is made for beans, and that's not so far from the truth. The spicy, slightly bitter flavour is a winner with starchy pulses of all kinds. To turn a dish of plain boiled beans into a feast – vegetarian, as it happens – add a handful of speedily fried celery batons (even those who are suspicious of celery will probably like it cooked this way), fresh juicy tomato and salty feta cheese.

Serves 4

340 g (12 oz) dried borlotti beans
1 onion, chopped
1 celery stick, chopped
3 tablespoons olive oil
1 garlic clove, chopped, plus 5 whole garlic cloves, peeled
1 bay leaf
2 sprigs of parsley
2 generous sprigs of summer or winter savory
½–1 tablespoon chopped savory
salt and pepper

For the garnish

4 celery sticks, cut into 5 cm (2 inch) lengths, then lengthways into narrow batons
well-seasoned flour
sunflower or olive oil for deep-frying
3 ripe tomatoes, skinned, deseeded and diced
150 g (5 oz) feta cheese, crumbled

Soak the borlotti beans overnight, then drain. In a large saucepan, fry the onion and celery in the olive oil until lightly coloured. Add the chopped garlic and fry for a further minute or so. Make a bouquet garni of the bay leaf, parsley and sprigs of savory by tying them together with string. Add it to the pan with the beans and the whole garlic cloves. Pour in enough water to cover by about 4 cm (1½ inches). Do not add any salt. Bring up to the boil and simmer for about 1–1½ hours, until tender, adding extra water only if necessary. By the time the beans are tender, the liquid should be reduced to a relatively small amount and slightly thickened. If not, let it boil hard for a few more minutes. Remove the bouquet garni. Crush some of the beans into the liquid to thicken it a little more, then stir in the chopped savory and season generously with salt and pepper. Taste and adjust seasoning.

Toss the celery in well-seasoned flour. Deep-fry, a small handful at a time, in hot oil until golden brown (they'll sizzle a fair amount, so be careful). Drain briefly on kitchen paper, then season with salt. Meanwhile, reheat the borlotti beans and ladle into individual shallow bowls or plates. Top with the deep-fried celery, diced tomatoes and feta cheese and serve straight away.

Opposite
Bay-scented Baked Custard with Apricot Jam and Clotted Cream
(page 34)

bay leaf
Laurus nobilis

The bay laurel (not to be confused with the cherry laurel) originated in Asia Minor but took such a shine to the Mediterranean so long ago that everyone thinks of it as a native. Certainly it was well established, growing wild all around the great sea's shores, by the time the ancient Greek civilizations were at their zenith. In fact it was so familiar that it had entered their mythology. Legend has it that the great Apollo, the sun god, fell head over heels in love with the stately nymph Daphne. Fired with lust, he set off to pursue her. Daphne, not at all keen on this state of affairs, fled from his advances and was magically transformed into the first bay tree. Ever since, the bay tree has been sacred to Apollo, and as he was also the god of poetry it was only natural that a crown of bay or laurel leaves should be awarded to fine poets and masters of rhetoric. The principle, preserved verbally if nothing else, has lingered on to this day, in the form of our very own poet laureate (though I have difficulty imagining Ted Hughes wreathed with a titfer of bay leaves).

In optimum circumstances the bay tree can grow as high as 20 metres (60 feet) but here in Britain it is unlikely to scale such impressive heights. I'm not sure that most of us would want it to, anyway. Though it is tough enough to survive the winter in the south of the country, as long as it is sited in a sheltered spot, further north it needs protection from the worst ravages of frost and more. Actually, I just love the look of container-grown bay trees, and growing them in large pots makes a good deal of sense as they can be brought in away from ice and cosseted when the temperature threatens to drop too low. I long to own a brace of standard bay trees, pruned lovingly into perfect spheres, to stand guard on either side of our front door. Perhaps, by the time you read this, I may have made this one small fantasy come true. If not, and meanwhile, I make do with the small bay bush that sits snugly under one of the outer walls of the garden. The leaves are a mite too small for my liking but their scent, with its balsamic crisp tones and hints of almond, is as true as that of any larger leaf.

There is some debate over the value of fresh bay leaves. It is true that when first picked they have a bitter note, and if at all possible it is best to let them 'ripen' on the branch or in a small open bowl in the kitchen for a couple of days before using. The tough leaves, with their waxy exterior, can take this treatment without deteriorating one mite. The bitter taste alone is lost. However, I think it is probably true to say that this is one of the few herbs whose flavour improves with drying. I remember well, in Portugal, being instructed by an excellent cook never to use anything but newly dried bay leaves, as their taste is so vastly superior.

Fresh or dried, bay leaves are immensely important to the European cook. No kitchen should be without them, as they are quite indispensable to an enormous array of relatively slow-cooked dishes, from béchamel sauce, to tomato soups and sauces, to terrines and pâtés, stews of practically all kinds (fish, fowl, meat or vegetable), stocks, marinades, pickles and even puddings. Yes, puddings, and there's nothing modern and newfangled about that. In the past, when imported spices such as cinnamon and vanilla were phenomenally costly (vanilla, don't forget, has only been with us since the eighteenth century), bay leaves were the natural flavouring for all kinds of milk puddings, either infused first in the milk or stewed long and slow in something like a rice pudding. As long as it is done with a modicum of discretion (bay is powerful stuff and must be treated with a little caution), it is a habit well worth reviving.

Bay provides the essential base note of a classic bouquet garni (see p. 35), complemented by sprigs of parsley and thyme, and many of us may rarely think of using it all on its own. Why not, though? Try adding two or three leaves of bay to a stew instead of majoring on some other herb and you will notice a very pleasant difference. If you own a bay tree you might also like to try slipping bay leaves between the cubes of meat or fish as you string up kebabs for the grill or, better still, the barbecue. If the leaves are dry, then soak them in warm water for an hour or two first to make them more malleable and less inclined to incineration. As the leaves char in the heat, they impart a delicious scent to neighbouring ingredients.

If you are ever in Italy, particularly in the south, look out for figs packed in small wooden boxes lined with bay leaves. Originally the bay leaves served to deter weevils but these days the flavour is more important. I once bought a garland of dried figs interspersed with bay leaves in the market of Dubrovnik, long before war took its toll. I wonder whether they are being threaded up again now, or whether the aftermath of violence has driven them into obscurity. I do hope not, for those skeins of brown, plump figs, shoulder to shoulder with noble bay leaves, were a delicious and beautiful living tradition that must have been handed down through the centuries.

Storage and Preservation

Fresh bay leaves will keep happily in a bowl on the kitchen side, on or off the branch but without water, for several days, losing any bitter taste they may have. If you want to dry them properly, then it is best to tie branches together with string and hang them up in a *dark*, airy, dry place until they are brittle and fully dried. Darkness helps to set their rich green colour. Strip the leaves off the stems after they have dried and store in an airtight container – again, in the dark, if possible. If the leaves you have are already stripped from the stem when fresh, you can thread them up on white thread or fine string to dry.

Bay-infused Oil
Chef Alastair Little likes to make a bay-infused oil, by gently warming 500 ml (16 fl oz) good extra virgin olive oil with 2 finely shredded bay leaves, 12 small dried chillies that have been rehydrated by soaking for 10 minutes in warm water, then dried and chopped, 1 sprig fresh rosemary, 4 sliced garlic cloves and if he can lay his hands on them, 2 finely shredded kaffir lime leaves. He lets the whole lot infuse gently over a low heat for half an hour, before cooling and bottling. Store in the fridge and beware...he says it is addictive.

This dish of eggs, coloured and lightly spiced with turmeric, paprika, cumin and coriander, comes bathed in a thick tomato and red pepper sauce, heartened by a triple helping of bay leaves – enough to make their presence clearly felt but not so much that they overwhelm. It is a great dish for vegetarians, and indeed for anyone who likes eggs. This is the kind of thing I like to eat with a green salad and hunks of good bread but you could spoon it over rice, flecked with plenty of finely chopped parsley, and accompany it with spinach or mangetout.

Serves 4–6

6–8 eggs, just barely hard-boiled
¼ teaspoon ground turmeric
½ teaspoon paprika
½ teaspoon ground cumin
1 teaspoon ground coriander
⅛–¼ teaspoon cayenne pepper
2 tablespoons olive oil
1 onion, chopped
2 red peppers, deseeded and cut into strips
2 garlic cloves, chopped
2 x 400 g (14 oz) tins of chopped tomatoes
2 tablespoons tomato purée
½ tablespoon sugar
3 bay leaves, tied together with a piece of string
salt and pepper

Shell the eggs carefully. Mix the spices together and spread them out on a plate. Roll the eggs in them. Heat the oil in a roomy frying pan over a moderate heat. Fry the eggs in the oil until lightly patched with brown here and there. Don't worry that the spices float off into the oil – they'll add depth to the sauce and they will have already done a fair bit of good to the outside of the eggs. Scoop out the eggs and set aside.

Add the onion and red peppers to the pan and fry until tender. Stir in the garlic and fry for a further minute or two. Now add all the remaining ingredients and bring up to the boil. Cook for some 20–30 minutes, stirring occasionally to prevent catching, until the sauce is good and thick. Nestle the eggs down in the sauce and let it simmer for about 3–5 minutes to heat through. Pull out the bay leaves and discard. Serve with hunks of crusty bread, or spooned over rice or couscous.

Bay-scented Baked Custard with
Apricot Jam and **Clotted Cream**

Alastair Little's Winter Fruits cooked
in **Red Wine** with **Bay**

In this divinely rich pudding the custard is infused with
bay and topped with thin layers of apricot jam and clotted
cream. Bliss. Make the custards the day before they are
to be eaten, or at least in the morning for the evening, so
that they have time to cool and chill before anyone slips
their eager spoon down through the layers.

Serves 6

300 ml (½ pint) single, whipping or double cream
150 ml (¼ pint) milk
2 bay leaves
4 egg yolks
45 g (1½ oz) vanilla sugar (or caster sugar and ½ teaspoon
    vanilla extract)
2–3 tablespoons best apricot jam
85 g (3 oz) clotted cream

Pre-heat the oven to 140°C/275°F/Gas Mark 1.
    Put the cream, milk and bay leaves into a saucepan
and bring slowly up to the boil. Reduce the heat to the
merest thread and leave to infuse, stirring once or twice,
for 15 minutes or longer. Whisk the egg yolks with the
sugar until pale and thick. Gradually whisk the hot cream
mixture into the egg yolks, then stir in the vanilla extract if
you are not using vanilla sugar. Strain into 6 ramekins or
small ovenproof bowls, filling them almost but not quite
to the brim. Stand the dishes in a roasting tin and pour
enough hot water around them to come about half way
up their sides. Very carefully place in the oven and bake
for 45–60 minutes, until just set and slightly crusty. Take
out of the roasting tin and leave to cool, then chill for
several hours or overnight.
    Warm the apricot jam, without boiling, until runny.
Spread thinly over the surface of each baked custard,
then return them to the fridge for half an hour. Beat the
clotted cream lightly to loosen the consistency, then
spoon large dollops on top of the apricot jam and
smooth it over even more carefully. Chill again. If you
wish, decorate each pot with a bay leaf before serving.

Alastair Little is a keen fan of using bay leaves in sweet
dishes. Here he slips one into a spiced compote of fresh
and dried fruit. Delicious. Make the compote at least one
day before you need it.

Serves 4

1 lemon
500 ml (16 fl oz) red wine
450 g (1 lb) caster sugar
1 vanilla pod, halved
3 bay leaves
1 cinnamon stick
12 black peppercorns
4 small pears (firm but not rock-hard – not ripe enough to
    eat uncooked)
12 no-soak prunes
12 no-soak apricots

Pare a strip of the zest from the lemon. Halve the lemon.
    Put the lemon zest, wine, caster sugar, vanilla pod,
bay leaves and spices into a large non-reactive saucepan
and bring to the boil, stirring. Skim off the froth that
comes to the surface. Simmer for 30 minutes to infuse
and set aside to cool.
    Peel the pears and rub with the cut face of the lemon
to prevent discolouration. Bring the red wine syrup back
to the boil, turn down to a gentle simmer and add the
pears. You need to keep the fruit beneath the surface of
the liquid and the easiest way to achieve this is to lay a
piece of greaseproof paper over the pan and cover this
with the lid from a smaller pan to hold them down.
Simmer the pears until they're tender (about 30 minutes)
and remove from the heat.
    Add the prunes and apricots to the pears. Replace
the lid and allow to cool completely before refrigerating
overnight.
    Serve with vanilla ice cream or crème fraîche.

bouquet garni

A bouquet garni is just a little bundle of herbs, dropped into a simmering sauce, stew or soup to give a full, rounded, complementary flavour to boost the appeal of the basic, more substantial ingredients. The idea is that no single herb predominates, and that means achieving some kind of balance when you select the herbs. If this sounds offputting, don't panic. The balancing act has already been sorted out long ago, and the classic all-purpose bouquet garni, particularly good for meaty stews and sturdy soups, is a straightforward enough affair. At its simplest, all you need are parsley, bay leaves and thyme and a length of string. Made with fresh parsley and thyme (it's fine to use a dried bay leaf), this takes only a minute or so to put together and is infinitely better than most of the ready-made sachets of dried bouquet garni.

Not that the fun of a bouquet garni stops there. You can make all sorts of variations on the basic trio – maybe just to refine and add extra flavour in the form of a length of celery or the outer leaves of leek, which will hold the bundle more snugly and securely, or to add a strip of dried orange peel to bring a hint of Provence to a beef stew, or to include herbs like fennel or dill in a bouquet to perfume a sauce for fish or a fish soup. Besides choosing herbs that will work with what you are cooking, don't forget that they must all have staying power; there's little point in including herbs such as coriander and basil, which lose so much of their flavour when they are cooked for a long time. Save those for stirring in right at the end of the cooking period.

The simplest way to hold your bundle of herbs together is with a few twists of kitchen string, firmly knotted. Try to remember to leave one long trailing end, which can be tied on to the handle of the saucepan or casserole so that you can just pull the bouquet out swiftly and neatly before serving, without having to fish around for it in the hidden recesses of the pan. If you wish to include a few whole spices such as juniper berries or allspice, swaddle your collection of aromatics in a square of muslin (available from kitchen shops and, at a better price, from fabric retailers) to keep them all together. Make the square larger than you think you need at first, so that the ends can be tightly gathered up and either knotted together or secured with a piece of string, again long enough to tie on to the handle.

Here are a few selections of herbs for particular bouquets garnis, to give you a feel for the business:

All-Purpose Bouquet Garni
1 bay leaf (fresh or dried), 2 sprigs of thyme, 2 or 3 parsley stems or sprigs (you can save the leaves for something else if you wish)

Fancy All-Purpose Bouquet Garni
2 sprigs of thyme, 1 bay leaf (fresh or dried), 2 or 3 stems or sprigs of parsley, all tucked inside either a 5–7.5 cm (2–3 inch) length of celery or the outer layer of a leek

Winter Bouquet Garni for Tomato-based Stews and Sauces
1 sprig of hyssop, 1 sprig of rosemary, 1 bay leaf (fresh or dried), 1 sprig of celery leaf or a short length of celery stick

Provençal Bouquet Garni for Beef and Red Wine Stews
2 sprigs of savory or thyme, 1 bay leaf (fresh or dried), 2 sprigs of parsley, 1 strip of dried orange zest, all tucked inside either a 5–7.5 cm (2–3 inch) length of celery or the outer layer of a leek (optional)

Bouquet Garni for Lamb
1 sprig of rosemary, 1 bay leaf (fresh or dried), 2 sprigs of marjoram or oregano, 2 sprigs of parsley

Bouquet Garni for Pork
1 or 2 sage leaves, 1 bay leaf (fresh or dried), 2 sprigs of thyme, celery leaf, or a short length of celery stick into which the other herbs can be tucked

Bouquet Garni for Fish
2 sprigs of dill or fennel, 1 strip of lemon zest, 2 sprigs of parsley, a small piece of lovage leaf

Two Bouquets Garnis for Chicken
1 sprig of tarragon, 2 sprigs of marjoram, 2 sprigs of parsley, 1 strip of lemon zest

2 sprigs of lemon thyme, 1 sprig of lemon balm, 1 sprig of fennel, 1 bay leaf (fresh or dried)

Bouquet Garni for Game
1 sprig of rosemary, 4 juniper berries, 1 strip of orange zest, 1 sprig of thyme, 1 sprig of parsley

Exotic Bouquet Garni for Fish, Chicken or Other White Meats
lower part of 1 or 2 lemon grass stems, bruised, 1 kaffir lime leaf, three or four 10 cm (4 inch) lengths of Chinese chives

Sopa de Frijoles
(Latin American Bean Soup)

This soup is based on the wonderful bean soups of Latin America, with elements stolen from one country and another. Melded together they create what is, paradoxically, my idea of the perfect cold-weather, winter comfort food, filling and richly flavoured with a flurry of fresh garnishes that lift it from mere starchy warmth into a joy of a dish.

Sometimes I flavour the soup with tomato but I love it, too, made with coconut milk, which blends gently with the soft beans. The results are different but both are very good. The soup can be made a day in advance and tastes all the better for being reheated. The quantities below make a filling main course for six or a less substantial but still sturdy first course for 8–10, which could simply be followed with good bread, a salad and some well-chosen cheese, or cured meats and sausages.

Serves 6–10

500 g (1 lb 2 oz) pinto beans, or mixed dried beans
110 g (4 oz) pancetta, bacon or *lardons*, diced
2 onions, chopped
2 large carrots, diced
2 celery sticks, diced
4 garlic cloves, chopped
3 tablespoons sunflower or vegetable oil
1 heaped tablespoon cumin seeds
1 tablespoon dried oregano
either 2 x 400 g (14 oz) tins of chopped tomatoes or
    600 ml (1 pint) coconut milk (see p. 14)
4 tablespoons dry sherry
juice of 1 lime
salt and pepper

For the bouquet garni
3 sprigs of parsley,
2 sprigs of savory or thyme
2 bay leaves
1 small sprig of rosemary

To serve
150 ml (¼ pint) soured cream or crème fraîche
1 avocado, peeled, stoned and diced at the last minute
6 spring onions, thinly sliced
2 red chillies, deseeded and very finely chopped
a small bunch of coriander, roughly chopped
2 limes, cut into wedges

Herbes de Provence

Tie the herbs for the bouquet garni together with string. Soak the beans for 4 hours, then drain thoroughly. Sweat the pancetta, onions, carrots, celery, garlic and bouquet garni in the oil over a low heat for 10–15 minutes. Now add the beans and enough water to cover by about 7.5 cm (3 inches). Bring up to the boil and boil hard for 10 minutes, reduce the heat and simmer gently, covered, until the beans are very tender – around 1–2 hours.

Now add the cumin, oregano, tomatoes or coconut milk, sherry, lime juice, salt and pepper. Simmer for another 30 minutes, stirring occasionally with a wooden spoon and crushing some of the beans against the side of the pan, until you have a thick soup, studded with whole beans. Remove the bouquet garni. Taste and adjust the seasoning (starchy beans appreciate plenty of salt).

Reheat the soup thoroughly when ready to serve, adding a splash of water if it seems overly thick. Put all the serving bits and bobs into small bowls and arrange them in the centre of the table. Ladle the hot soup into bowls and pass around, encouraging people to help themselves from the selection of garnishes in the bowls.

This is a heady mixture of herbs from the South of France, made up of a variable group chosen from savory (*sarriette* in French), the wild thyme known as *serpolet*, rosemary, marjoram, oregano, hyssop, basil, bay and possibly even lavender flowers. In home territory in the hot summer months, they may be added fresh to meat stews, game, tomato dishes and braised vegetable dishes, but they are also dried, crumbled and mixed for winter cooking, which is how we usually get them abroad, packaged in jaunty little jars at vast expense. One of the easiest ways to capture that scent of a hot Mediterranean summer is to rub the herbs into chicken, fish or chops before cooking, along with a touch of olive oil, freshly ground pepper and coarse sea salt. If you grow your own herbs, it will be a pleasure to create your own 'Provençal' mixture, either for yourself or to give as presents when cold weather comes.

wild garlic
Allium ursinum

Have you ever, while strolling through damp woods or narrow lanes in spring or early summer, suddenly been assaulted by the reek of garlic? Quite likely, as wild garlic grows prolifically throughout the British Isles. With its dazzling clusters of white star flowers and broad, bright-green leaves, curved like those of a tulip or lily of the valley, it is one of our most beautiful woodland plants, and also one of our most useful, though it is often overlooked. Its other name, as pretty as the flowers themselves, is ramsons, which has given us many a country place name: Ramsbottom (wild garlic valley) and Ramsey (wild garlic island), for instance.

In French it is known as *ail des ours*, in German *Bärlauch*, and even in Latin it is *Allium ursinum*, all three of them meaning bear garlic. Why? For the obvious reason – bears, real wild bears, just can't get enough of it. Over the past few years the big bears of the smarter restaurant kitchens have wised up to it, too. Nowadays finding wild garlic on the menu comes as little surprise. It can be used raw, though the scent is fairly pungent so it pays to be a little cautious. Spring leaves are the mildest and tenderest and this is the best time for using it raw. Try adding some shredded or chopped leaves to a mixed green salad to get a feel for the taste. Later on they toughen up a little and it makes more sense to cook them, though only the lightest heat will be necessary when they are chopped. Chopped leaves, or the whole small early leaves that push up in March or April, are excellent stirred into scrambled eggs or sautéed briefly in butter to fill an omelette. Wild garlic goes well, raw or cooked depending on your preference and the time of year, in buttery mashed potatoes. I love a simple potato and wild garlic soup, made roughly along the same lines as a potato and leek soup. The fresh garlicky scent goes admirably with lamb – try the sauce on p. 40, or simply sweat the leaves in butter or stir-fry them and serve alongside the lamb. Try it, too, stirred into haricot beans that have been cooked with a bouquet garni, then liquidized in part with some of their cooking juices.

Opposite
**Clockwise from top left: chives; wild garlic leaves and flowers; Chinese chives with buds; garlic; elephant garlic
Centre above: smoked garlic**

Add plenty of wild garlic and a big knob of butter, season well and you have something along the lines of the famous French dish of garlic beans, but prettier with its streaks of vivid green.

I love wild garlic with fish. You might wrap the leaves round fillets of mackerel or trout and then steam them (see p. 42), or whizz it up in a food processor (young leaves only) with lemon zest, a few squirts of juice, a little parsley and some butter, then chill to form a garlic leaf butter to perch on grilled tuna or monkfish. Thrown into stir-fries it adds a delicious flavour, rather like a garlicky spinach leaf. Dipped into batter (try the one on p. 26) and deep-fried, ramsons fritters make a pretty and unexpected first course (serve them with wedges of lemon and a finely diced tomato and basil salsa). In fact, once you've located a sure source of wild garlic and got a taste for it you will find that it marries well with all sorts of foods. Just one note of warning, though: when you go gathering, doublecheck every time that what you are picking is genuine wild garlic – there's no mistaking the smell but if you are in any doubt at all, leave well alone.

Storage and Preservation

Wild garlic is best used within a day or two of being picked. If you do have to keep it, pop it into an airtight container or wrap in clingfilm and store in a cool place to prevent the pungent aroma bursting out and contaminating other things. If you can avoid putting it in the fridge, so much the better. Garlicky milk in your tea is not one of the world's great treats.

It is not, I think, a herb that looks to be preserved. Part of the pleasure of using wild garlic, besides the flavour it imparts, is its immediacy, following a stroll in the fresh air to harvest it. Look forward to it in the spring, enjoy the fact that it is free, and return to ordinary bulb garlic when the season is over.

From Sue's excellent book, *Fruits of the Forest*, which contains many inspiring recipes for using wild foods, comes this simple, delightful recipe for a spring green garlic sauce to serve with lamb or fish.

Serves 4

about 80 g (scant 3 oz) wild garlic leaves, roughly chopped
25 g (scant 1 oz) butter
250 ml (8 fl oz) chicken or fish stock
125 ml (4 fl oz) whipping or double cream
salt and pepper

Soften the garlic leaves in the butter over a low to moderate heat. Add the stock, cream and a little salt and pepper. Bring up to the boil and simmer for 15–20 minutes. Liquidize, then rub through a sieve. Taste and adjust the seasoning, then reheat when needed.

Wild Garlic Bubble and Squeak

'When midst the frying Pan, in accents savage
The Beef so surly, quarrels with the Cabbage'
wrote Dr William Kitchiner back in 1817. In those days,
bubble and squeak was made of cold roast beef, onion
and cooked cabbage all fried up together. Potato didn't
get a look in until near the end of the century, and
eventually the beef disappeared altogether. What we
think of now as classic bubble and squeak is composed
largely of potatoes and cabbage. Replacing some or
all of the cabbage with wild garlic, gathered from the
hedgerows, is my new version of this classic dish,
updated for the end of another century.

Serves 4

300 g (10 oz) green cabbage, Savoy cabbage or kale, cored
    and chopped
2–3 tablespoons beef dripping, bacon fat or butter
1 onion, chopped
about 60 g (2 oz) wild garlic
60 g (2 oz) prosciutto or pancetta, cut into thin strips (optional)
salt and pepper

For the mash
600 g (1 lb 5 oz) floury potatoes (give or take)
30 g (1 oz) butter
2 tablespoons milk

Either bake the potatoes in their skins until tender or
cook them in the microwave (pierce the skins with a
skewer or a fork, then place, uncovered, on a plate and
microwave for 8–12 minutes, turning the plate several
times, until tender). Halve the potatoes and scoop out the
flesh. You should have about 500 g (1 lb 2 oz) – leftover
skins could be saved for the recipe on p. 112. Put the
potato flesh in a saucepan and mash thoroughly while
still hot. Add the butter and some salt and place over a
low heat. Beat thoroughly, gradually working in the milk
to give a moderately stiff mash.

Meanwhile, bring a pan of salted water to the boil and
add the cabbage or kale. Simmer for about 4–5 minutes,
until just tender, then drain and squeeze out all the water
with your hands.

Shortly before serving, mix the potato with the
cabbage or kale, then taste and adjust the seasoning.
Heat half the dripping, bacon fat or butter in a wide frying
pan until it foams or sizzles. Add the onion, wild garlic
and prosciutto or pancetta and fry gently until the onion is
tender and the garlic miserably limp. Scrape out and mix
with the potato and cabbage. Add the remaining fat to
the pan, heat through, then dollop in the potato mixture,
and smooth down.

Fry over a moderate heat for about 8 minutes, until
the underneath is browned. Carefully slide the bubble
and squeak out on to a dish, then return the pan to the
heat. Invert the bubble and squeak on to another plate,
then slide back into the pan. Cook until lightly browned
underneath and then serve piping hot.

Wild Garlic Wrapped Mackerel Fillets with Red Pepper Marmalade

A real star of a dish this, gloriously pretty with its reds, fresh green and yellow, and very good to eat too. The added bonus is that it is rather cheap. Mackerel are very good value, the wild garlic is free, onions are hardly exorbitant and the one small extravagance is the brace of red peppers. Serve it either as a very stylish first course or as a main course.

If you don't have a purpose-made steamer you can rig up a replacement with a wide saucepan (to take the water), a large sieve (to act as the steamer basket) and a large sheet of silver foil (the essential lid).

Serves 4 as a first course, 2 as a main course

2 fine mackerel, filleted
a couple of handfuls of wild garlic leaves
salt and pepper
4 lemon wedges, to serve

For the red pepper marmalade
15 g (½ oz) butter
1 tablespoon sunflower oil
2 red peppers, deseeded and cut into thin strips
1 onion, halved and thinly sliced
½ star anise
1 dried bird's eye chilli
2 tablespoons caster sugar
1 tablespoon red wine vinegar

The marmalade can be made in advance and reheated when needed. Melt the butter with the oil in a heavy pan over a low heat. Add the peppers, onion, star anise and chilli. Stir to coat lightly in the fat, then cover and leave to sweat for about 25 minutes, stirring once or twice, until both onion and pepper are limp and tangled. Now remove the chilli and discard, then add the sugar, vinegar and a little salt. Stir, cover again, and continue to cook for 7–8 minutes, stirring once. Taste and adjust the seasoning, then reheat gently when required.

Now for the mackerel. Choices, choices. Do you want a) to swaddle the fillets individually in blanched garlic, which will take a little longer to prepare but looks by far the most fetching, or b) to cook them on a bed of garlic leaves, which requires almost zilch preparation but looks rather messier?

If the answer is a), proceed as follows. Cut the mackerel fillets in half lengthways, slicing on either side of the central line so that the row of fine bones can just be thrown straight out. Season with salt and pepper. Bring a pan of water to the boil (I use the bottom of the steamer – saves on washing up), and drop a handful of garlic leaves into it. Scoop out swiftly after 8–10 seconds and lay on kitchen paper or a clean tea towel to sop up excess water. One by one, wrap the garlic leaves around the long, thin pieces of mackerel, enclosing them entirely. Blanch a second handful of leaves once the first have been used up. Lay the swaddled fillets in the steamer basket set over boiling water, making sure that the water does not bubble up over them, cover tightly and steam for 5 minutes and no more.

And if the answer is b), just line the steamer basket with a blanket of garlic leaves, lay the fillets, seasoned with salt and pepper, on top, then cover with another snug blanket of leaves. Steam for 5 minutes over boiling water, tightly covered, until just cooked through.

To serve, reheat the pepper marmalade, then either spread out in a warm serving dish or divide between warmed serving plates, mounding it up in the centre. Lay the mackerel and garlic leaves on top of the marmalade, then perch the lemon wedges on top of that. Serve immediately.

Opposite
**Wild Garlic
Wrapped
Mackerel
Fillets with
Red Pepper
Marmalade**

garlic
Allium sativum

Is garlic a herb? Well, that's highly debatable and depends largely on how you define a herb in the first place. We batted the possibilities about, argued, and in the end decided that garlic, fresh garlic, was such a quintessential, universal flavouring for food that we would include it anyway.

Not long ago, I eavesdropped – accidentally, of course – on two grey women out shopping one Sunday morning. They were choosing frozen pizzas. 'Ooh, has that one got garlic on it? Ooh, nooo, no, no, then I don't want that one. Have a look at the others for me.' This went on for some while, these poor women scared stiff by the very thought of beastly foreign garlic. What an anachronism in this day and age. Garlic-fearers are a dying breed. At the time I longed to butt in and ask them why on earth they wanted pizzas if they didn't like garlic. Wouldn't something a little more British have been easier to deal with? But I didn't. I left them to it and wandered away, intent on laying in a stock of whole heads of garlic so that I could roast them in their entirety that evening to smear on toasted bread.

I can still remember the first time I presented friends with this as a first course at a dinner party. It was in the early eighties, before the greater part of the country was at ease with the stuff. My friends hesitated but, being loyal and true, they tucked in and discovered what bliss slowly roasted garlic is, mellow and creamy with an underlying pungency that tickles gently as the taste fills the mouth.

And there, of course, is the sheer glory of garlic, something that the uninitiated have yet to understand. It does not have to be the devilishly exciting foreigner that induces fear. Mind you, in my book, the powerful flavour of raw garlic is something to be relished anyway, but it is only one facet of this multi-purpose, multi-form member of the Allium clan. Fried in thin slices until just golden brown, it becomes crisp, nutty and fragrant. Chopped more finely and then fried, it can meld its power with onions, tomatoes, spices and what-have-you, tickling all it meets into form, without necessarily taking over. When

it is cooked slowly and gently in whole cloves, garlic tastes utterly different, as mild and mellow as finely chopped raw garlic is raucous and pungent. Take poached garlic – if you simmer the whole peeled cloves in water for a few minutes, then drain and finish poaching in a little milk until tender, what you end up with has no bitterness at all. Use it to make a caressing garlic sauce to go with fish, perhaps, by using the poaching milk to make a white sauce, then puréeing the poached cloves into it. Or you might process them with a little of the milk and some onions that have been slowly sweated to a sweet tenderness with a small knob of butter.

When I was researching recipes for my book *Fish* (written with my husband, William Black) I came across an extraordinary recipe for fish served with a purée made from candied garlic, olive oil and parsley. The whole cloves of garlic are simmered in a sugar syrup for almost an hour, until tender and translucent. The result is fabulous, and reveals yet another dimension to the flavour of garlic.

The key to manipulating the pungency of garlic lies in its chemistry. You will notice that an untampered-with raw head of garlic does not smell. If you break off a clove without tearing the skin away to expose the insides, your nose will remain unassaulted. Peel it and you are bound to break into the interior in some small way, releasing a little of the juice. The smell is minimal. It's only when you start to cut into the clove that the familiar waft rises up.

This is because what we think of as the characteristic smell of garlic comes into existence only when the cell walls are damaged. A virtually instant chemical chain reaction takes place, releasing amongst other minor elements a powerful sulphurous compound...and the pungent scent of garlic is on the loose. The more the clove is cut into, the stronger the smell becomes.

The lesson to be learned from all this chemistry is simple. If you want lots of garlicky flavour but want to keep it unaggressive, leave the garlic cloves whole. Sliced garlic gives a gentle hit of pungency, while for a more insistent dose, chopped garlic does the business. And when you want to shout garlic loud and strong, crush the cloves brutally. It is sometimes said that garlic crushed with a garlic-crusher is more bitter than garlic crushed with a knife. I'm not entirely convinced that this is so, except perhaps that the crusher is more efficient than the knife, so more of the all-important enzyme is released.

There is a large number of different types of garlic around, which is one of the reasons I like to stock up when I am in France, where vendors can usually tell me which ones will keep well and which are for immediate use. When I run out of my French garlic I take pot-luck at the supermarket, hoping for larger, less fiddly cloves, though smaller ones can often be just as finely flavoured and pungent. Pink-skinned, purple-skinned, white-skinned – in the end it is a simple matter of personal preference, allied to what is available.

Most of the garlic that we buy has been cured – in other words, semi-dried – so that it keeps at least for a few months, but in the summer, around about June, look out for fresh garlic that has just been harvested. The fat cloves will be very juicy, mild and a little sweeter in taste. It can be used in just the same ways as cured garlic but takes longer to cook, particularly if you are roasting it whole. Elephant garlic has, as you might well imagine, enormous cloves, which beg to be treated more as a vegetable than as seasoning – poached or roasted whole, or sliced and fried to a crisp, literally. Smoked garlic is becoming increasingly available in supermarkets, though I have to say that I am not greatly enamoured of it. The smoky scent is nice enough but not an improvement on the original, and not that noticeable when the garlic is used in relatively small quantity in sauces. The best use I've found for it is mashed in generous quantity to a paste with sea salt and olive oil, then smeared between the skin and flesh of a chicken before roasting.

And finally, two quick tips on peeling garlic, which is a sticky job if you have to tackle more than one or two cloves. If the garlic is to be chopped up, then you will find that the easiest way to remove the skin is to top and tail the clove first, then lay it on the work surface, place the flat of a knife blade over it and give it a good bash, smashing the garlic down. After that the papery skin just falls away. When you want to keep the cloves whole, what you need is a garlic-peeling tube. Watch out for them in good kitchen shops – they look something like wobbly plastic cannelloni. The clove goes inside, you roll it around briefly and Bob's your uncle, the little dear is soon stark naked.

Storage and Preservation

Since most of the garlic we buy has been cured, it should keep well, as long as you treat it right. Small earthenware garlic pots, pierced with holes, are brilliant for the head of garlic that is in current use, keeping it in good condition for a week or two, despite the humidity of a kitchen. Otherwise, don't keep your garlic anywhere near the kitchen or it will soon moulder and rot. It needs to be stored in a cool, dry place (I hang plaits of garlic up in our porch) but away from frost. Depending on the type of garlic, it should last perfectly well for months.

Baked Garlic and Goat's Cheese Custards

Sweet-Sour Garlic and Oil Preserve

This is about as subtle as you can get with a dozen cloves of garlic. I bet that even fervent garlic-o-phobes would be hard put to identify the delicate flavour of these savoury baked custards. Serve them as a first course, with a little mixed leaf salad if you wish to dress them up.

Serves 6

12 garlic cloves, peeled but left whole
300 ml (½ pint) milk
1 bay leaf
1 small sprig of thyme
125 g (4 oz) goat's cheese, crumbled
150 ml (¼ pint) double cream
1 egg
2 egg yolks
salt and pepper

Pre-heat the oven to 150°C/300°F/Gas Mark 2.

Cover the cloves of garlic with cold water, bring to the boil and simmer for 1 minute. Drain thoroughly, then repeat. Now simmer the garlic in the milk (uncovered) with the bay leaf and thyme until very tender – about 15 minutes. Fish out the bay leaf and thyme stalk and discard. Put the garlic and about half the milk into a food processor with the crumbled goat's cheese and whizz to a cream. Beat in the remaining milk, the cream, egg, egg yolks and some salt and pepper.

Pour into 6 small ramekins and stand them in a roasting tin. Pour in enough hot water to come about half way up their sides. Bake for about 35 minutes, until set but still slightly wobbly in the middle. Serve hot or warm.

Opposite
**Three Allium
Tart**
(page 57)

These pickled garlic cloves are so very good that I've just had to include the recipe, although it has already been published in a previous book. Nutty, tender, juicy, they are lovely eaten with cheeses or cold cured meats but I also like to use them in cooking – maybe adding some to stir-fries or stews. They take a couple of weeks to mature in their oil and will continue to improve if left for a month or two longer. If you have the patience to peel all those cloves, they make a good present for garlic-loving friends. Straight extra virgin olive oil gives the best flavour but if you prefer something lighter (on the purse as well as the mouth), then mix it half and half with sunflower oil. Don't waste the oil, either, since it will have taken on a fine flavour of its own. Use it for cooking, making salads or as a condiment to drizzle over a simple vegetable soup.

Fills one 500 ml/17 fl oz jar

4 large or 8 small heads of garlic
300 ml (½ pint) white wine vinegar
300 ml (½ pint) water
150 g (5 oz) caster sugar
2 teaspoons cumin seeds
2 teaspoons coriander seeds
2 whole star anise
2 dried red chillies
extra virgin olive oil
sunflower oil (optional)

Separate the cloves and peel the whole lot of them. Put the vinegar, water, sugar, and spices into a pan and bring up to the boil, stirring until the sugar has dissolved. Simmer for 5 minutes, then add the garlic cloves and reduce the heat. Simmer very gently for 10–15 minutes, until the garlic is barely tender. Lift the cloves out with a slotted spoon, bringing as many of the spices with them as you can. Leave to drain in a sieve.

Pack into sterilized, but cold, jars (see p. 150). Pour in enough olive oil, or olive oil mixed with sunflower oil, to cover completely. Let them stand for an hour or so to settle, then top up with oil if necessary. Seal tightly, label, then store in a cool, dark cupboard for at least 2 weeks before using.

Antonio Carluccio's Stracciatella all'Aglio (Garlic Soup)

Stracciatella is a marvellous Italian soup made with a good, flavourful stock and then lightly thickened with eggs and cream. Antonio Carluccio, who uses garlic with gleeful abandon, showed me how to make his favourite version of stracciatella, subtly or outrageously scented with garlic depending on your personal taste for the stuff. Antonio disapproves strongly of mucking about with this most essential of flavourings and was rather sniffy about the merits of elephant garlic or, worse still, smoked garlic. I didn't dare suggest that you could possibly use smoked garlic, or one giant clove of elephant garlic, but I am tempted to try in the secrecy of my own home. The quantity of garlic used here makes a moderately garlicky soup. For more pungency, add another couple of cloves.

Serves 4–6

1 litre (1¾ pints) very good chicken or vegetable stock
6 garlic cloves, very finely sliced
4 egg yolks
2 whole eggs
6 tablespoons double cream
salt and pepper

To serve
4–6 slices of country or ciabatta bread, I.5 cm
     (about ½ inch) thick, well toasted
2 garlic cloves, cut in half
extra virgin olive oil
freshly grated Parmesan
1 small bunch of chives, snipped

Bring the stock to the boil in a saucepan, then add the slices of garlic and boil for 3–5 minutes. While the stock boils, rub each slice of bread with the cut side of a clove of garlic, then drizzle about 1 teaspoon of olive oil over it. Pile the slices of bread up on a warm plate.

In a bowl, beat the egg yolks and whole eggs together, then whisk in the double cream. Season. Pour the egg mixture into the boiling soup, whisking the soup constantly. Quickly draw the pan off the heat, whisk for a few seconds more, and the soup is done.

Pour the soup into individual serving bowls and sprinkle thickly with Parmesan. Place the bread on the soup, pressing it down a little so that it soaks up some of the broth. Sprinkle with the chives and serve immediately.

Algerian Garlic Meat Balls in Garlic Broth

This is a richly flavoured main-course stew, redolent of slow-cooked mellow garlic and very restorative on a cold day. The meat balls jostle for space with chickpeas (if you have time, soak and cook your own rather than using tinned ones) and rice. Serve with rounds of Arab pitta bread and scoop up straying chickpeas.

Serves 4–6

1 head of garlic
4 tablespoons olive oil
1 large onion, finely chopped
1 cinnamon stick
3 sprigs of thyme
1 bay leaf
1 litre (1¾ pints) chicken or meat stock
2 tomatoes, skinned, deseeded and chopped
1 carrot, sliced
2 tablespoons tomato purée
4 tablespoons long grain rice, rinsed
250 g (9 oz) cooked chickpeas
a couple of squeezes of lemon juice
salt and pepper

For the meat balls
500 g (1 lb 2 oz) minced beef or lamb
1 small bunch of coriander, finely chopped
½ onion, grated or finely chopped
1 teaspoon ground cinnamon
1 egg, lightly beaten

Break the head of garlic up into cloves and peel them, then process the whole lot roughly. Heat the olive oil in a large pan and fry the onion until tender. Add two-thirds of the garlic and the cinnamon stick and stir around for a few minutes. Now add the herbs, stock, chopped tomatoes, carrot and salt and pepper and bring up to the boil. Simmer gently for 40 minutes.

Meanwhile, make the meat balls. Mix the remaining garlic with the minced meat, coriander, onion, cinnamon, some salt and pepper and enough beaten egg to bind. Roll into walnut-sized balls. Once the broth has been simmering for its allotted 40 minutes, add the tomato purée, meat balls and rice. Simmer for 15 minutes, then add the chickpeas and simmer for a final 3–4 minutes to heat through. Stir in a couple of squeezes of lemon juice, then taste and adjust the seasoning. Serve immediately.

Slow-roast Leg of Lamb with Whole Heads of Garlic

Garlic lovers will take to this dish with enthusiasm but, in truth, it does not turn out impossibly strong, since most of the garlic is cooked whole and so remains fairly mild and creamy (and avoidable for the really nervous, though the garlic is actually the best bit). The recipe is inspired by Catalan ways of cooking lamb and my usual way of roasting garlic. Choose nice, plump heads of garlic and don't be tempted to rush things along. The whole point is that both the lamb and the garlic should end up meltingly tender.

Serves 6

1.5–2 kg (3 lb–4 lb 8 oz) boned leg of lamb, cut into
    6 sizeable chunks
8 garlic cloves, peeled and cut into slivers
125 ml (4 fl oz) olive oil
6 whole heads of garlic
2 sprigs of rosemary
3 sprigs of thyme
300 ml (½ pint) sweet sherry
salt and pepper
chopped parsley, to garnish

Pre-heat the oven to 220°C/425°F/Gas Mark 7.

Make slits in the chunks of lamb with a small knife and push in slivers of garlic, using up about a third of them. Brown the chunks of lamb, two or three at a time, in a third of the oil over a high heat. As they brown, transfer them to a large oiled roasting tin or ovenproof dish. Nestle the whole heads of garlic and the rosemary and thyme sprigs amongst them, then scatter over the remaining slivered garlic. Drizzle the remaining oil over the whole lot.

Roast in the hot oven for 20 minutes, then pour over the sherry, season generously with salt and pepper and cover the dish tightly with foil. Return to the oven and reduce the heat to 180°C/350°F/Gas Mark 4. Roast for a further 3½–4½ hours, basting frequently with the pan juices. If the pan threatens to dry out, add a splash or two of hot water and then make sure that the foil really is covering the dish properly. The lamb is done when it is so tender that a fork just slides through it like softened butter. Remove the foil, sprinkle with parsley and take to the table.

Give each diner a chunk of lamb and a whole head of garlic, moistened with some of the pan juices. To eat the garlic, squeeze the cloves with the flat of a knife and the softened flesh will ooze out like toothpaste from a tube. Either smear it on to the lamb or scoop it up with good bread.

chives
Allium schoenoprasum

Chives are one of the first herbs to poke their heads up into the cool air of early spring. Brave and determined, the small tufts of thin, green spears follow hard on the heels of snowdrops, a sign that winter is on its way out and that lighter, fresher foods are on the horizon. A joyful sight. For such slender stems they are unexpectedly sturdy, withstanding the cold of spring and thriving, with the minimum of attention, right through to the first stiff frosts of autumn. They are amiable garden companions, growing happily in most soils and in most locations, in the garden in light shade or sun, in pots on the patio, in windowboxes. They can withstand dry patches, though they prefer a modicum of damp, and will be quite happy near ponds and rivers.

Chives just love to be cut. The more you use them, the happier they will be and the longer they will last into the dark days of the year. Jolly good news, for chives are the easiest, sweetest, lightest way to introduce the scent of onions, without viciousness, into salads, soups and egg dishes. Snipped (it is generally so much easier to cut bunches of chives with scissors) straight over the bowl, they tumble down in a rich green shower to invigorate what lies below. Even a plain green salad will be improved by a generous scattering, though they make a bigger impact still on cucumber, tomato, beetroot or potato salads (add loads of them to mayonnaise-dressed potato salads to spike the starchiness of the potatoes). Talking of potatoes, chives are brilliant stirred, again with generosity, into buttery mash. For sandwiches, stir chopped chives into cream cheese or young goat's cheese. To make a dipping sauce or a fresh, light relish for grilled fish, stir them into thick Greek yoghurt with chopped mint.

Any composite dish crowned with a poached egg takes well to a helping of chives. For a quick, luxurious lunch or supper, stir snipped chives into soft, creamy scrambled eggs, together with a dash of lemon juice, and dish them up with smoked salmon on toasted bagels or brioche.

Those same scrambled eggs make a light, summery first course, piled into hollowed-out tomatoes and lightly warmed through in the oven. Then there is that classic of French home cooking, the omelette, which should be cooked only until the top is nearly set, but still a mite creamy and runny – *baveuse*. Stir the chives into the eggs before they are added to the pan. If you want to take the French route, then mix the chives with parsley, tarragon and chervil to make *fines herbes*, the quintessential Gallic herb blend. The amount of cooking they get in an omelette is about their limit. Chives are not kitted out for the rigours of long, slow braising, or even violent brief bursts of heat. They wilt and waste away to nothingness. Small amounts of relatively gentle heat can help release their flavour but that is about the limit. What it boils down to, if you will excuse the poor pun, is that chives are a last-minute herb, by and large, which is why they are so good sprinkled over soups and sauces, the pretty flashes of green and gentle onioniness animating the whole very nicely, thank you.

The purple pom-poms of the flowers are lovely to see and they are every bit as edible as the hollow-stemmed chives themselves. If you are partial to the sight and taste of them in salads and what-have-you, it pays to grow two distinct groups of chives, the first for the stalks themselves, the second for the flowers. This is the only way to get good supplies of both, for if you leave the plant to flower you will find that the stems weaken and die back more quickly.

Storage and Preservation
Chives wilt and turn floppy speedily once cut. By all means wrap them in dampened kitchen paper and tuck them into a plastic bag in the vegetable drawer of the fridge but don't expect them to last much more than a day or two in prime form. Though you can buy freeze-dried chives, and you could in theory dry your own, I really can't see any point in attempting to preserve them. Chives should be used fresh.

Beetroot, Potato, Apple and Chive Salad

A salad of home-cooked beetroot (always so much nicer than the ready-cooked stuff), dressed with a mustardy vinaigrette and sprinkled copiously with chopped chives, makes a perfect first course with hunks of good bread to mop up the scarlet juices. This is a more substantial salad, with potato and sweet nuggets of apple, too, dressed with mayonnaise or soured cream. More complicated it may be but the chives still play an important role in seasoning the combination of flavours and textures. Serve as a first course, or with smoked chicken or smoked fish – particularly eel if you can get it.

Serves 4–6

300–325 g (10–11 oz) raw beetroot (or cooked if you are short of time)
1 crisp apple
lemon juice
250 g (9 oz) new potatoes or waxy salad potatoes, cooked in their skins and sliced
3 tablespoons chopped chives, plus a few extra to garnish
4 tablespoons mayonnaise (or 4 tablespoons soured cream and ½ tablespoon tarragon vinegar or white wine vinegar)
salt and pepper

To cook the beetroot, trim off the stalks about 2.5 cm (1 inch) away from the beetroot itself. Do not cut off the long tapering root. Wash the beetroot clean as necessary, trying not to pierce the skin. Wrap each sphere in silver foil. Place in a roasting tin and roast in a slow oven, around 170°C/325°F/Gas Mark 3 (though the exact temperature is not something to worry about – a little warmer or cooler, if you happen to be using the oven for other things as well, will not matter too much) for about 1½–2 hours, depending on their size, until the skin scrapes easily away from the root end of one of the largest spheres. Cool slightly, then peel and cut into 1 cm (½ inch) chunks.

Quarter and core the apple (but do not peel), then dice and toss in a little lemon juice to prevent browning. Mix together the apple, beetroot, potatoes, chives, mayonnaise (or soured cream and vinegar), salt and pepper. Taste and adjust the seasoning, then sprinkle with chives. Serve at room temperature.

Zwiebelkuchen

This German tart-come-pizza, like the similar *zewelwai* from across the border in Alsace, takes onions, chives and bacon bathed in cream and eggs as its topping. *Zwiebelkuchen* is made with a yeasted dough whereas *zewelwai* comes closer to a quiche Lorraine with its shortcrust. I love the bready base but if you fancy something more refined, put much the same oniony mixture into a shortcrust pastry case, increasing the quantity of eggs and cream to fill it up.

Serves 6

90 g (3 oz) good back bacon (or *lardons*), cut into strips
45 g (1½ oz) goose fat, lard or butter
3 large onions, very thinly sliced
2 large eggs
250 ml (9 fl oz) crème fraîche or soured cream
1 teaspoon caraway seeds
2 tablespoons chopped chives
salt and pepper

For the dough
450 g (1 lb) strong white flour
7 g sachet of easy-blend yeast
2 teaspoons salt
90 g (3 oz) goose fat, lard or butter, softened
175 ml (6 fl oz) milk
175 ml (6 fl oz) water

To make the dough, put the flour, yeast, salt and fat into a food processor and process briefly to mix. Mix the milk and water together. Set the processor running and gradually trickle in enough liquid to form a soft, slightly sticky dough. Take out and knead on a lightly floured board until smooth and elastic. Place in a clean bowl, cover with a cloth and leave in a warm place for 30 minutes or until about doubled in bulk.

Pre-heat the oven to 220°C/425°F/Gas Mark 7.

For the filling, fry the bacon in half the fat until lightly browned. Now add about half the onions to the pan and put the remainder in the remaining fat in a second pan (unless you have an extra large frying pan, in which case fry the whole lot together). Fry both for about 10 minutes, until limp. Mix them all together and allow to cool slightly.

Punch the dough down, knead lightly and scrape out on to a greased 30 x 20 cm (12 x 8 inch) baking sheet. Press it out to the edges with your hands. Spread the onions and bacon over it, leaving just a narrow bare border. Beat the eggs with the cream, caraway seeds and plenty of salt and pepper. Spoon over the onions and bacon. Bake for 25 minutes or until the border is browned and crisp and the gooey mixture just about set. Scatter over the chives, then serve hot, cut into bite-size wedges or squares.

Theoretically, this is to be partnered with sauerkraut but I like it better with a tomato or rocket salad.

Chinese chives
Allium tuberosum

Chinese chives are, as you would expect, closely related to ordinary chives, both members of the powerful, ubiquitous Allium clan, which includes their big, bulbous brothers onions and garlic. Where ordinary chives echo the raunchy vitality of the onion, Chinese chives present a softened version of raw garlic, hence their alternative name, garlic chives. Sturdier looking, flattened and long, with pretty white flowers, they can claim close kinship with the most ancient of chives, which were recorded almost 5,000 years ago in China. One of the earliest recipes for chives, cooked with scrambled egg, appears in a sixth-century manuscript, and later the intrepid explorer Marco Polo was to remark upon their use.

In China, where relatively few herbs are used in cooking, Chinese chives are employed with considerable enthusiasm as both flavouring and vegetable combined, a tip that we might well consider. Like ordinary chives, they are not suited to prolonged cooking, though they can take a little more exposure to heat without losing their character. They can be used in all the same ways as garden chives, making allowances where necessary for their garlicky presence, but they also slide happily into a wok, where they make a delicious partner for chicken, pork, seafood, tofu, aubergine, courgettes and other vegetables. A brief spurt of stir-frying brings them to their sweetest and most exalted state. The key is to use them with a generous hand. In their native land they are also added to the fillings for steamed dumplings and pasties and stirred generously into soups.

As well as the flat green leaves, you may well come across two other forms of Chinese chives if you are rootling around in a Chinese supermarket. The flower buds, little fat tips on long, strong, juicy green stems, are usually sold separately (special varieties are grown for their flowering stems alone) and can be used in much the same way as Chinese chives, though they are particularly suited to stir-frying. When preparing them, discard the lower part of the stem if it is at all tough and stringy, as it may well be.

Even more highly rated are the tender, floppy, light-deprived Chinese yellow chives, grown in the dark. They are quite a delicacy and are usually reserved for special occasions. So delicate are they that they are stir-fried all on their own, so that they cannot possibly overcook, then mixed with other ingredients. If you want to try them, mix the cooked chives with briefly stir-fried scallops or prawns scented with ginger, a shake or two of rice wine or sherry and a dash or two of soy sauce and sesame oil. I rather like to add a little lemon grass too, for extra fragrance. Naturally, you can use them raw as well, chopped and scattered into salads, egg dishes or anywhere else you might want to employ a light, chivey scent.

Storage and Preservation

Chinese chives should be used up fairly swiftly though they have more staying power than ordinary chives. To extend their life to all of a couple of days, wrap them in dry kitchen paper, slip into a plastic bag and slide into the vegetable drawer of the fridge. I've found that the flower buds on their strong stems will keep far more happily, for a week or more, stored in the same way. Yellow chives are an altogether different matter, and really must be used up within 24 hours before they start to degenerate into an unsightly, costly state of no return.

In some parts of China, Chinese chives are salted for long conservation but that's not something I'd suggest undertaking at home. Enjoy Chinese chives when you find them, or grow your own, and be content with that.

I can never resist a big plateful of noodles and these ones, dressed Chinese style with Chinese chives and oyster sauce, are very satisfying. They make an excellent meat-free meal (for vegetarians, make sure you buy the special vegetarian versions of oyster sauce) on their own or you can serve them with some simply cooked poultry or fish.

Serves 3–4

400 g (14 oz) fresh flat or ribbon egg noodles
2 tablespoons groundnut or sunflower oil
1 tablespoon sesame oil
4 cm (1½ inch) fresh root ginger, very finely chopped
1 bunch of Chinese chives (about 30–45 g/1–1½ oz), cut into
    1cm (½ in) lengths
175 g (6 oz) fresh or frozen sweetcorn kernels, thawed
    if frozen
3 medium tomatoes, deseeded and diced
4 tablespoons oyster sauce
1 tablespoon soy sauce

Cook the noodles according to the packet instructions. Drain and toss with ½ tablespoon of the groundnut or sunflower oil. Heat up a wok over a high heat until it smokes. Add the remaining groundnut or sunflower oil and the sesame oil and, as soon as they've heated through, throw in the ginger. Give it a quick stir, then add the chives and sweetcorn. Stir-fry for about 40–60 seconds, then add the tomatoes. Stir-fry for a further 30 seconds or so, then tip in the noodles. Stir and mix lightly for about 30 seconds, then spoon in the oyster sauce and soy sauce. Toss until the sauces are mixed in evenly and the noodles heated through. Taste and adjust the seasoning and serve immediately.

Opposite
**Chinese
Chive,
Tomato and
Sweetcorn
Noodles**

Chinese Chive and Ginger Dipping Sauce

This is a powerfully flavoured, quickly made dipping sauce that is usually served with poultry (it transforms plainly steamed or poached chicken into a feast), though I like it with fish just as much. As the boiling hot oils are poured on to the other ingredients, their flavours are instantly released and flattered.

Serves 4

2 tablespoons chopped Chinese chives
1 tablespoon finely chopped fresh root ginger
½ teaspoon caster sugar
2 tablespoons groundnut or sunflower oil
1 tablespoon sesame oil
2 teaspoons soy sauce

Mix the chives, ginger and caster sugar together. Heat the oils together until they smoke, then pour them over the chive mixture. Stir, then add the soy sauce. Serve straight away.

Parchment-baked New Potatoes with Chinese Chives

This neat, pretty way of cooking new potatoes in a wrapper of greaseproof paper is something of a classic, and it produces gloriously buttery, tender little mouthfuls. The flavour of Chinese chives (particularly the flower-bud stems) is very good with them, though thyme, rosemary and parsley can all be used instead.

Serves 3–4

500 g (1 lb 2 oz) small new potatoes (around 16–20 potatoes)
45–60 g (1½–2 oz) butter
2 tablespoons roughly chopped Chinese chives
coarse salt

Pre-heat the oven to 190°C/375°F/Gas Mark 5.
Cut out 2 large, heart-shaped pieces of greaseproof paper (they should be around 32 cm (13 inches) across at the widest part and around 28 cm (11 inches) in length). Lay each one half-on a baking tray. Put half the potatoes on each piece of paper. Dot with the butter, sprinkle with the chives and season with coarse salt. Fold the other half of the heart over to form a skewed semi-circle. Starting at the pointed end, seal the edges pressing them over and over again. Work your way around each package to enclose the potatoes neatly and snugly. Bake for 35 minutes, by which time the potatoes will be tender and buttery. Serve immediately in their parcels, so that they can be opened at the table.

Three Allium Tart

Three Alliums, Chinese chives (or ordinary chives if you can't get Chinese ones – they can just survive the slow, moist cooking in cream and eggs), garlic and red onions, are all brought together in one savoury tart. I like the contrast of the rich creamy filling against the complexities of the three allied garlic-onion flavours but if you prefer something a little lighter, replace half the cream with milk.

Serves 6–8

For 340 g (12 oz) shortcrust pastry
225 g (8 oz) plain flour
Pinch of salt
110 g (4 oz) chilled butter, diced
1 egg yolk, beaten
Iced water

For the filling
1 head of garlic separated into cloves and peeled
250 ml (8 fl oz) single cream
200 ml (7 fl oz) milk
2 egg yolks
1 egg
2 red onions, sliced
2 tablespoons olive oil
2 tablespoons chopped Chinese chives
85 g (3 oz) Taleggio or dolcelatte cheese, cut into cubes
salt and pepper

First make the pastry. Sift the flour with the salt. Rub the butter into the flour until it resembles fine breadcrumbs. Make a well in the centre and add the egg yolk and enough iced water to form a soft dough – 1½–2 tablespoons of water should be enough. Mix quickly and lightly, and knead very briefly to smooth out. Wrap and chill for at least 30 minutes in the fridge. Bring back to room temperature before using.

Pre-heat the oven to 190°C/375°F/Gas Mark 5.

Roll the pastry out and line a 23 cm (9 inch) tart tin with it. Rest, then prick the base all over with a fork and line with foil or greaseproof paper. Weight down with baking beans, then bake blind for 10 minutes. Remove the beans and paper and return the pastry case to the oven for 5 minutes or so to dry out.

Blanch the cloves of garlic in boiling water for 1 minute. Drain. Heat the cream and milk in a roomy saucepan until simmering. Add the garlic cloves and poach gently until very tender – 10–15 minutes. Lift out with a slotted spoon. Mash to a paste, then work in the egg yolks and egg. Whisk in the cream and milk and plenty of salt and pepper. Reduce the oven temperature to 170°C/325°F/Gas Mark 3.

Sauté the onions briskly in the olive oil until tender and browned. Scoop out and drain on kitchen paper. When cool, spread out in the pastry case. Scatter over the chives and cheese. Pour over the garlic cream. Return the tart to the oven for 30–40 minutes, until just set but still with a slight wobble in the centre. Serve warm or cold as preferred.

sweet basil
Ocimum basilicum

And she forgot the stars, the moon, the sun,
And she forgot the blue above the trees,
And she forgot the dells, where waters run,
And she forgot the chilly autumn breeze;
She had no knowledge when day was done,
And the new morn she saw not: but in peace
Hung over her sweet Basil evermore.

'Isabella', John Keats

Poor Isabella, mourning the death of her lover, his head buried in the pot of basil. At least the scent of the leaves must have been some comfort, though heaven knows how she coped with the winter months. Basil likes warmth, and though cosseting and comforting it in a warm place will lengthen the life of its magic leaves it will, in the end, give up the ghost. Now that really would be grim – dead lover and only a few barren dry twigs to gloom over. Let's hope that, forgetfulness not withstanding, she had had the forethought to bring on some small seedlings in the greenhouse, to replenish supplies the following year.

Presumably the basil that her tears watered was the common sweet basil that has made its primary home around the northern shores of the Mediterranean (she was an Italian heroine, so that seems more than likely), though it hailed originally from India. To us in our chillier climate, basil appears to be the most characteristic herb of Italian cooking, though actually parsley, rosemary and mint could all lay a claim to that title. But basil is such a charismatic herb, so heady and peppery and pungent, so very evocative of sunshine and the throbbing heat of southern skies, that it dominates the rest with consummate ease. Scatter leaves of basil over a salad of ripe, scarlet tomatoes and there it is...Italy on a plate. Tomatoes and basil, one of the greatest double acts of all time, in salads and raw salsas (take the salsa recipe on p. 81, replace coriander with basil, lime juice with lemon juice or red wine vinegar, and drop the chilli altogether and hey presto, you have the Mediterranean salsa cruda, wonderful on steaming hot pasta or as a relish with fish or chicken), in sauces, soups and stews.

Opposite
Clockwise from top left: basil; hyssop; methi; sweet marjoram; oregano; coriander; purple basil

Basil's most famous tomato-free incarnation is that near-miraculous unguent for pasta, pesto, for which I give a recipe on p. 65. Closely related is the Provençal pistou, which is stirred into soup to give an instant last-minute glamour. A little basil in a salsa verde (with lots of parsley, garlic, capers, anchovies and olive oil) gives it an underlying scented peppery note, while on a similar theme, an emerald-green basil vinaigrette can be made by processing lots of basil leaves with wine vinegar, oil, salt, pepper and a touch of sugar. Basil marries well not only with tomato but also with grilled and sautéed red peppers, fried courgettes, grilled aubergine, some chicken dishes and so on. In the form of pesto, almost anything goes with it these days – use it in large sandwiches, smeared over the bread to take a filling of grilled aubergine or barbecued chicken, or fish and sliced tomato; stir it into dressings for hot and cold food, or into yoghurt or fromage frais to make a snappy sauce for anything from rice dishes to baked potatoes. The possibilities are endless, and if you have a taste for the stuff, I dare say you already keep a pot of it in the fridge ready to raid at every possible occasion. If you have never tasted home-made pesto you will be amazed at how easy it is to produce, and how vibrant it is in comparison with bottled pesto.

I've often read that cooking intensifies the flavour of basil, but have never found this to be true. With cooked dishes, though you may add a few sprigs of basil to the pan to stew down slowly into the body of the preparation, for a real starburst of peppery basil aroma you must add fresh leaves right at the end of the cooking period, torn, shredded or whole as recipe and mood dictate. Another myth accompanies basil and is ripe to be debunked; shredding or chopping basil with a knife is not a heinous crime. The scent of the leaves is just the same whether they are torn or cut, though the aesthetics of tearing them up with your fingers are infinitely finer. And you don't have to wash the knife or the chopping board, which counts for something in my book.

I'll never forget the pleasure of walking through a basil field near Genoa one scorching July day, the smell rising up from the green leaves as intoxicating as any alcohol. You won't quite get that in the UK but a ray of sunshine direct on the leaves will do a basil plant a power of good. Given the variable nature of our weather, it is advisable to grow basil in a pot, like Isabella but without the lover's head, on a sunny windowsill. Then, on a good day, you can wheel it out to bask in the warmth like an elderly relative. Or you may just prefer to throw the windows open wide and rely on the basil to ward off flies, which it does moderately well for something so inanimate. Since basil is a herb to use in generous quantity and summer flies are infuriating and numerous, it makes sense to have not just one lone plant but a collection of pots ranged along the sill, each with its own healthy, green-leaved basil plant thrusting forth. I reckon two is the minimum for the occasional basil user, but anyone with more than a passing taste for the herb will require at least three to see them through the season.

Such is the popularity of basil that plant nurseries will often stock a welter of different varieties. They divide neatly into three categories. The first is the group of basils with a true, sweet Mediterranean aroma, the essential culinary group, which includes common basil (*Ocimum basilicum*), the impressive large-leaved lettuce leaf basil (*Ocimum basilicum* var. *crispum*), and the tiddly-leaved bush or Greek basil (*Ocimum minimum*). They all taste very similar. For those who like to cook Asian food, there are holy basil and Thai basil, and you can read more about them on p. 139. The third group is the largest and the most frolicsome and frivolous – none of them essential but fun to play with now and again. These are the many different scented basils and the startling purple-leaved ones – opal basil and purple ruffles basil. Among the scented plants, you may come across lemon basil, anise basil, ginger basil, cinnamon basil and even camphor basil. Take your pick.

Storage and Preservation

Basil leaves are very tender, so do not expect a long life from cut basil. Stored in a plastic bag, wrapped loosely in damp kitchen paper, they should keep for up to three days but after that they will hardly be worth using. If you are lucky enough to have a good haul of basil that you want to preserve, the best method is to make a big batch of pesto, which can be stored in the fridge, covered with an extra layer of olive oil, in a sealed jar for a week or two, or can be frozen for three months or so, to emerge almost as good as new. Alternatively you can purée the leaves with olive oil alone or with water and freeze in ice-cube trays. There has been a muted vogue lately for olive oil ice cubes in cool soups, so you could go one step further and pop olive oil and basil ice cubes into very hot winter soups so that they gently release their scent as they melt in. If you want a touch more of the old-fashioned Italian mamma, layer the leaves in jars, sprinkling with salt between layers and filling up with olive oil. Seal tightly and store in the fridge. The leaves will turn black but the flavour is captured in the oil, which is marvellous as a condiment, drizzled over hot or cold foods just before serving, or in salads.

Salad of Marinated Mackerel, Tomatoes, New Potatoes and Basil

This salad comes out of disappointment. A menu listed marinated sardine salad and I ordered it only to discover that the sardines were actually salted anchovies. The thought of fresh, lissom, silvery fillets of marinated fish stayed with me, and a week or two later, when I had some beautiful pearly fresh mackerel to hand, I concocted my own marinated fish salad.

Serves 4–6

3 plump mackerel, filleted
250 g (9 oz) small new potatoes
3–4 ripe plum tomatoes, cut into chunks
1 bunch of watercress
2 oranges, peeled to the quick and cut into chunks
a handful of basil leaves, roughly torn

For the marinade
juice of 2 lemons
4 tablespoons olive oil
6 basil stems, roughly chopped
coarse salt and plenty of freshly ground pepper

For the dressing
1 tablespoon lemon juice
1 teaspoon Dijon mustard
1 teaspoon caster sugar
5–6 tablespoons olive oil
salt and pepper

Mix the marinade ingredients together and pour them over the mackerel fillets in a shallow non-corrosive dish. Turn the pieces, then cover and leave in a cool place for at least 2 hours, turning once, until they take on an opaque look, almost as if they had been cooked.

Make the dressing: whisk the lemon juice with the mustard, caster sugar, salt and pepper. Gradually whisk in the olive oil, then taste and adjust the seasoning.

Boil the potatoes in their skins until tender. Drain, then immediately halve them and toss in a little of the dressing. Leave to cool.

Toss the tomatoes, watercress and oranges in just enough dressing to coat lightly. Arrange on plate(s) with the potatoes. Take the mackerel out of its marinade, pat dry, then cut each fillet in half diagonally. Lay the fish across the salad and scatter with basil leaves. Serve at once, with plenty of good bread.

Conchiglie with Basil, Tuna, Olive and Caper Sauce

Basil on more basil here, and in two distinct forms. The first batch is stirred into a gently stewed sauce of tuna, made piquant with olives, capers and sun-dried tomatoes. The second is deep-fried until crisp and fluttered over the pasta with a flurry of shavings of Parmesan (make them with a vegetable peeler, dragging it along the thinner side of the wedge). Pasta shells, by the way, are particularly good for a bitty sauce like this one, because they capture nuggets of sauce in their curved interiors.

Serves 4

400–450g (14–16 oz) conchiglie (pasta shells) or other pasta shapes
salt

For the sauce
1 small onion, roughly chopped
6 tablespoons extra virgin olive oil
1 x 185g (6½ oz) tin of tuna, drained and flaked
2 tablespoon capers, rinsed and soaked if salted, roughly chopped
60g (2 oz) black olives, pitted and roughly chopped
75g (2½ oz) currants
45g (1½ oz) pine-nuts
2 tablespoons chopped parsley
3 garlic cloves, chopped
4 sun-dried tomatoes, roughly chopped
150 ml (5 fl oz) water
2 tablespoons shredded basil
salt and pepper

For the garnish
16–20 large unblemished basil leaves
olive oil and/or sunflower oil for deep frying
plenty of Parmesan shavings

To make the sauce, sauté the onion lightly in the oil in a saucepan, then add all the remaining ingredients, except basil and salt. Stir, then leave to simmer very gently for 25–30 minutes, stirring occasionally, until the water has more or less evaporated leaving a moist, richly flavoured sauce. This can be prepared in advance and reheated when needed. Shortly before serving, stir in the basil. Taste and adjust seasoning, adding salt only if really needed.

Put a large pan of salted water on to boil for the pasta. When it reaches a rolling boil, tip in the pasta, bring back to the boil and cook until *al dente*.

While the pasta is cooking, pour enough oil, either olive or sunflower or a mixture of the two, into a small pan to give a depth of about 3 cm (1 inch). Heat until good and hot and test by dropping a small cube of bread into the oil. If it sizzles furiously and browns within 30 seconds, the oil is hot enough. Fry the basil leaves in the oil, three or four at a time. Make sure they are quite dry before they go in, don't be surprised by spitting and sizzling as they hit the oil, and then fish them out within 5–10 seconds, while they are still bright green. If they are a sludgy darkish olive green, then the oil is *too* hot. Let it cool slightly and then try again. Drain the leaves on kitchen paper and repeat with the remaining basil.

To serve, drain the pasta thoroughly then tip it into a large, warmed serving bowl, pour in the hot sauce and toss to mix well. Top with the deep-fried basil leaves and shavings of Parmesan. Eat immediately.

Opposite
Salad of Marinated Mackerel, Tomatoes, New Potatoes and Basil
(page 61)

Tomato, Sweetcorn and Basil Soup with Pesto Croûtons

This soup can serve as a first course but I usually make it the mainstay of a light lunch or supper. The sweetcorn gives substance and sweetness to what is really a fairly standard tomato soup, but what sets it apart are the croûtons, smeared with pesto and topped with a little crème fraîche. It looks very pretty indeed and is immensely satisfying.

Serves 4–6

3 ears of corn, or 340 g (12 oz) frozen sweetcorn kernels,
    defrosted
1 large onion, chopped
3 garlic cloves, chopped
3 tablespoons olive oil
6 fresh anchovy fillets, roughly chopped
    (optional, but a good idea)
2 x 400 g (14 oz) tins of chopped tomatoes
2 tablespoons tomato purée
1 bouquet garni of thyme, bay leaf and parsley sprigs tied
    together with string
1 litre (1¾ pints) water or stock
a handful of basil leaves
salt and pepper

For the pesto croûtons
½ stick of French bread, sliced into rounds about
    1 cm (½ inch) thick
olive oil
3 tablespoons pesto (see p. 65)
about 3 tablespoons crème fraîche (optional)

Pre-heat the oven to 190°C/375°F/Gas Mark 5.

If using fresh corn, stand the ear upright on the work surface and slice downwards with a sharp knife to take off the kernels.

To make the soup, gently fry the onion and garlic in the olive oil until tender. Add the anchovies, if using, and fry for a few minutes longer until they have collapsed down. Now tip in the tomatoes, tomato purée, sweetcorn and bouquet garni. Bring up to the boil, then simmer until reduced by about a third. Now add the water or stock, salt and pepper and bring up to the boil. Simmer gently for 10 minutes or so.

Meanwhile, brush both sides of the slices of bread with olive oil and place on a baking sheet. Bake for about 20 minutes, turning occasionally, until golden brown. Keep warm until needed, then spread with pesto and top each one with a small dollop of crème fraîche, if using. Shortly before serving, shred the basil finely.

When the soup is ready, remove the bouquet garni and liquidize about half the soup for a slightly chunky, knobbly texture or the whole lot for a smooth(ish) texture. Taste and adjust the seasoning, then reheat and stir in the shredded basil. Serve immediately, with the pesto croûtons in a bowl so that people can float their own on top if they want to, or keep them separate.

Pasta alla Genovese

On my first visit to Genoa I wanted above all to taste real pesto in its native territory. We found a small restaurant with a terrace, sipped ice-cold Campari soda, and then revelled in big bowlfuls of *trofie* – small, thick, hand-made pasta gnocchi – sozzled in the brilliant green nectar. Some years later, I was introduced to another, equally authentic version of pasta with pesto. This time it was ordinary spaghetti (dried, not fresh) cooked with pieces of carrot, potato and green bean in the same pan, then drenched in pesto.

Serves 4

400–450 g (14 oz–1 lb) dried spaghetti (not quick-cooking)
1–2 large potatoes, peeled and cut roughly into 2 cm (¾ inch) chunks
2–3 carrots, thickly sliced
125 g (4 oz) green beans, cut into 4 cm (1½ inch) lengths
plenty of salt
freshly grated Parmesan or pecorino cheese, to serve

For the pesto
75 g (2½ oz) basil leaves
60 g (2 oz) hard pecorino or Parmesan cheese, or a mixture of the two, broken into chunks
60 g (2 oz) pinenuts
2–3 garlic cloves, roughly chopped
100–125 ml (3½–4 fl oz) olive oil

To make the pesto, put the basil leaves, cheese, pinenuts and garlic into a food processor and process to a paste. With the blades still running, trickle in the olive oil to give a creamy sauce.

If you want to do it in a less machine-driven way, get out a large mortar or a heavy bowl. Pound the garlic to a paste with a pinch or two of salt, using a pestle or the end of a rolling pin. Add the basil and nuts and keep pounding until you have a green paste. Grate the cheese and add that too, working it in with the pestle. Then work in enough olive oil to give a creamy sauce.

Bring a large pan of well-salted water to the boil and add the spaghetti, potatoes and carrots. About half way through the cooking time, add the beans. By the time the pasta is *al dente* the vegetables will be cooked. Drain well, toss with the pesto and serve with the cheese.

Raspberry and Basil Ice-cream

Basil is used almost exclusively in savoury dishes, yet it has a distinct sweetness for all its peppery nature, and a strong echo of cloves. Having tried it in sweet, creamy dishes, which I liked very much, I moved on further afield to partnering basil with fruit. It is especially nice with raspberries, I discovered. Try macerating a few roughly torn-up leaves with fresh raspberries, sugar and a little lemon or lime juice or a shot of gin. And then go one step further, with this deep-pink ice-cream.

Serves 4

450 g (1 lb) raspberries
175 g (6 oz) caster sugar
a handful of basil leaves, chopped
juice of ½ orange
lemon juice, to taste
300 ml (½ pint) double cream

Sieve the raspberries, then stir in the sugar, basil and orange juice. Let the purée stand for half an hour at room temperature, stirring occasionally to dissolve the sugar. Now add lemon juice to balance the sugar but don't go overboard – there's still the cream to come, and then the chill of the freezer will dampen the sweetness, too. I reckon a couple of tablespoonfuls, give or take, should be adequate.

Whip the cream lightly and fold in the raspberry mixture. Churn in an ice-cream maker, if you have one. If you don't, pour the mixture into a freezer container and leave in the freezer, turned to its coldest setting, until the sides begin to solidify. Break them up and push towards the centre of the container. Repeat once. This time leave the ice-cream until it is just about solid but not rock hard, then either process quickly or scrape into a bowl and beat vigorously to break up the larger ice crystals. Return to the freezer and leave to freeze fully. Transfer from the freezer to the fridge some 30–45 minutes before serving, to soften.

sweet marjoram
Origanum majorana

*Indeed, Sir, she was the sweet marjoram of the
Salad, or rather the herb of grace.*

'All's Well That Ends Well', William Shakespeare

Sweet marjoram, or what most of us call merely
marjoram, is one of the quieter herbs, which doesn't
proclaim its virtues as loudly as thyme or rosemary. Quiet
it may be in some ways, but it is undoubtedly one of
Europe's essential herbs. It is a perennial that survives
the light winter chills in the warmer parts of the Continent
with ease. Not here, though, on the whole. Most
gardeners treat it as an annual, replanting or re-sowing
every spring. Our marjoram must be the exception that
proves the rule. Despite the location of its site, in a
windswept garden, it has made it through three winters,
though admittedly none of them has proved at all severe.

I tend to think of marjoram as a soft-leaved, tender
version of thyme. It is less harsh but has some of that
same soft spiciness backed by a touch of bitterness. It is
sweeter, that's for sure, but again, there is the echo of
camphor that you find in thyme. Unlike thyme, marjoram
is not a herb for prolonged, harsh cooking. Its flavour is
at its best when it is shown a considerate, caring hand.
It has long been thought a brilliant herb for stuffings,
where it is protected by the carcass of the bird, fish or
vegetable, as well as by the starchy content of most
stuffings, so it is never hit too hard by direct heat. Try it
particularly in the stuffings for vegetables – tomatoes,
peppers, courgettes – mixed perhaps with rice or
couscous. Its delicate nature makes it even more
appropriate for lightly cooked eggy dishes – omelettes,
soufflés and the like, or in the egg and cream or milk
filling for a quiche. Any dish with thyme cooked slowly
into it (such as a meaty stew) will probably benefit from a
final addition of some chopped marjoram, supposing that
you want to enhance the thyme-like scent.

The purple-white knots of flowers (from which it derives
the name knotted marjoram) are a pretty addition to
salads, along with some of the leaves. I particularly like
them with a composed salad of grilled peppers,
quartered hard-boiled eggs, cherry tomatoes and black
olives, or on a salad of sliced orange, thinly sliced sweet
red onion and again black olives.

Pot or Sicilian marjoram is a very close cousin, but a
different species, *Origanum onites*. It has a similar scent
to common marjoram, though less sweet. You may also
come across highly decorative golden or curly-leaved
marjorams, again similar to common marjoram though
milder in flavour. Oregano is wild marjoram (*Origanum
vulgare*), and for more on that turn to p. 69.

Storage and Preservation

Marjoram has fairly tender leaves, so a short shelf-life.
Stored in an airtight plastic box or bag in the vegetable
drawer of the fridge, it can be expected to last for some
four or five days. To dry, pick just before flowering and
hang up in a dry, airy place. Once dried, store in an
airtight container, but don't expect it to retain its scent for
more than a couple of months. Marjoram is a good herb
for flavouring olive oil, but don't leave fresh marjoram in
the bottle for too long or it will disintegrate and begin to
look unsightly.

Chez Nous Shepherd's Pie

This is basically a classic shepherd's pie, made with cooked lamb (though you can also use raw minced lamb if that is more convenient) but flavoured liberally with fresh marjoram and garlic and moistened with red wine and tomatoes, just to give it a little more zip. It is a great favourite of ours and perfect comfort food on a cold day.

Serves 4 very hungry people, 6 ordinary mortals

1 onion, chopped
1 red pepper, deseeded and finely diced
1 large carrot, finely diced
2 tablespoons sunflower oil
2–3 garlic cloves, chopped
340–400 g (12–14 oz) rare roast lamb, thinly sliced then finely
    diced, or minced raw lamb
1 small sprig of rosemary (optional)
400 g (14 oz) tin of chopped tomatoes
150 ml (¼ pint) red wine
1 tablespoon Worcestershire sauce
2 tablespoons chopped marjoram or 1–1½ teaspoons
    dried oregano
salt and pepper

For the topping
1 kg (2 lb 4 oz) large potatoes in their skins
45 g (1½ oz) butter
150 ml (¼ pint) milk

Either bake the potatoes in their skins or microwave them until tender, in which case remember to prick the skins first so that they don't burst all over the microwave. Cut in half while still hot and scoop out the insides. Save the skins to make fried potato skins (see p. 112). While it is still hot, mash the potato with two-thirds of the butter and some salt, gradually working in the milk to give a smooth mash.

Fry the onion, pepper and carrot in the oil over a moderate heat until the onion and pepper are tender. Add the garlic and continue cooking for a minute or two. If you are using roast lamb, add to the pan now. If you are using raw minced lamb, raise the heat high, then add the lamb and fry for 5 minutes or so, at a rollicking heat, breaking up the lumps, until it is lightly coloured all over. Now add the rosemary if you are using raw mince, or did not flavour the roast with rosemary. Stir in the tinned tomatoes, wine and Worcestershire sauce and season well. Bring up to the boil and then leave to simmer gently for at least 45 minutes if it was roast lamb or at least 1 hour if it was raw lamb. If necessary, add a little hot water to prevent it drying out. Stir in the marjoram when the sauce is more or less cooked. By the time it is done, the mixture should be moist, rich and a darkish brown, and definitely not swimming in liquid. Taste and adjust the seasoning.

Pre-heat the oven to around 220°C/425°F/Gas Mark 7 (a little less won't hurt, if you have something else cooking in there at the same time).

Spread the mince out in an ovenproof dish to give a layer about 2–2.5 cm (¾–1 inch) thick. Dot the mashed potato on top, then smooth down carefully, spreading it right to the sides. Use the tines of a fork to make waves or swirls or whatever pattern takes your fancy on the top of the potato. Dot with the remaining butter. Pop the dish into the oven and leave to reheat and brown for 25–30 minutes. Serve steaming hot, and full of comfort.

Three-tomato Tart with Marjoram

Somehow this isn't quite a pizza, though it slides pretty close with its yeast dough and heavy complement of tomatoes. It is, in fact, constructed along the lines of a tart, with a bit more depth to it than a classic pizza. I like it just as it is, without any added cheese, but if you wanted a slight change, then try scattering a handful of Parmesan shavings (cut them from a block of Parmesan with a vegetable peeler) over the filling after it comes out of the oven. Either way it is delicious and substantial. I originally created it, minus cheese, for the vegan boyfriend of a very dear old friend. As it happens, he had given up on veganism by the time he got to try it, but no matter – we all loved it anyway.

Serves 4

2½ tablespoons sun-dried tomato purée or red pesto
3 tablespoons fine cornmeal or polenta
8 plum tomatoes, sliced
10 medium-sized cherry tomatoes, halved
½ teaspoon thyme leaves
½ teaspoon caster sugar
olive oil
a small handful of marjoram, oregano or basil leaves
salt and pepper

For the yeast pastry
225 g (8 oz) strong white flour
125 g (4 oz) plain flour
1 teaspoon salt
7 g sachet of easy-blend yeast
1 generous tablespoon olive oil

To make the pastry, sift the two flours into a bowl with the salt and stir in the yeast. Make a well in the centre and add the olive oil and enough water to make a soft dough. Knead vigorously for 5–10 minutes, until satin-smooth and elastic. Place in an oiled bowl, turn to coat in oil, then cover with a damp tea towel and leave in a warm place to rise until doubled in bulk. If you want to slow its progress down (the tart is nicest served warm from the oven, not reheated), then pop it into the fridge.

Oil a 25 cm (10 inch) tart tin. Punch the dough down and knead briefly, then spread the dough out thinly in the tin with your hands, pushing it up the sides. Spread the sun-dried tomato purée or red pesto over the base. Sprinkle 1½ tablespoons of the cornmeal evenly over the purée (this will sop up some of the juices from the fresh tomatoes). Now arrange the sliced plum tomatoes and halved cherry tomatoes, cut-side up, haphazardly over the tart, covering the base completely and thickly. Sprinkle with the remaining cornmeal plus the thyme leaves and sugar. Season with salt and plenty of pepper, then drizzle with 1½ tablespoons of olive oil. Let the tart sit for 10 minutes while the oven warms up.

Place a baking sheet in the oven and heat to 230°C/450°F/Gas Mark 8. Pop the tart onto the hot baking sheet and bake for 15 minutes, until the edges are puffed and golden brown. Brush the pastry with a little extra oil, then return to the oven for 5 minutes. Serve hot or warm, scattering over the fresh marjoram, oregano or basil just before taking the tart to the table.

Sabzi Khordan (Persian Herb Salad)

In Iran it is traditional to serve a fresh herb salad with every meal to refresh, cleanse and invigorate. In her book *The Legendary Cooking of Persia*, Margaret Shaida suggests serving it as an appetizer with Persian bread and salty feta cheese.

Choose as many of the following as you can get: basil, chives, spring onions, tarragon, mint, marjoram, coriander, radishes, flat-leaved parsley and any other tender-leaved herbs that you have a taste for. Pick off all the leaves, or tear or chop as appropriate. Toss together and serve, without any dressing, with feta cheese and warm Arab bread. I quite like to add a squeeze of lemon juice, olive oil, salt and freshly ground pepper, but then I'm not Iranian.

Antony Worrall Thompson's Herb Fritters with **Yoghurt, Mint** and **Apricot Dip**

oregano (wild marjoram)
Origanum vulgare

The herb garden created by Antony Worrall Thompson and his wife, Jay, is a joy to behold. Here he grows one of his favourite herbs, marjoram, along with a host of others, including parsley, sorrel, tarragon and basil. This particular dish of herb fritters is one that he created for Sense, a charity working with deaf and blind people. The fritters are easy to make – crisp on the outside, melting and herby inside. Delicious on their own, they are even better dipped in the yoghurt-based sauce.

Serves 6

3–4 eggs, lightly beaten
150 g (5 oz) mozzarella, grated
85 g (3 oz) freshly grated parmesan
125 g (4 oz) fresh breadcrumbs
½ red onion, finely chopped
¼–½ teaspoon red chilli flakes
2 tablespoons roughly chopped fresh marjoram
2 tablespoons roughly chopped chives (and a few of their
    flowers, torn into segments, if available)
5 tablespoons roughly chopped flatleaf parsley
a handful of rocket leaves, roughly chopped
a handful of baby spinach leaves, roughly chopped
salt and pepper
sunflower oil and a generous knob of butter for frying

For the dip
500 g (1 lb 2 oz) tub Greek yoghurt
12 ready-to-eat dried apricots, finely diced
2 garlic cloves, crushed
2 tablespoons chopped fresh mint
salt and pepper

Mix together all the ingredients for the fritters, except the cooking oil and butter, until thick and fairly solid; if it seems too damp, add a few more breadcrumbs to bind. Refrigerate for half an hour or more.

To make the dip, mix all the ingredients together shortly before using.

Pour 1 cm (½ inch) of oil into a frying pan, add the butter and heat until slightly hazy. Use a tablespoon to mould oval-shaped fritters, pressing the mixture together firmly with your hand to compact it. Slide them into the hot oil and fry for 2–3 minutes on each side until brown and crisp. Drain briefly on kitchen paper. Serve hot with the yoghurt dip.

The smell of warm summer mornings in France comes to me from my childhood – slowly walking back up the hill, a long loaf of still-warm bread under my arm, its oven-baked aroma entwining with my every step and mingling with the scent of the wild marjoram that covered the banks on either side. I still love that smell and return to it with pleasure every year. But I can't lay any special claims to it, for the pairing of bread and spicy warm herb, brought together in the early-morning sunshine, is one that belongs to huge numbers of small villages, not only in France but also in Italy, Greece, Spain and wherever freshly baked bread is an essential start to a day in the countryside. Oregano, or wild marjoram, is a common plant on the Continent – and in Britain, where dawn-baked daily bread is harder to track down.

The flavour and intensity of wild marjoram vary tremendously from one spot to another. Heat undoubtedly improves it: our wild marjoram is good enough, but tramp through the marjoram-strewn hills of Italy or Greece and the scent is miraculous. Though we may cull our own to use in cooking, we actually do better to buy dried oregano grown in hotter climates. Oregano is one of those rare herbs that is improved by drying, bringing out its true, pungent, peppery, almost bitter spiciness, so unlike its tamed cousin, sweet marjoram, though you can smell the family likeness. The only time that I think it worth buying commercially grown fresh oregano is when you need marjoram but can't get hold of any.

Dried oregano is a marvellous herb, possessing a natural affinity with tomatoes and garlic, lemons, olives, olive oil, and all things southern. Some years ago, while filming in Italy, we bought an enormous bunch of dried oregano for a song in the backstreets of a small town in Sicily. We took it across to the island of Favignana, home of the last Sicilian *matanza*, the dramatic and bloody tuna hunt. They'd fought and caught some of the noble fish the day before and a giant of a fisherman had offered to cook some for us. He marinated it briefly in a *salmoriglio*, a mixture of lemon juice, extra virgin olive oil, salt, pepper and our dried oregano. Quickly seared over a small fire, it was then dressed with more of the same.

Italian oregano is the crucial pizza herb, surviving the fierce heat of the pizza oven – indeed, blessed by it – to spice the garlicky tomato sauce, the cheese and other pungent toppings. It is what gives the tomatoey *pizzaiola* sauce its energy. Dried oregano can even hold its own against chilli, as it does so often in the cooking of Calabria down in the toe of the Italian boot.

Across the Aegean, in Greece, oregano is even more ubiquitous. Here it is at its most exuberant; the name comes from the ancient Greek *oros* (mountain) and *ganos* (joy), which describes it so perfectly, a real joy of the mountains. In ancient Greece the herb was planted over graves to send the departed off on their last journey in a joyous state of mind. They even said that it was created by their goddess of love, Aphrodite, as a token of happiness, and they massaged wild marjoram oil into their hair after bathing.

Greek dried oregano is known as *rigani*, and may include several different species of wild oregano. If you holiday in Greece it is one of the choicest of souvenirs to bring back with you, as the scent will endure unscathed for a year and more. Unlike sweet marjoram, the flavour of dried oregano actually develops and deepens with prolonged cooking. Use it as they do in Greece, sprinkled over lamb to be braised long and slow in the oven until the meat falls away from the bones, or cook it in the meat sauce of a moussaka. Even in marinated or briefly cooked dishes it brings a powerful dose of pungent sunshine – add it to a marinade for kebabs of meat or fish, or sprinkle it over oven-roast fish, burnished with best olive oil. Not that it needs heat at all – unlike most dried herbs, it doesn't seem musty or dusty in a salad, and it goes almost without saying that one of the things that makes a good Greek salad, besides plenty of sweet, crisp lettuce, scarlet tomatoes, cool cucumber, salty feta cheese, freshly squeezed lemon and olive oil, is a healthy complement of aromatic *rigani*.

If you are partial to oregano, then lay in stocks of the dried herb from different countries to taste the difference. The *rigani* of Greece is not the same as the oregano of southern Italy, nor does it equate with the wild marjoram of France, which is different, yet again, from what you may come across in the UK. Use fresh wild marjoram only if you come across it on a walk and can pick it yourself, and while you're at it, try drying a little to see how it compares with oregano from hot countries.

Storage and Preparation

To dry wild marjoram, or oregano, cut just before flowering and hang up in an airy, dry, dark place. Either wrap the whole dried bunches in plastic bags or rub the leaves off the stems and stash in airtight containers. Dried oregano is a brilliant flavouring for olive oil. Submerge several branches in a bottle, add a clove or two of garlic, if you wish, and perhaps a dried chilli, then fill up with good olive oil. Leave for a week or two before using.

Onion, Aubergine and Pak Choi Frittata

Italian-style frittatas, or Spanish tortillas which are rather thicker, are wonderful ways of using up a medley of vegetables that have collected in the bottom of the fridge, as long as they are not treated as too much of a dustbin dish. A bit of restraint pays dividends. None the less, you can make either of these substantial omelettes with practically any vegetable you care to name, seasoning them if you will with pancetta, bacon, chorizo or other cured meat products. This is one version that I came up with recently. What I particularly liked was the texture of the pak choi against the softer aubergine and eggs, and the caramelized brown sweetness of the onions.

Serves 4

1 red onion
4 baby pak choi
4 tablespoons olive oil
4 streaky bacon rashers, or slices of pancetta, cut into strips
½ large aubergine, cut into 2.5 cm (1 inch) cubes, salted and rinsed if you have time
3 garlic cloves, sliced
½ red chilli, deseeded and sliced into thin strips
2 tablespoons sun-dried tomato purée
1 teaspoon dried oregano or 1 tablespoon chopped fresh oregano or marjoram
6 eggs, lightly beaten
30–45 g (1–1½ oz) Parmesan cheese, cut into paper-thin shavings
salt and pepper

Peel the red onion and cut it in half, then cut each half into 6 wedges. Cut each pak choi in half, slicing through the heart from the white base to the green leaf. Heat 2 tablespoons of the oil in a heavy-based frying pan over a high heat. When it is good and hot, lay the onion wedges in the pan, cut-side down. Leave for 2–3 minutes, then turn. The underneath should be well browned – if not leave them for a minute or two longer. When the other sides are lightly browned too, add the bacon and aubergine to the pan and toss and stir, still over a high heat, until the aubergine is patched with brown, too, and the bacon is cooked through.

Reduce the heat to moderate and add the pak choi, garlic and chilli. Stir to coat in the oil, then cover tightly and leave to cook in its own juices for 5–10 minutes, until the pak choi is tender and wilted, stirring once or twice. Now stir in the sun-dried tomato purée, oregano, remaining oil and a little salt and pepper.

Meanwhile, pre-heat the grill thoroughly and beat the eggs with salt and pepper. Pour the eggs over the vegetables and leave to cook, pulling the sides away from the edge of the pan every now and then to let runny egg seep down and cook, until the egg is three-quarters set but still runny in the centre. Scatter the Parmesan shavings over the top, then rush the omelette under the grill and grill until it is just set and the top is lightly browned. Serve hot, warm or cold (probably the nicest), straight from the pan.

Souvlakia

hyssop
Hyssopus officinalis

I first tasted souvlakia, the ubiquitous Greek kebab, on a train rumbling slowly down to Athens in blazing heat. We'd leaned out of the window to buy them hot from a smoking brazier at a small station. Flavoured with coriander seeds and pungent *rigani*, they tasted sensational as the train swung and bumped its way on towards the capital.

Serves 4–6

1 tablespoon coriander seeds, coarsely crushed
2 teaspoons dried oregano
150 ml (¼ pint) olive oil
4 tablespoons red wine vinegar
1 onion, grated
2 bay leaves, roughly torn up
1 kg (2 lb 4 oz) boneless leg or shoulder of lamb, trimmed and cut into 2 cm (¾ inch) cubes
salt and pepper
lemon wedges, to serve

Mix together the coriander seeds, oregano, oil, vinegar, onion, bay leaves and salt and pepper and pour them over the lamb. Turn to coat, then cover and marinate for at least 2 hours, better still a full 24 hours.

Thread the meat on to brochettes or small wooden skewers. Grill on a barbecue, close to the heat, until browned but not cooked to death, turning and brushing with the marinade. Serve with lemon wedges.

My first encounter with hyssop was on a trip to the Holy Land. One of my many food-related souvenirs was a box of dried hyssop, which I foisted on my mother. We made a few attempts at sprinkling it on bread, which seemed suitably biblical, found it quite intriguing and then forgot all about it. The packet languished for several years at the back of a cupboard and finally met its end in the dustbin. Only now do I discover that the hyssop referred to in the Bible ('thou shalt purge me with Hyssop, and I shall be made clean') was probably a form of oregano. Maybe we should have attempted something less scriptural.

These days, I am the lucky possessor of a bush of fresh hyssop, which is quite another matter. For a start, I am reminded of its presence every time I wander up to the herb garden – the bees adore it and buzz around it excitedly when it is in flower. And secondly, I have discovered what an exciting herb it can be and how very well it does, in fact, work in bread doughs, biblical or not. Its thin leaves have an immensely pleasing flavour, with a mild bitterness overlaid by a warm, spicy veneer carrying echoes of rosemary and mint. In June the purple-blue flowers begin to bloom (there are also white and pink-flowered varieties), their scent a delicate version of that of the foliage, which is excellent sprinkled into salads or over egg dishes.

One of the great advantages of hyssop is that it is in leaf throughout the winter, when other aromatics are on the wane. Roughly chopped and scattered over wintry tomato salads it energizes the flavour of dull hot-house specimens, but it has even more value as an addition to winter stews, and in particular rabbit and game stews – it is surpassingly good with venison. I like it, too, with pulses and lentils, or mixed into stuffings for vegetables and meat. It comes as more of a surprise to discover that it is rather pleasant with fruit, particularly tender tree fruit such as plums and peaches. Add a small sprig (it is fairly powerful stuff) to syrups for fruit compotes, for making sorbets or for moistening cakes. If you've overindulged at the table, then a brew of hyssop leaves, dried or fresh, may soothe a troubled stomach and dispel flatulence.

Storage and Preservation

The fresh herb is pretty sturdy, so it keeps well in a tightly sealed plastic box or bag in the vegetable drawer of the fridge. If you want to dry hyssop, pick the branches just as they are coming into flower, then hang up in an airy, dry place.

It may seem radical and modern but slipping a sprig of hyssop into the syrup for marinating peaches is actually an old trick. The scent of the herb and the sprightliness of lemon does wonders for ripe but dull peaches, and naturally is even better with fragrant fruit. If you don't have access to a bush of hyssop you can replace it with rosemary, which shares some of hyssop's characteristics and goes very well with fresh peaches.

The marinated peaches make a refreshing pudding on their own, but for something a little more jazzy try partnering them with a slice of rich chocolate cake and a scoop of crème fraîche.

Serves 4–6

4 ripe peaches, skinned
juice of ½ small lemon
60 g (2 oz) granulated or caster sugar
2 strips of lemon zest
1 sprig of hyssop, plus 1 more sprig to garnish
90 ml (3 fl oz) water

Halve the peaches and discard the stones, then slice. Turn the slices in the lemon juice to stave off browning for a little while. Put the sugar, lemon zest and hyssop into a pan with the water and stir over a moderate heat until the sugar has dissolved. Bring up to the boil and simmer for 3 minutes. Pour the mixture over the peach slices and leave to cool, by which time they should have formed enough syrup to submerge them. Pick out the bedraggled hyssop sprig. Cover the peaches with clingfilm and chill until needed (a few hours at most). Stir again to disguise the inevitable browning of the upper layer, garnish with a new sprig of hyssop and dish up.

Fresh Hyssop and Cornmeal Focaccia

Based on recipes for Italian focaccia, this bread takes on a golden yellow hue from the cornmeal in the dough and an aromatic warmth from the fresh hyssop. If you can't get fresh hyssop, use dried, about half the amount, either worked into the dough or sprinkled on top before the final rising and baking.

The bread is brilliant with cheese (particularly goat's cheese or blue cheeses) and also makes lovely chunky sandwiches, split in two. If you have any left over, it toasts very nicely indeed.

Makes a 30 x 20 cm (12 x 8 inch) flat loaf

450 g (1 lb) strong white flour, plus extra for kneading
500 ml (18 fl oz) warm water
7 g sachet of easy-blend yeast
2 teaspoons light muscovado sugar
250 g (9 oz) cornmeal or polenta
1 tablespoon salt
6 tablespoons olive oil, plus extra to finish
4 tablespoons chopped hyssop leaves
coarse sea salt, to scatter over the dough

Sift one third of the strong flour. Put the warm water into a large bowl and whisk in the sifted flour, the yeast and sugar. Keep whisking until smooth, then cover with a damp tea towel and leave in a warm place for at least 30 minutes and up to 2 hours.

Now mix in the remaining flour, cornmeal and salt. Stir to make a wet dough. If you have a mixer with a bread hook, now is the time to get it out. If you don't, then get ready to get messy. With a mixer, scrape the dough into the bowl and add 3 tablespoons of the olive oil. Knead slowly, adding a little flour here and there, until the dough begins to stretch and develop elasticity – usually after about 5 minutes.

With no mixer to hand, leave the dough in the bowl and pour over 3 tablespoons of the olive oil. Oil your hands, then plunge them under the wet dough, scooping it up and stretching it damply, then turning it over and letting it back down. At first it will just be soggy lumps but soon the gluten will start to develop and it will begin to stretch. Sprinkle the dough with a little flour as you knead to flesh it out, and keep going for about 5 minutes, turning and stretching the dough. When the dough feels smoother and elastic, cover again with a damp tea towel and leave in a warm place for about an hour, until doubled in bulk.

Come back to the dough, drizzle over the remaining olive oil and sprinkle over the hyssop. Repeat the same sort of kneading, again dusting lightly with flour as you go, for 5 minutes or so. Now tip the dough into an oiled 30 x 20 cm (12 x 8 inch) baking tin and spread and tease it out to the corners with freshly oiled hands. Smear a little more oil over the top, then push your fingers down into the dough here and there to make nice dimples. Scatter with coarse salt and then leave to rise again for another hour or so, covered with a damp tea towel.

Pre-heat the oven to 220°C/425°F/Gas Mark 7.

Bake the bread for 25–30 minutes, until golden brown and cooked through. Run a knife round the edge, then turn out on to a wire rack. For best eating, serve warm from the oven.

Opposite
**Fresh
Hyssop and
Cornmeal
Focaccia**

methi (fenugreek)
Trigonella foenum-graecum

Years ago I was sent on a mission to Southall in west London, to report on an Indian restaurant there in one of the country's largest Indian communities. What fascinated me that day (and on many occasions since) were the marvellous food stores, packed inside with spices and cooking implements galore and displaying swathes of verdant, vigorous greenery on stands outside. The restaurateur said proudly that in Southall you can buy Indian vegetables and herbs in better condition than in many parts of India, for they are a mere stone's throw from Heathrow, where the planes land with fresh produce picked only a matter of one or two days earlier. Certainly the bunches of silvery, olive-green fenugreek, with delicate oval leaflets and pale ivory flowers, were as lively and fresh as you could hope for. It was the first time I'd come across fresh fenugreek greens and I was quickly seduced by the delicate perfume of curry that wafts from the blossoms as you brush your hand across the bunch.

Strangely enough, fenugreek is actually native to the Mediterranean – *foenum-graecum* means literally Greek hay, because it was used by ancient civilizations as fodder for cattle – but its use as a herb and a leafy vegetable is mainly confined to the Indian sub-continent and Iran. Though the leaves and flowers smell sweetly of curry, their flavour is less aromatic, but with a delicious mild bitterness. It sits particularly well with potatoes and chickpeas. Fenugreek is often cooked with spinach or chopped finely and added to puris and other Indian breads. The trick is to use just the tender upper portion and leaves, discarding the tougher lower stems. Taste the leaves and, if you like the flavour raw (I do, very much), add a small handful to green salads as well, or chop and stir into raw salsas based on tomatoes or on fruit such as mango or pineapple.

Look out for bunched fresh fenugreek, sold as *methi*, or *methi bhaji*, in Indian food stores, or in Iranian shops, where it will be sold as *shambaleeleh* – in Iran it is used in a herb *koresh* (stew) and *kuku*, a form of thick omelette. Dried fenugreek leaf, again available from Indian shops, is called *kasoori methi*, and can be used instead of fresh fenugreek, though it isn't quite so fragrant.

It is quite easy to grow your own fenugreek, straight from the fenugreek seeds that you buy as a spice. Sow liberally in a sheltered, well-drained corner of the herb garden and harvest when the plants are around 10–20 cm (4–8 inches) high. The sprouted seeds (sprouted indoors on flannels or in jam jars, just as you would mustard and cress) are lovely in salads and sandwiches.

Storage and Preservation
If you buy big, bouncy, perky bunches of fenugreek, then store in an airtight box or plastic bag (the aroma being rather too pervasive and not so enjoyable when it taints cream or milk) in the vegetable drawer of the fridge. You should find that it will keep for up to six or seven days. Dried fenugreek leaves should be stored in airtight jars, away from the light.

Methi Chicken

I left the chicken in the oven to cook as I bathed the children. By the time they were in their pyjamas the whole house was wreathed in heavenly smells of roasting chicken, garlic and, above all, fragrant curry with a leafy green edge to it. And by the time they were sound asleep, our supper was done, and dragging me downstairs by the nose.

This was the first non-Asian dish that I had cooked with *methi*, and it made me realize just what a marvellous herb fresh fenugreek is, and how very adaptable. The preparation is simplicity itself – a matter of a few minutes only – and the effect is quite out of proportion to the work involved. Potatoes and, if you can get them, Jerusalem artichokes are cooked in the same dish as the chicken, so all you need add is a good green salad to follow.

Serves 4–5

1 large chicken, preferably free-range
5 tablespoons olive oil
1 lemon, cut in half
8–10 garlic cloves, unpeeled
250 g (9 oz) small new potatoes, scrubbed but not peeled
250 g (9 oz) Jerusalem artichokes, scrubbed but not peeled (optional)
½ bunch of *methi* (fenugreek) leaves (discard stalks)
coarse salt and pepper

With a pair of poultry shears, a stout pair of scissors or a sharp knife, spatchcock the chicken by cutting along its backbone (i.e. the underneath, opposite the breast) from neck to tail end and trimming off extraneous flaps of fat. Now press down along the breast bone with the flat of your hand, flattening out the chicken like a squashed toad. Smear about 1½ tablespoons of the olive oil over the base of a roasting tin with room to take the flattened chicken and a little more to spare. Lay the chicken in it.

Squeeze the lemon juice over it with your hands, or in a juicer if you prefer, but why make extra washing up when it isn't really necessary? Rub the juice in, then season with coarse salt and pepper. Spread the garlic, potatoes and Jerusalem artichokes, if using, in a single layer on either side of the chicken and wherever there is room for them. Season with salt and pepper. Scatter the *methi* over the whole lot, then drizzle over the remaining olive oil. Turn the potatoes and artichokes so that they are coated in oil. Cover the tin with foil.

Bake for 30 minutes at 220°C/425°F/Gas Mark 7, then uncover, baste the chicken and turn the vegetables. Return to the oven, uncovered, for a further 20–30 minutes, basting once, until chicken and vegetables are cooked through. Serve immediately, cutting the chicken up into large chunks with scissors or a knife.

methi

coriander
Coriandrum sativum

Tastes change with the times, and the taste for coriander leaf more than most. These days we can't get enough of it. Even the supermarkets have begun to bow to pressure and are selling coriander in generous, sexy, gorgeously ample bunches. And yet, until some twenty years ago, and possibly even later than that, it was barely acknowledged that the leaf was edible. The seed was accepted and even appreciated in northerly Britain – the Romans had introduced it to us long ago – but the leaf…aah, the leaf was definitely considered non-U, even downright disgusting. Certainly only fit for the palate of peculiar foreigners.

Flicking through a handful of books on herbs and flavourings written before 1978, I found that if coriander leaf was mentioned at all it was at best in passing and more than likely in a disparaging tone: it has a 'fetid and unpleasant smell' (Colin Clair, 1961); 'As the seeds ripen, about August, the disagreeable odour gives place to a pleasant aroma' while 'The inhabitants of Peru are so fond of the taste and smell of this herb that it enters into almost all their dishes, and the taste is often objectionable to any but a native' (Mrs M. Grieve, 1931); and, a few centuries earlier, '…coriander is a very stinking herbe, smelling like the stinking worme…' (John Gerard, 1597).

Let me declare a passion for this 'very stinking herbe'. If I could take only one herb with me to my desert island, then I think it would have to be coriander for there is no other herb to match it. It works a singular magic on foods of all kinds (oh okay, perhaps not puddings), spiriting them from the realms of the dull and dependable up into the celestial spheres of delight. Am I getting a little carried away here? Well, maybe, but I'm not exactly alone in this fondness for coriander. It is, apparently, the most widely and enthusiastically used herb in the world, and even in our own little islands it is the second-bestselling fresh cut herb in supermarkets, superseded only by parsley. Over the past decade, after centuries of loathing, we have taken coriander to our hearts, following belatedly in the footsteps of the Chinese, Indians, South-east Asians, Latin Americans, Arabs, Africans and Portuguese.

Now there is a strange thing – the Portuguese like coriander leaf and have done for centuries, the only European nation to take any interest in it. Maybe that's something to do with their trading colonies in the East, though funnily enough coriander is actually native to southern Europe. Its name is derived from the Greek word *koris*, meaning bed bug, because the smell was said to be similar. So there we are – we Europeans thought it worthless, passed it on to other nations who recognized its true value, and now we are welcoming it back with open arms.

If you have never tried coriander before, you may at first find it a little unexpected in flavour, but go back for more because it is addictive and, as addictive things go, relatively good for you. If only it worked as a substitute for nicotine… Once a taste for the herb is acquired, you will find no shortage of ways to use it. A few leaves thrown into salads or scattered over gentle soups is only a beginning. Try it on grilled meats and fish; in vinaigrettes of all kinds; on roast or barbecued vegetables; in herb-heavy sauces; in dips based on yoghurt, soured cream, puréed vegetables such as aubergine, pulses such as hummus, or seeds such as tahini. It is absolutely the herb for fresh salsas (mix with finely diced tomatoes, spring onion, garlic, chilli and lime juice, or replace the tomato with papaya, mango or pineapple, omitting the garlic). Sprinkle it over chicken and tomato stews, add a shot to braised red meat and go wild with it on fresh tuna.

Coriander and spices are a blessed union, which is why it is so very popular in India and China; on curries and stir-fries, on piled-high plates of noodles, in clear soups…the list goes on and on. Mix coriander, chilli and lime and you have captured the flavour of Latin America, a combination that electrifies comforting bean dishes and floury tortillas. That same starry trio is reunited in the dishes of Thailand and Indonesia, right on the other side of the world, while in Vietnam they use it almost as a salad leaf (see p. 197).

Opposite
Methi Chicken
(page 77)

Guacamole

Coriander is a herb that must be used with generosity. A mean teaspoon or two of chopped greenery will get you nowhere. These days it is easy to get it all year round in decent quantity from both small ethnic groceries and some of the larger supermarkets, which have at last stepped beyond measly little flat packlets. Ignore the weedy, spindly tangles of adolescent greenery that are sold as 'growing herbs' – they taste of practically nothing. If you have space enough, then consider growing your own in the summer months, and look out for varieties like 'Cilantro', which are less inclined to bolt. To keep the green leaf going for as long as possible, pick hard and frequently, removing flowering stems quickly. The little ferny upper leaves are a bit fiddly to pick and use but still taste okay, though perhaps a little less enticing than the larger flat lower leaves. Incidentally, the roots are not to be wasted. They have a deep, earthy coriander scent and are used extensively in Thai cooking, pounded to a paste with other aromatics.

Storage and Preservation

Coriander is not blessed with longevity. Store the cut leaves in an airtight plastic box or bag lined with dry kitchen paper in the vegetable drawer of the fridge. Before you stash it, pick off any yellowing or damaged leaves and stalks, and do the same every day that you keep it. If it is in a good state when you buy it, it should last for up to four days and maybe a little more if you are lucky and attentive. Wash the leaves only just before using. If there are roots, you can slice them off and pop them into the freezer wrapped in clingfilm until you have the time and the inclination to cook Thai food. The leaves can also be frozen. Chop them finely and pack into small paper or plastic cups or containers (ice-cube trays are too small and mean for big-hearted coriander), adding enough water to cover them. You can also freeze sauces like the Coriander Salsa Verde on p. 81 or coriander-based versions of pesto (see p. 65).

Guacamole, essentially mashed avocados gleefully spiced up, is an incredibly useful sort of a food. It is a great starter with nothing more than strips of warm pitta bread and raw vegetables to dip into it, but it slides easily into the role of sauce or relish, to serve with grilled or roast poultry or fish or to dollop on burgers or into warmed tortillas with spiced minced beef or chicken (see p. 161) and a chilli-hot tomato salsa. It is also very good spooned on to baked potatoes.

Serves 4 (or more if it is an incidental rather than a mainstay)

¼ red onion, chopped
2 garlic cloves, chopped
3 tablespoons roughly chopped coriander, plus a few leaves
    to garnish
1–2 green or red chillies, deseeded and chopped
2–3 avocados, depending on size
2 tomatoes, skinned, deseeded and finely chopped
juice of ½–1 lime
a pinch of sugar
salt and pepper
a sprinkling of cayenne pepper, to serve

Mix the onion, garlic, coriander and chillies on a chopping board and chop together very finely (or whizz them together in brief spurts in a food processor, watching that you don't end up with a purée). Peel and stone the avocados and mash with a potato masher or fork (but don't put them in the processor, since you want to end up with a slightly uneven mush, though it shouldn't be positively lumpy). Mix the avocados with the chopped flavourings, tomatoes, juice of ½ a lime, a pinch of sugar and salt and pepper. Taste and add more lime if needed. There should be just enough to take the edge off the richness of the avocado without making it too tart. Scoop into a bowl, smooth down and cover the surface of the guacamole with clingfilm to keep the air out as much as possible and so delay browning. Just before serving, give it a light stir to reveal the vivid colour of the purée, then scatter with a little extra coriander and a very light dusting of cayenne.

Coriander Salsa Verde

Goat's Cheese and Courgette Quesadilla with Avocado, Mango and Coriander Salsa

Salsa verde, at least the one that this is based on, is a piquant Italian sauce, traditionally served with boiled meats. Italian salsa verde is made with copious amounts of parsley and perhaps a handful of basil or mint thrown in for good measure. This salsa verde, which I first made in an emergency when unexpected guests turned up for lunch, is dominated by a great big beautiful bunch of coriander leaves, with their inimitable fragrance. That first time, I served it with wedges of roast winter squash, roast baby beetroot and roast onions, together with a big spoonful of crème fraîche, alongside a salad of rocket. It was a most delicious meal, quite unintentionally vegetarian.

Coriander salsa verde also goes very well with pale meats such as rabbit or chicken, or veal, or indeed with quickly seared or grilled fish. You can even smear it in sandwiches, with slices of grilled aubergine or chicken and salad. No doubt, if coriander is your kind of thing, you can come up with any number of permutations. Exact quantities of coriander and parsley are at your discretion – it is the bunch that counts, and I give approximate weights only as a rough guide.

Serves 6

1 bunch of coriander (around 75 g/2½ oz leaves)
½ bunch of flat-leaf parsley (around 30 g/1 oz)
6 anchovy fillets
2 tablespoons capers
2 garlic cloves, roughly chopped
1 slice of bread, crusts removed, torn up (about 60 g (2 oz) after the crusts have been cut off)
½ teaspoon sugar
2 tablespoons white wine vinegar
150–250 ml (5–9 fl oz) olive oil
pepper

Slash the leaves from the coriander and parsley. Put them into a food processor with all the other ingredients except the olive oil. Process in short bursts, scraping down the sides, until finely chopped. Keep the blades whirring as you trickle in enough olive oil to give a thickish, creamy sauce. Taste and adjust the seasoning – the anchovies and capers should make it salty enough, so only add extra salt if it really needs it.

A quesadilla is a stuffed, cooked tortilla, or, in this instance, a stack of tortillas sandwiched together with an unctuous filling and baked in the oven until the outer edges of the tortillas are crisp as a wafer and the inner cheese is molten.

Serves 2 as a main course, 4 as a starter.

3 x 17–20 cm (7–8 inch) flour tortillas

For the filling
1 shallot, sliced
2 courgettes (around 330g/12 oz), cut into matchsticks
1 red pepper, cut into narrow strips
2 tablespoons olive oil
2 garlic cloves, chopped
2 tablespoons chopped coriander
½ tablespoon balsamic vinegar
90g (3 oz) goat's cheese, crumbled
140g (5 oz) taleggio or fontina, rinds removed then thinly sliced, or 125g (4½ oz) grated medium Cheddar
salt and pepper

For the salsa
1 avocado, peeled, stoned and finely diced
1 small–medium mango, peeled, stoned and finely diced
2 shallots, finely chopped
3 tablespoons chopped coriander
juice of 1 lime
1–2 red chillies, deseeded and finely chopped
salt

To make the salsa, mix all the ingredients, then cover and store in the fridge until needed.

To make the filling, sauté the shallot, courgettes and pepper in the oil over a brisk heat until limp and patched with brown (about 8–10 minutes). Add the garlic and sauté for a few minutes more. Draw off the heat and stir in the coriander, vinegar, salt and pepper.

Lay one tortilla on a baking tray. Spread half of the vegetable mixture over it, then sprinkle over half the goat's cheese and half of the taleggio or fontina or Cheddar. Lay a second tortilla over it and repeat the filling. Cover with the last tortilla and press down firmly, but not too forcefully, to even out the levels. Bake at 240°C/450°F/Gas Mark 8 for 8–12 minutes until the tortillas are crisp at the edges and the cheese has melted. Cut into wedges and serve immediately with the avocado and mango salsa.

rocket

Eruca vesicaria subsp. *sativa*

Call it what you will – rocket, arugula, rucola, roquette, rokka – this remains the kingpin salad herb of the nineties, here, there and everywhere, as garnish, component, mainstay, from the smallest bistro with a yen for smarter things to the most chichi of London restaurants. Such is its power and allure that there can be little doubt that it will hold on to its starring role well into the new millennium. In fact, what is so bizarre is how unfashionable and neglected a salad herb it has been for most of the twentieth century and some years before. We used to grow rocket in this country – Evelyn mentioned it in his seventeenth-century *Salad Calendar*, among many other references – but then we stopped caring for it and forgot all about it. I imagine that this may be at least in part due to the Victorians, so handy for such blame, who found rocket too pushy and headstrong for their taste. It eclipses namby-pamby flavours with consummate ease, stamping out the subtle glory, of, say, a blanquette of chicken, or even the delicate pallor of nursery food.

Still, rocket was not lost. In Italy, Cyprus and other warm-weather pockets, they never lost sight of the jump-for-joy vivacity of their arugula or rokka. It quietly carried on pleasing and at last foolish Northerners rediscovered what they had been missing. These days we take pleasure in big flavours – garlic and sun-dried tomatoes, anchovies, chargrilled meats and marinated fish – and rocket is having a ball. It has presence and substance, where other lettuce leaves are merely sweet and insubstantial. It does have the pungency of a herb, but a particular peppery pungency that is not unpalatable by the mouthful.

Well, I say not unpalatable, though that does depend on the variety and maturity of the rocket in question. Younger, more delicate rocket (often labelled roquette, which I find irritatingly pretentious but don't mind me), with fine, perky little green leaves, and inordinately fashionable spikey-leaved wild rocket, are brilliant served as a salad all on their own without the softening mercy of other leaves and ingredients. Middle-of-the-road, middle-sized rocket is fine for salads, too, though some may find it a tad domineering, preferring to mix it with lamb's lettuce

Opposite
Clockwise from top left: rocket; dandelion; garden sorrel; Buckler leaf sorrel; summer purslane; wild rocket Centre: salad burnet

(mâche), say, or a few leaves of mollifying Cos. It does a fine job as a backdrop to other flavours, from the joy of an oozy poached egg to strips of roast red pepper, sweet summer tomatoes or little warm boiled potatoes. Put it with a steak of rare chargrilled or seared tuna and a tomato and black olive salad and you can't fail. Then there is the coarser sort of rocket, the type that is sold impressively cheaply in Cypriot and Turkish greengroceries, in deliriously big bunches – a lovely sight indeed. Now, this sort of rocket lets you know clearly that it belongs to the crucifer family, with that familiar whiff of sulphur that you find in Brussels sprouts and their ilk. A confirmed rocket fan, such as me, will have no difficulty with that, but even I think it best softened in a mixed leaf salad, or clamped between two bits of bread, along with some Parma ham or shavings of Parmesan and a shake of vinaigrette. It really comes into its own, however, when it is cooked. That's right. Rocket is not to be consigned to the salad bowl alone. Down south, in Italy and other Mediterranean locations, they are much more inventive. I have a particular yen for a Pugliese rocket and potato soup but it is also a dream stirred into hot pasta with tomato sauce or chopped finely to make a filling for ravioli and the like. The heat tames it to a degree but what remains is a deep, proud flavour that comes as a bit of a revelation.

The price of the more refined forms of rocket is monstrously high considering how easily it grows – mint probably gets the bunny of the herb universe award, but rocket thrusts up like billy-oh and even a not-too-green-fingered, lazy-as-sin gardener like me can reap a decent crop with indecent haste and idleness. If you do grow your own, remember to plant in succession, in other words a little and often, so that you can reap the rewards over a period of weeks rather than having to live on nothing but rocket and bore your friends rigid with bags of it for a mere fortnight or two. When buying rocket, ignore the tiny packs that are lodged with other herbs and search through the salad shelves for more bountiful bagfuls. For cooking, your best bet is to search out a Greek or Turkish greengrocer's, where it will be sold as rokka in generous bunches.

This rocket and potato soup is a soothing one, with the flavour of the rocket softened by its brief exposure to heat. What makes it really sing, however, is the final addition of a dollop of rich mascarpone, and a scattering of fried capers and crisp, golden nuggets of garlic.

Serves 4–6

1 onion, chopped
675 g (1½ lb) potatoes, peeled and cut into cubes
3 garlic cloves, chopped
4 tablespoons olive oil
1.5 litres (2½ pints) light chicken stock
125 g (4 oz) rocket leaves, roughly chopped
2 teaspoons balsamic, white wine or sherry vinegar or lemon juice
salt and pepper

To serve
2 generous tablespoons vinegar-pickled capers, rinsed and drained
3 tablespoons olive oil
2 large garlic cloves, chopped
2–3 tablespoons mascarpone cheese
cayenne pepper (optional)

To make the soup, put the onion, potatoes, garlic and olive oil in a large pan, stir about, then cover and sweat for 15 minutes. Uncover and add the stock, salt and pepper. Bring up to the boil and simmer for 15–20 minutes, until the potatoes are tender. Stir in the rocket and cook for another minute. Liquidize or process in batches, then rub through a sieve. Stir in the vinegar or lemon juice, then taste and adjust the seasoning. Any glueyness from processing the potatoes will slink away if you leave the soup to rest for an hour or two.

Just before you reheat and serve the soup, dry the capers thoroughly. Heat the oil in a small frying pan over a moderate heat. Add the capers and garlic and fry until the garlic is golden. Draw off the heat. Beat the mascarpone lightly to loosen the texture. Either ladle the soup into individual bowls, adding a spoonful of mascarpone and a scattering of capers and garlic with a little of their oil, or pour it into a tureen and dot with dollops of mascarpone, then spoon over the capers, garlic and oil. If you like its colour and heat, dust the soup lightly with cayenne pepper.

Spaghetti with Tomato Sauce and Rocket

The simplest of pasta and rocket recipes, where the green of the rocket is matched by the scarlet of a simple tomato sauce. The intensity of the sauce is perfect with the rocket that has just been wilted in its heat. In the height of tomatoey summer in Italy, it is traditional to make vats of basic tomato sauce to be bottled and stashed away for Christmas. Though the bottled tomato sauces that we get here aren't quite the same, many of the latest generation of cooked semi-puréed tomatoes are similar, with a pleasing scattering of chunks of tomato to relieve the smoothness. I use a lot of one brand called Sugo Casa, which has an excellent texture and flavour without the addition of herbs, making it the perfect base for simple sauces to be flavoured as I desire, not as the manufacturers fancy.

Serves 4

400–450 g (14 oz–1 lb) tagliatelle or spaghetti
a little olive oil
60–85 g (2–3 oz) rocket, tougher stems removed and leaves roughly chopped
freshly grated Parmesan cheese, to serve

For the tomato sauce
2 large sprigs of thyme
1 bay leaf
1 sprig of rosemary
700 g (1 lb 9 oz) jar of Sugo Casa, or other semi-puréed plain tomato sauce or passata
2 garlic cloves, crushed
2 tablespoons olive oil
1–2 teaspoons sugar
salt and pepper

For the sauce, tie the herbs together in a little bundle with a piece of string, then put into a pan with all the remaining sauce ingredients. Bring up to the boil and simmer gently for 25–30 minutes, stirring occasionally. Taste and adjust the seasoning. Reheat when needed.

Cook the pasta in plenty of boiling salted water until *al dente*. Drain thoroughly, toss with a little olive oil to lubricate, then pile into a hot serving bowl or individual bowls. Quickly ladle over some of the hot tomato sauce, scatter over the rocket and serve straight away, tossing everything together at the table. Pass around a bowl of freshly grated Parmesan to sprinkle over the pasta.

Rocket and Spiced Salmon Salad with Honey, Lime and Chilli Dressing

This recipe serves as a good example of how to use rocket as a sturdy but harmonizing support for other ingredients with a strong presence. It serves as a cushion for wedges of salmon, coated in crushed spices and then fried. Together the rocket and salmon make an excellent quickly prepared first course, or even the main course of a light meal.

Serves 6 as a starter, 4 as a main course

450 g (1 lb) skinned salmon fillet
1½ heaped tablespoons freeze-dried green peppercorns
1½ heaped tablespoons coriander seeds
olive oil
125 g (4 oz) rocket leaves
4 pieces of sun-dried tomato in olive oil, cut into long, thin strips

For the dressing
2 tablespoons runny honey
juice of 1 lime
1–2 teaspoons chilli sauce
1 tablespoon sesame oil
1 tablespoon fish sauce
2 tablespoons water

To make the dressing, put all the ingredients into a small pan and stir over a low heat, without letting them boil, until smoothly mixed. Leave to cool.

Cut the salmon into 4–6 portions, depending on how many people you are feeding. Crush the green peppercorns and coriander coarsely in a mortar, then spread out on a plate. Brush the salmon pieces lightly with olive oil on both sides, then coat in the crushed peppercorns and coriander. Heat about 1 tablespoon of oil in a wide frying pan over a high heat. Fry the salmon pieces for 1–2 minutes on each side until cooked to your liking (I think it best slightly underdone and translucent in the centre, but not everyone agrees).

As the fish cooks, quickly toss the rocket with enough of the dressing to coat it nicely, then arrange on individual plates. Lay the salmon on the salad, scatter over the sun-dried tomato strips, then drizzle a little more dressing over the salmon. Serve straight away.

summer and winter purslane

Portulaca oleracea, Portulaca sativa and
Claytonia perfoliata (or *Montia perfoliata*)

'This plant is so well known that a short description may serve...' That's what the herbalist Nicholas Culpeper wrote in the seventeenth century. Purslane was a commonplace plant then, grown widely in Britain for its fleshy leaves with their peculiar, sharp, slightly astringent juiciness. Every herbal praises it to high heaven and old cookery books include many a recipe for salads of purslane and other leaves, or pickled purslane leaves and stems. It was also much loved in France, Italy and, further afield, in the Middle East. Over there the fondness for a spot of purslane has not waned. Here we've forgotten about it altogether.

Well, almost altogether. You can buy purslane seeds relatively easily, which suggests that somebody somewhere is growing it, and if you choose to scan the offerings in Cypriot or Arab greengroceries you are more than likely to stumble across bunches of purslane flown in from warmer shores. Most of the purslane grown from seed will be the red-stemmed variety (*Portulaca oleracea*) but occasionally I have bought larger-leaved purslane with green stems, which I think must be golden purslane (*Portulaca sativa*). The two of them taste very similar, and the difference in leaf size is probably more to do with maturity than anything else. These two are both forms of summer purslane. Winter purslane is quite different and you may well have it thrusting forth in your garden. This is claytonia, or spring beauty (*Claytonia perfoliata*), a quaintly pretty import from the west coast of North America which, despite its name, flowers in the winter. The tiny flowers push up through the centre of the leaves like some ready-made miniature nosegay. They are entirely edible and make an attractive addition to a mixed leaf salad. In Britain we also have, growing wild on our southern and eastern coasts, a fourth plant known as sea purslane, with beautiful silvery leaves which can also be added to salads.

The summer purslanes, though, are the really interesting and valuable culinary plants. When the stems are slender and the leaves young they can be tossed into salads, adding a very particular flavour which is much appreciated in the Middle East. John Evelyn recommended eating it alone with 'Oyl and Vinegar'. And again in the seventeenth century, Giacomo Castelvetro wrote that back home in Italy 'purslane is eaten a lot as a salad on its own, or with other herbs; we always add pepper and finely chopped onion to counteract its coldness'. That coldness is an oft-repeated quality attached to purslane and, with its fleshy lobes, like a more elegant, spine-free version of some decorative cactus, you can see why. This cold herb was 'good to allay the heat of the liver, blood, veins, stomach and hot agues'. It was also reckoned to do wonders for gonorrhoea and to be most efficacious in cases of blasting by lightning or planets and burning by gunpowder. I'm so glad I wasn't born 300 years ago...

As the plant grows, the leaves become more noticeably astringent, and from then on they are better blanched in a pan of boiling salted water (they need only 10 seconds or so to do the trick) before use. This brings out their mucilaginous quality, something like the slipperiness of okra but less pronounced. Served as a hot vegetable, all they need is a little melting butter and some salt and pepper; or you can dress the hot cooked purslane with olive oil, a squeeze or two of lemon, salt and plentiful pepper to serve as a cold salad. For a more substantial cold salad (handy when your purslane harvest is rather smaller than anticipated), mix the cold cooked purslane with strips of grilled red pepper and anchovy or crumbled feta cheese, or toss lightly with rocket and nasturtium leaves, then sprinkle with chopped hard-boiled egg and black olives.

Opposite
**Rocket and
Spiced
Salmon Salad
with Honey,
Lime and
Chilli
Dressing**
(page 85)

Fattoush

Purslane is a hot favourite in Mexico, where it is used enthusiastically as a cooked vegetable, briefly blanched. One way to prepare it is to sauté onion and garlic with a little chilli in olive oil until tender, then add a few chopped, skinned and deseeded tomatoes (or the wonderful green tomatillos that are so hard to find in the UK). When this is softened, stir in the blanched purslane and serve as it is – or (even nicer) spoon it over fried eggs, or pile it into a taco or tortilla with a spoonful of soured cream, some diced cheese or sautéed potato cubes. It also goes particularly well with fatty meats such as pork.

If you do decide to grow purslane, sow plentifully as the plants are on the small side. It's a very thirsty plant, so in hot weather remember to water it regularly. When harvesting, cut the stems right down to encourage a vigorous new crop.

Storage and Preservation

Though at its best when newly picked, robust and fleshy summer purslane will survive moderately well in the fridge. Stash in an airtight container and regularly pick off any damaged leaves. It should still be quite edible after five days or so. To preserve purslane, blanch first in salted water, then pickle in spiced, sweetened vinegar. Winter purslane is best used on the day it is picked.

Fattoush is a Middle Eastern salad, an orchestra of ingredients that come together in a carefully thought-out harmony. One of the players should, by rights, be fleshy-lobed purslane. Its astringency is balanced by all the other bits and bobs but it adds a crucial note to the whole. If purslane is quite out of the question, the salad will still be enormously enjoyable, even if it is missing out ever so slightly.

Serves 6–8

1 cucumber, diced
1 pitta bread
juice of 1 lemon
4 tomatoes, deseeded and diced
6 spring onions or 1 red onion, chopped
leaves of 1 small bunch of purslane, chopped if large
4 tablespoons chopped parsley
2 tablespoons chopped mint
2 tablespoons chopped coriander
2 garlic cloves, crushed
6–7 tablespoons olive oil
salt and pepper

Spread the cucumber dice out in a colander and sprinkle lightly with salt. Leave for 30 minutes to drain, then rinse and dry on kitchen paper.

Split open the pitta bread and toast with the opened side to the heat until browned and crisp. Break up into small pieces and place in a salad bowl. Sprinkle with about a third of the lemon juice. Now add all the remaining ingredients, including the cucumber. Turn with your hands to mix. Taste and adjust the seasoning, adding more lemon juice if needed.

purslane

salad burnet
Sanguisorba minor (Poterium sanguisorba)

I'm sorry but I really can't get excited about salad burnet, at least not as a culinary herb. I do grow it, but merely for the sight of the very pretty foliage. In his *Newe Herball* of 1551, William Turner described it thus: 'It has two little leives like unto the wings of birdes, standing out as the bird setteth her wings out when she intendeth to flye'. The pairs of little tooth-edged oval leaves ranged along the tender stem are lovely to look at, and the crimson bobbles of flowerheads add a gay splash of colour. The rather curious thing about them is their multi-sexual orientation. At the top the tiny flowers are female, in the middle they are hermaphrodite and at the very bottom they are male. Far more interesting, I think, than the taste of the herb itself. Usually it is described as cucumbery, which is not entirely untrue but none the less rather misleading. There is a note of cucumber in there, but there is also a slight bitterness and a hint of old hazelnut, which makes it sound much more intriguing than it really is.

Not for nothing is this called salad burnet. Salads are about the best place for it, in relatively small quantity. To be fair, it makes a pleasant enough addition, especially in early spring and late autumn when interesting salad greens are few on the ground. Chopped finely, it can be added in moderation to eggy dishes or stirred into soft, creamy cheese, together with chives, tarragon, parsley or chervil. If you are making a hot or cold sauce ravigote and you happen to have burnet growing nearby, add a little for sterling authenticity. The seventeenth-century herbalist Nicholas Culpeper recommended adding a few stalks with leaves to a 'cup of wine, especially claret... to quicken the spirits, refresh and clear the heart and drive away melancholy' – a habit that lives on to this day, though probably not for those reasons. These days burnet gets to float on cooling wine cups and long summer drinks, supposedly for the flavour it brings, though I suspect that people really just like it because it looks cute, jostling with a few borage flowers and a slice or two of strawberry. Quite jolly enough to drive away summer twilight melancholy.

Probably the best of all recommendations, though, came from Sir Francis Bacon, who suggested that it should be grown along garden paths and alleys with wild thyme and water mint 'to perfume the air most delightfully, being trodden on and crushed'. Very wise, and quite the best place for it. Admire and appreciate, but don't expect any great culinary returns from it.

Storage and Preservation
Placed in a plastic bag or box, salad burnet will keep for a day or two in the vegetable drawer of the fridge. Capture its flavour, if you like it, in vinegar (see below) to dress salads and flavour cordials, but otherwise enjoy its prettiness while it is around and forget about it when the winter cold sets in.

Burnet Vinegar
A recipe that comes from Jason Hill's *Wild Foods of Britain* (A & C Black, 1939). Salad burnet grows liberally in the wild on chalky soil, so if you ever come across a good cache on a walk, or if your garden burnet is in need of a good picking over (the more you pick, the better it will grow), here's one way to exploit it to the full:

'Fill a stone or glass jar loosely with the leaves, fill up with vinegar, stand it in a cool place for a week and then pour the vinegar on to another lot of leaves; at the end of another week, strain and bottle.'

Reginette with **Spring Herbs, Poached Eggs** and **Pecorino**

I think salad burnet earns its keep best when mixed with other herbs, to add discreet notes to an orchestra of aromatics. This dish of flat pasta (reginette, sometimes called lasagnette, are wide bands of pasta with frilly edges) has a beguiling freshness about it, garnered from the plentiful mixture of herbs and the lemon zest.

Serves 4

400–450 g (14 oz–1 lb) reginette (lasagnette), or tagliatelle or taglierini
4 eggs, poached
3 tablespoons extra virgin olive oil
finely grated zest of 1 lemon
3 tablespoons freshly grated pecorino cheese
1½ tablespoons chopped salad burnet
1 tablespoon chopped chives
2 tablespoons chopped parsley
1 tablespoon chopped chervil or sweet cicely
1 tablespoon chopped lovage
1 tablespoon chopped lemon balm
salt and pepper

Bring a large pan of water to the boil, adding 1 level tablespoon of salt for every 600 ml (1 pint) water. Add the pasta and boil until just *al dente*. Poach the eggs while the pasta is cooking. Drain the pasta thoroughly and toss with all the remaining ingredients except the eggs (but don't add any more salt). Taste and adjust the seasoning. Pile into bowls and top each one with a poached egg. Serve immediately, with extra pecorino for those who want it.

Opposite
Reginette with Spring Herbs, Poached Eggs and Pecorino

dandelion
Taraxacum officinale

...Dandelion this,
A college youth that flashes for a day
All gold; anon he doffs his gaudy suit,
Touch'd by the magic hand of some grave Bishop
And all at once, by commutation strange,
Becomes a Reverend Divine.
'The Village Curate', James Hurdis (1788)

Common, pesky weeds, that's what dandelions are, with tenacious roots that are the very devil to yank out. The lawn that can boast not a single dandelion is quite something. And yet, and yet...it has been known for respectable gardeners to cultivate those very weeds, in neat military rows, absolutely and undeniably on purpose. I'm not talking about some bizarre foreign practice, either, but one that survived in this country until the end of the last century. Richard Mabey in his riveting *Flora Britannica* quotes the son of a Cambridge seed merchant who remembered that 'it was customary for the gentry to grow dandelions in their unheated greenhouses for winter salads...it helped to prevent the rich port-drinking inhabitants from getting gout. Dandelion salads were very popular in those days; also sandwiches of thin brown bread and butter filled with dandelion leaves were served by the ladies for afternoon tea.' And why not? What a wonderful way to get your own back on a wayward weed, by taming it and regimenting it, then dishing it up on the dinner table.

Dandelion leaves, when they are young and newly grown in the spring, or tempted up out of the ground under glass in late winter, are really very good to eat. They have a pleasing bitterness at this stage, which can be subdued even further by blanching – the horticultural sort of blanching or, in other words, covering the young plants with upturned flower pots, a stone placed over the drainage hole, and letting them grow, pale and yellow, in the dark, rather like chicory or forced spring rhubarb. You occasionally still see this in those lovely, orderly French vegetable gardens that pepper the countryside. In the spring, rows of tender young dandelion leaves are hidden by an army of brick-red terracotta pots, in readiness for the salad bowl. Though the leaves may be mixed in with

other saladings, in the early months of the year there are relatively few to be picked in the garden. Instead, the bowl will be filled with the tender dandelion leaves which are coated with a sizzling dressing of hot lardons (thick batons of bacon), red wine vinegar and oil, perhaps with a little garlic or some croûtons for good measure. Delicious.

Those dainty Victorian sandwiches of dandelion leaves are also rather good, especially if you add a squeeze or two of lemon juice and grind over lots of black pepper. Not that dandelions are only to be enjoyed raw. Sweated in a little butter, they make a good filling for an omelette. Mrs Grieve suggested in her *Modern Herbal* (1931) that they should be cooked with spinach to soften the bitterness, then enriched with butter and seasoned with grated nutmeg (you could also add a little cream and leave it at that) or garlic, a teaspoonful of chopped onion or a little freshly grated lemon zest.

If you do cook dandelions, be prepared for a fairly pronounced flavour, which needs to be softened in some way (with eggs, cream, rice, potato and so on) or serve in small quantities almost as a relish. But beware of over-enthusiastic consumption of a weed that is to be had for nothing. Long, long folk experience has established that dandelions are not only a diuretic but also a laxative. Just look at their common names – in French they are called *pissenlit*, which translates directly into an old English name, piss-a-bed. Then there's wet-the-bed, pissy-bed, mess-a-bed and the lengthy but equally graphic 'one, two, three pee-a-bed'. I can't say that I've ever had direct proof of this, but then there's a limit to how many dandelions I can be bothered to pick at one fell swoop.

Storage and Preservation

Don't store dandelions for more than a day or two, stashed in a plastic bag at the bottom of the fridge. The leaves are not suitable for drying, though I have read of pickling the young flower buds. The dried root is used for medicinal purposes and as a coffee substitute.

Dandelion is not only good as a salad, but also delicious cooked and used with eggs. The hearts only are used, all the coarser, big leaves should be removed and only a small portion of the root, carefully scraped, left, just enough to keep the small leaves together. They should be well washed, then well dried...

Another quote. This time from *120 Ways of Cooking Eggs* by Marcel Boulestin and Robin Adair, first published in 1932.

Serves 2

6 dandelion hearts (see above)
4 eggs
1 tablespoon double cream
50 g (a scant 2 oz) unsalted butter
salt and pepper

Prepare the dandelion hearts as above. Beat the eggs with the cream, salt and pepper. Heat 30 g (1 oz) of the butter in a frying pan until foaming. Add the dandelions and season with salt and pepper. Cook for a few minutes until wilted and tender. Keep warm.

Melt the remaining butter in a saucepan over a very low heat (or, for the best scrambled egg ever, in a bowl set over a pan of simmering water – a slower method, but it pays in terms of taste), then add the eggs. Stir, scraping up any egg stuck to the bottom or the sides, until the mixture is thick and creamy. Take off the heat and divide between 2 plates. Lay the dandelions on top and pour over their juices. Eat immediately.

Dandelion and Chorizo Salad

This variation on the classic French warm dandelion salad theme replaces the bacon with spicy Spanish chorizo sausage. If you can, buy the thinner, semi-dried ones that are meant to be cooked. The salami-like fully dried chorizo can be used but will need to be diced rather than sliced and will be drier and chewier. Avoid anything that is labelled 'Spanish-style' as it is usually nothing like the real thing.

To turn the salad into a more substantial main course, place a whole poached egg on top of each serving. If you wish, soften the bitterness of dandelion by mixing it with other leaves.

Serves 4

a salad bowl of young dandelion leaves
2 slices of bread, cut 1 cm (½ inch) thick
4 tablespoons olive oil
150 g (5 oz) chorizo, thickly sliced or diced, or *lardons*
2 garlic cloves, chopped
1 tablespoon red wine vinegar
salt and pepper

Pick over the dandelion leaves, rinse and then dry in a clean tea towel. Pile into a serving bowl. Cut the crusts off the bread, then cut into cubes. Heat half the olive oil in a frying pan and fry the croûtons over a moderate heat, turning frequently, until fairly evenly browned. Drain on kitchen paper.

Wipe out the pan and add the remaining oil. Fry the chorizo or *lardons* over a high heat until browned. Add the garlic and fry for a few seconds longer, then draw off the heat. Let it cool for a minute, then stir in the vinegar and pour everything over the salad. Scatter over the croûtons, season with salt and pepper, toss and serve immediately.

Spring Herb Risotto

This is my springtime revenge risotto, the most delicious way I know of consuming dandelions. To make up the balance of greens, I add rocket, chives and parsley. Together these four greens make this one of the freshest of rice dishes. Later on in the year, even small dandelion leaves can be overly bitter so if you make this after mid-June, reduce the quantity to balance the risotto, or use blanched dandelion leaves.

Serves 4–6

1.2 litres (2 pints) chicken stock
3 shallots, chopped
2 garlic cloves, chopped
85 g (3 oz) butter
1 bay leaf
225 g (8 oz) risotto rice, e.g. arborio, vialone nano, carnaroli
1 glass of dry white wine
a handful of young dandelion leaves (around 30 g/1 oz), roughly chopped
a big handful of rocket leaves (around 60 g/2 oz), roughly chopped
4 tablespoons chopped chives
2 tablespoons chopped parsley
60 g (2 oz) Parmesan cheese, freshly grated, plus extra to serve
salt and pepper

Put the chicken stock in a pan and bring gently to the boil, then turn the heat down very low to keep it warm. While the stock is coming to the boil, gently fry the shallots and garlic in 60 g (2 oz) of the butter, without browning, until tender. Now add the bay leaf and rice and stir for 1 minute. Pour in the wine. Season lightly with salt and pepper. Stir until the wine has all been absorbed. Add a generous ladleful of hot stock and keep stirring until the stock has all been absorbed. Repeat until the risotto is almost cooked. The rice should be slightly *al dente*. Stir in one more ladleful of stock and all the dandelions and rocket and half the chives and parsley. Keep stirring until most of the stock has been absorbed, leaving a creamy but not dry risotto. Draw the pan off the heat and beat in the remaining butter, chives and parsley and the Parmesan. Taste and adjust the seasoning, then serve with more Parmesan for those who want it.

sorrel
Rumex acetosa and *Rumex scutatus*

For the cook, the two types of sorrel that matter are garden sorrel and buckler leaf sorrel, in that order. There's a third variety of minor culinary interest and that is wood sorrel, which pushes its pretty head up in woodlands in spring but is little more than a piece of frippery for garnishing. Technically speaking it is unrelated, but it has a sharpness that is similar to true sorrel. The three heart-shaped leaves that cluster at the tip of each stalk, bending backwards towards the ground, are lovely to look at but too delicate and tender for cooking, and besides, an abundance of wood sorrel could induce stomach pains. A few in a salad or on the side of the plate is about as far as it goes.

Garden sorrel (*Rumex acetosa*) is the sorrel for real cooking, for sauces, soups and the like. This is the sorrel that grows in every French kitchen garden, that pushes up its crown of long, bright, green leaves spring after spring, that offers a lively sharpness to refresh the heart, the palate and the stomach after the heavy comfort dishes of winter. If you don't have any in your garden, rush down to your nearest plant nursery and buy a pot or two straight away. It grows eagerly, easily and prolifically. Even I have never had any problems with it, and I've grown it in windowboxes, containers and straight in the ground. About the only thing I know of (from bitter experience) that will kill it is repeated showerings of cats' pee, but that does for just about anything. The more you pick, the better it will grow, so go for it with enthusiasm. You'll be doing yourself a favour, for sorrel houses healthy quantities of vitamins A and C. Oxalic acid is what gives it its tartness.

If you have room, add a couple of plants of buckler leaf sorrel (*Rumex scutatus*), which has tiny, squat, shield-shaped leaves and a more lemony, gentler acidity than its larger cousin. The shape of the leaves is charming, and they look and taste superb in a salad. Although he was more likely to have been referring to garden sorrel, John Evelyn's words seem particularly appropriate to buckler leaf sorrel: 'Together with salt, it gives both the name and the relish to sallets from the sapidity, which renders not plants and herbs only, but men themselves pleasant and agreeable'.

Garden sorrel is a little harsher, but in moderation the finely shredded leaves make a nicely tart addition to a green salad, or a mixed salad of cooked pulses, tomato and finely chopped red onion, chives or shallot. It goes by a whole host of other names, including common sorrel, broad-leaved sorrel and French sorrel, all for fairly obvious reasons. Its wild version gets an even more varied nomenclature: green sauce, sour grabs, cuckoo sorrow and cuckoos' meate, for it was once said that the cuckoo cleared his voice by nibbling on the tart leaves.

Sorrel makes one of the best of all spring sauces, lovely to serve with fish – it comes with perfect timing for the wild salmon season. The sauce begins with the essential simple cooking of the sorrel in a little butter. Remove the thicker, tougher stems, then make little piles of leaves, roll them up tightly like cigars and slice thinly (with a stainless steel knife) to release the fine shreds known as a chiffonade. Melt a generous knob of butter in a pan, add the chiffonade and stir for a few minutes, until the sorrel collapses to a dark green purée. This is the basis for a sauce – either add a generous helping of double cream and let it all boil up together, then season with salt and pepper or, for something a little lighter, pour in first a measure of fish or chicken stock, simmer for a few minutes and then enrich with cream.

Opposite
**Dandelion
and Chorizo
Salad**
(page 93)

For a soup, begin by making a basic potato, or potato and leek, soup, then stir in the shredded sorrel just before liquidizing to preserve its spring-green colour and freshness. Sorrel also goes nicely with fatty meats such as roast goose or pork (try a purée made with half and half sorrel and spinach or lettuce) and with veal and sweetbreads, while, to my mind, it is even more delicious with eggs. Fold shredded sorrel into the beaten eggs for an omelette or fill the cooked omelette with raw or puréed sorrel (and a spoonful of soft goat's cheese or mascarpone for a serious treat). A thin bed of sorrel purée is an unlooked for and very welcome discovery under a baked egg, and the shredded leaves can be stirred into scrambled eggs when they are just about done. Poached eggs bathed in a creamy sorrel sauce make a fine lunch dish.

One of my favourite ways of making the most of the first sorrel is to transform it into fritters: coat the leaves in flour, then egg and crumb them before deep-frying briefly in hot oil until golden.

Storage and Preservation

Once cut, sorrel soon begins to wilt. If you cannot use it more or less straight away, store in a plastic bag in the vegetable drawer of the fridge and use within a day or two at the outside. The best way to preserve sorrel is to cook it in butter until it collapses to a purée, then cool and freeze in small tubs.

The combination of cucumber and sorrel – not so much sorrel that it overwhelms the more delicate taste of cucumber but enough to liven things up – works well in a summer soup. I think it is best served hot but if you prefer to make a chilled version for a warm day, use a couple of tablespoons of oil instead of the butter. If you wish to enrich the soup a little, finish it with a swirl of whipped cream floating on the top, or a drizzle of single cream added as you serve.

Serves 4

1 onion, chopped
45 g (1½ oz) butter
1 large cucumber, peeled and diced
2½ tablespoons pudding rice
1 bay leaf
1 sprig of thyme
1.2 litres (2 pints) light chicken or vegetable stock
1 handful of sorrel (around 45–60 g/1½–2 oz), larger stalks removed, shredded
1 tomato, deseeded and diced
salt and pepper
chopped chives, to serve

Sweat the onion in the butter in a covered pan for 5 minutes, then add two-thirds of the cucumber, the rice, bay leaf and thyme. Stir, cover again and cook for a further 5 minutes. Add the stock and some salt and pepper, bring up to the boil and simmer for about 10 minutes, until the rice is tender. Pick out the bay leaf and thyme twig. Stir in the sorrel, then liquidize in batches to form a smooth cream. Taste and adjust the seasoning.

To serve, reheat gently, without boiling, then scatter the remaining cucumber, the tomato dice and some chopped chives over the top.

Pan-Fried Salmon Fillet with Green Butter

This sorrel butter really is the most superb bold green and it looks very pretty perched on top of a piece of pale pink salmon.

I particularly like to serve my salmon and green butter on a bed of little green or brown lentils, but a pile of mashed potatoes, speckled with chopped chives or flavoured with a little English mustard, would be almost as good, along with some purple sprouting broccoli if the time of year is right.

Serves 4

4 portions of salmon fillet, skin on, weighing
    around 175 g (6 oz) each
a little oil
salt and pepper
lemon wedges, to serve
a few sprigs of parsley and lengths of chive, to serve

For the green butter
a small handful of sorrel leaves (about 30–45 g/1–1½ oz)
1 tablespoon chopped parsley
1 tablespoon chopped chives
100 g (3½ oz) unsalted butter

First the butter. Put everything into a food processor and process. If you don't have a processor, chop the sorrel and other herbs finely, then beat into the butter. Either way, scrape the butter on to a sheet of silver foil, pat into a sausage shape, roll up and chill in the fridge until needed.

About half an hour before cooking, season the salmon fillets with salt and pepper. When you are nearly ready to eat, heat a little olive oil in a frying pan over a moderate heat. Cook the salmon skin-side up for 3–5 minutes, without moving it around at all. Then turn the fish over and leave to cook for a further 3 minutes or so, until it is cooked but still has a line of translucent, darker pink flesh in its centre. This slight 'undercooking' keeps the salmon moist and tender. Any more and it is dry, and much duller to eat.

Lay the salmon on warm serving plates and top with a slice or two of the green butter. Tuck a lemon wedge in on the side, add the parsley and chives and serve immediately.

Lesley Waters' Rustic Sorrel Omelette with a Warm Walnut Salad

Anyone who watches cookery programmes on television will know Lesley Waters and will have seen how she manages to embrace traditional dishes, giving them a new, simple twist to transform them into something stylish and special, without losing their identity. Nothing fits the category better than this classic omelette sharpened with sorrel, which sits atop a bed of salad tossed with balsamic vinegar and walnuts, still warm from the oven – the Lesley touch, which makes all the difference.

Serves 2

For the omelette
4 eggs
salt and pepper
25 g (1 oz) butter
2 handfuls of sorrel or rocket, roughly shredded

For the dressing
2 tablespoons balsamic vinegar
4 tablespoons olive oil
salt and pepper
55 g (2 oz) walnut halves, roughly broken up

For the salad
half a butterhead lettuce, washed
a handful or two of baby salad leaves

To make the dressing, whisk the vinegar with the oil, salt and pepper. Set aside until needed.

Crack the eggs into a small bowl and whisk to break up. Season well and add 1 tablespoon water.

Heat the butter in a large frying pan until foaming. Add the sorrel and cook gently until just wilted. Pour in the omelette mixture and cook until golden brown underneath but still slightly soft and runny on top.

As it cooks, spread the walnuts out on a baking tray and toast in a hot oven for 2–3 minutes until lightly coloured (be careful not to burn them). As soon as they're ready, toss the warm nuts with the lettuce, baby leaves and dressing. Arrange on two large dinner plates. Cut the omelette roughly into four long, wide strips, fold in half and place on top of the salad leaves. Serve at once.

cutting celery
Apium graveolens

Cutting celery is the cultivated version of the wild celery, also known as smallage, that was the ancestor of common celery and celeriac. This is not to say that cutting celery, celery and celeriac are all the same thing, although in one sense they are: they are all forms of *Apium graveolens*. They share a good number of characteristics but they swell and curve in very different places. Celeriac is a big, fat, gnarled bulbous lump, celery has thick, long, juicy half-moon stalks, whereas the cutting celery that is planted as a herb is slender stemmed and more or less the spitting image of the original wild celery.

So much for differences. There are two major similarities. The first is the look of the glossy, green-toothed leaves and the second is that unmistakable celery flavour. Those leaves and that flavour are the whole *raison d'être* of cutting celery. The leaves look rather like a cross between those of ordinary celery and flat-leaved parsley, but one sniff and you are left in no doubt that this is a member of the close-knit celery clan.

For a plant that is so steadfastly neglected these days, cutting celery has a noble past. Celery and celeriac weren't developed until the seventeenth century, so it had precious little competition up till then, apart perhaps from lovage. The Greeks and Romans both took a shine to wild celery, planting wreaths of the greenery square on the heads of the winners in the Greek Nemean games, held in honour of the mighty Zeus himself. Romans consumed it in all kinds of pungent herbal sauces and in stuffings for pork and other meats. It is quite possible that we were tucking into roasts flavoured with smallage at around the same time and even long before, as it is native to most of Europe, including our northerly isles.

Opposite
Clockwise from top left: fennel; bronze fennel; cutting celery; chervil; dill; tarragon; lovage

The cultivated version is a decidedly useful herb to have to hand, though you won't come across it in any supermarket. If you can find a pot or a corner of the garden for a plant of cutting celery, and you remember to keep it well watered (in the wild it has a preference for damp spots, near the sea or on squelching marshlands), you will not regret it, as it is one of those very useful background pot herbs. Use it wherever a stick of celery might be a contender for inclusion, to round out the background flavours. In other words, add to bouquets garnis for stews, soups and stocks. Slip a few leaves into a pan of simmering beans or tomato sauce, or include within the bed of vegetables underlying a comforting pot-roast of pork or guinea fowl.

Like lovage, a few chopped leaves of cutting celery (go gently at first since it is on the strong side) mixed into cream cheese makes a good filling for a sandwich, with some salad and maybe smoked mackerel or trout. Small whole cheeses are good marinated in olive oil with chopped celery leaf and other tender herbs, lemon zest and a little chilli. Included in salads dressed with mayonnaise or soured cream, it tempers the greasiness (try adding to a marinated herring, apple and potato salad dressed with mayo and sharpened with finely chopped shallot or red onion). Smallage soup, made along the lines of lovage soup (p. 110) is comforting and seductive, and really much more appealing than straight celery soup, which can risk a degree of dishwateriness.

Fatty meats such as pork or rich roast goose take rather well to a stuffing speckled with chopped celery leaf. Mixed with a little tarragon, a snip or two of chives and parsley, it makes an alternative form of *fines herbes* that sits as well in simple egg dishes as the classic foursome.

Just because you can't get hold of any true smallage, or cutting celery, doesn't mean you will have to ignore its possibilities. It is still just about possible to buy straight celery complete with leaves, though all too often they have been shorn off before they get anywhere near the consumer. When you do get a head in full leaf, make the most of it by using the foliage as a herb, just like its cultivated wild alter-ego.

Storage and Preservation

Since you are highly unlikely to come across smallage unless you grow it yourself, or know someone who does, it is probably best to cut it as you need it, avoiding the thorny question of longevity altogether. If you do get landed with a bouquet of the stuff, wrap it in a tea towel, pop into a plastic bag and store in the vegetable drawer of the fridge, where it should stay bright and lively for four or five days. Leaves cut from a head of celery will be a little more delicate, but if they are given the same treatment you should be able to use them over a period of three or four days.

Smallage dries quite well, retaining a more than adequate degree of celery savour. Toast the leaves very slowly in an extremely low oven until bone dry. Cool completely, then store in an airtight container for up to three months.

Caramelized Chicken Livers with Smallage Latkes

I adore these thin, grated potato pancakes, soft and melting at the centre, crisp and whiskery at the edges. They are best eaten crisp and hot from the pan, or at least warm. They can also be made an hour or two in advance and reheated in a single layer on a baking sheet at 220°C/425°F/Gas Mark 7 for 10–15 minutes.

Serves 4

450 g (1 lb) peeled and coarsely grated potatoes
2 onions, coarsely grated
2 garlic cloves, crushed
2 tablespoons finely shredded cutting celery or 3 tablespoons finely shredded celery leaves
1 tablespoon plain flour
1 egg
salt and pepper
oil for frying
4 sprigs of cutting celery to garnish

For the chicken livers
450 g (1 lb) chicken livers
15 g (½ oz) butter
1 tablespoon sunflower oil
1 tablespoon caster sugar
4 tablespoons Marsala, Madeira or sweet sherry
1 tablespoon balsamic vinegar

Squeeze the potatoes hard to remove as much water as possible, then spread out on a clean J-cloth or fine tea towel. Fold the towel over the potato, then roll up and wring out all the water over the sink – you will be surprised by how much comes out. Place the potato in a mixing bowl. Dry and squeeze the grated onions in the same way, then mix with the potato, garlic and cutting celery. Add the flour, egg and plenty of salt and pepper. Mix thoroughly.

Pick over the livers and remove any tubes or yellow-green patches. Quarter larger pieces of liver. Melt the butter with the tablespoon of oil in a frying pan. Fry the chicken livers over a fairly brisk heat for about 3 minutes. Sprinkle over the sugar and turn to mix in. Fry for a further minute before adding the Marsala, Madeira or sherry and some salt and pepper. Simmer for 2 minutes or so until the liquid is reduced slightly. Draw off the heat and stir in the balsamic vinegar. Taste and adjust the seasoning, then reserve. Reheat briefly when needed, adding a splash of water if the liquid is in danger of boiling away altogether.

Heat a 0.5 cm (¼ in) layer of oil in a large frying pan until hot. Take heaped tablespoons of the potato mixture, place in the pan, then flatten down as thinly as you can with the back of the spoon or a fish slice, without actually breaking it up. Make 2 or 3 more fritters in the pan at the same time. Turn each fritter carefully as soon as the underneath is browned, about 1–2 minutes, and brown the other side. Drain on kitchen paper and keep warm. Continue until all the mixture is used up.

Arrange several pancakes on each person's plate, then spoon over the chicken livers. Garnish with an extra sprig of cutting celery and serve immediately.

cutting celery

dill

Anethum graveolens

According to the seventeenth-century herbalist, Culpeper, not only does dill strengthen the brain but – oh, joy of joys – it is also 'a gallant expeller of wind'. Now there's a fine selling line for a herb if ever I saw one. Quite how true this is I can't tell, though I've downed a fair amount of dill in my time.

Dill is a herb that has taken some countries by storm but barely left a mark on others as it passed through. In its native Iran it is a big cheese, in a culture that embraces herbs with considerable devotion. Here they cook it with rice or spinach, they add it to herby soups and spoon it generously into their wonderful, thick omelettes known as *kuku*. Of their many celebrated ways of exploiting dill, I think my favourite is probably with fresh spring broad beans. If you have never sampled the two together, then don't delay: cook up some broad beans, slit open their tough grey skins and squeeze out the startling bright green beanlet inside, then toss in hot butter with chopped dill. Good enough to eat just as it is, with a warm, crusty roll. Or toss the beans with lemon juice, olive oil and dill while still hot, then leave to cool and serve as a salad, with feta cheese and sweet, juicy cherry tomatoes.

I suspect that the Iranians may also have some claim to the invention of dill pickles. Certainly their dill and gherkin preserves can rival anything that comes out of America. Mind you, we were pretty much ahead of the game on that score, for around about the time that the Pilgrim Fathers were settling in across the Atlantic our dill and cucumber pickles were already well established, and being written about with an unmistakable degree of licking of the lips. Awards, though, must go to Jewish communities, particularly in the States, for keeping a brilliant tradition alive and kicking.

Dill is well employed in Russia and parts of Eastern Europe, to which it is also native, but as is so often the way, a new territory is where it has been taken up with unbridled glee. You just can't imagine Scandinavian food without dill. Dill with herrings, dill with potatoes (a great combination for a potato salad dressed with either soured cream or mayonnaise) and, above all else, dill with salmon. If it weren't for dill, Swedish gastronomy would be very much the poorer. Dill grows well there, despite the cold, and it brings instant vivacity to what was certainly in the past a very limited range of foodstuffs, particularly in the chilly, snowbound midwinter: fish, fish, fish, a slice of lamb or reindeer and an infinity of root vegetables. I exaggerate but none the less, dill is the flavour that I associate most strongly with Scandinavian food, and if it weren't for that particular flavour I doubt very much whether so many of our supermarkets would be selling gravad lax, ready-made and ready-sliced.

It is even suggested that the name dill comes from the Old Norse word *dylla*, to lull or to soothe, another allusion to the carminative properties of the plant. In other words, it soothes away the pain of a windy stomach, which is back where we began. Certainly, many of the proprietary gripe waters made for babies are based on dill. My two both loved the taste of them when they were small, though they didn't seem to relieve their type of colic one iota.

Dill looks rather similar to fennel but has lusher, silkier foliage and is far smaller. If you grow dill it is best to raise it from seed in situ, in a sunny position, as it really doesn't like to be transplanted. It is an annual, so you will need to resow every year, and if you are especially partial to its fresh, sweet caraway vigour, interlaced with a hint of citrus, then it may well pay to plant in several batches, separated by a few weeks, so that you can raid the plants continuously. Don't plant it near fennel as the two are terribly keen on cross-pollinating. It is reputed that carrots and tomatoes are not overfond of dill either, in the garden at any rate, so keep it well away from them too.

Opposite
Salmon Quarter Pounders with Dill and Capers
(page 104)

Salmon Quarter Pounders with
Dill and **Capers**

When using dill, chop and add it near the end of the cooking time to preserve its flavour. Be bold and use lots of it, but remember that prolonged cooking does it few favours. Dill leaves are often known as dillweed, to distinguish them from dill seeds.

Storage and Preservation

Luxuriant dill will keep for up to five or six days in a plastic bag in the vegetable drawer of the fridge. Dried dill holds a good deal of the flavour of fresh, and is often and successfully used in such dishes as gravad lax (for which you will find a recipe in my book *Fish*, co-written with my husband, William Black). Wherever possible, add it to a liquid, or use it where it will be able to absorb moisture, so that it softens and rehydrates.

Salmon Quarter Pounders with Dill and Capers

These salmon burgers are a great hit with children and adults alike and an excellent way of introducing fish to the wary. Serve them with deliciously crisp shoestring chips and proper coleslaw.

Serves 4

450 g (1 lb) skinned salmon fillet, very finely diced
  (about 3 mm (⅛ inch) cubes)
2–3 tablespoons chopped dill, fennel or chives
45 g (1½ oz) shallot, grated or very finely chopped
1½–2 tablespoons small capers, roughly chopped
1½ tablespoons mayonnaise
a good squeeze of lemon juice
salt and pepper

To serve
4 ciabatta rolls or other good-quality rolls, halved
mango chutney
lemon wedges
2 tomatoes, sliced
2–3 crisp lettuce leaves, finely shredded
mayonnaise

Mix together all the ingredients for the burgers, then chill the mixture for at least half an hour to firm it up. Divide into 4 portions and form each portion into a 'burger' about 1 cm (½ inch) thick. Keep cool until needed.

Prepare all the accompaniments. Pre-heat the grill thoroughly. Line the grill rack with silver foil. Grill the burgers and the bread rolls about 5–7.5 cm (2–3 inches) away from the heat. Allow about 4–5 minutes for the burgers and don't turn them over – they'll cook through anyway, and the more you handle them the more likely they are to collapse before they are fully cooked. Once they are done, they will be a little sturdier. You will, of course, turn the halved rolls over to toast both sides.

Spread a litle mayonnaise on the base of each roll, then top with shredded lettuce. Lay a salmon quarter pounder on top, smear over a little mango chutney, then top with a few rings of tomato. Spread a little mayonnaise on the cut side of the tops and clamp them on firmly. Press down with the heel of your hand, then dish up, with lemon wedges on the side, and eat.

Mushrooms with Mascarpone, Lemon and Dill Sauce

This is a recipe that I came up with when I was making supper for my children one night. At first, all I was aiming for was a simple dish of mushrooms in a white sauce, but there was only enough milk left for next morning's essential parental cuppa. There was, however, the remains of a small tub of rich mascarpone, lurking in the back of the fridge, and a couple of sprigs of dill, which goes particularly well with mushrooms. In they went, and the resulting dish, with its generous amount of sauce, was highly appreciated by the lucky infants, with enough salvaged to serve on rice for our adult supper. Fortuitous serendipity.

Serves 4

½ onion, chopped
30 g (1 oz) butter
250 g (9 oz) button mushrooms, sliced
1 tablespoon plain flour
2–3 tablespoons mascarpone
1–2 tablespoons chopped dill
1 or 2 good squeezes of lemon juice
salt and pepper

Fry the onion gently in half the butter in a saucepan, without browning, until tender. Add the mushrooms, fry for a minute or so more, then add just enough water to almost cover the mushrooms. Season and then simmer for 10 minutes.

Meanwhile, mash the remaining butter thoroughly with the flour to make a *beurre manié*. Gradually add small knobs of the *beurre manié* to the mushrooms until the liquid thickens to your liking (you may only need about half of it). Stir in the mascarpone and dill and continue to cook gently for about 3 minutes, until you have a sauce of a good consistency. Stir in the lemon juice, then taste and adjust the seasoning. Serve immediately.

fennel
Foeniculum vulgare

So gladiators fierce and rude,
Mingled it with their daily food.
And he who battled and subdued,
A wreath of fennel wore.

Henry Wadsworth Longfellow

Roman soldiers put great faith in fennel. They consumed it to keep them healthy and fighting fit. Meanwhile, back at the ranch, or rather the villa, the Roman womenfolk toyed delicately with sprigs of fennel in the belief that it would help them to shed excess pounds. Things really haven't changed that much … The belief in fennel as the perfect diet food persisted well into the seventeenth century: 'The seeds, leaves and roots of our Garden Fennel are much used in drinks and broths for those that are grown fat, to abate their unwieldiness and cause them to grow more gaunt and lank,' assured William Coles in 1657, and contemporary herbalists all echoed his sentiments (though this may have some small connection with the recycling of facts, rather than fervent belief). Maybe I'll give it a try; after all, it sounds a darn sight more pleasant than popping bran tablets.

Fennel grows wild all around the village in France where I idled away a fair portion of my childhood. The fine, feathery leaves, which my father described as being like a 'tangle of green hair', are one of the favourite foods of the caterpillars of the swallowtail butterflies that float and glide so very beautifully across our garden in warm weather. In France, as elsewhere, the herb is primarily connected with fish. With its clean, crisp scent of liquorice, there can be no doubt that it was made to complement man's piscine haul. I trot off up the hill to snap off a few sprigs to stuff into the belly cavity of sea bass or bream, which we bake in mounds of salt or barbecue over hot charcoal. If there's time, it goes into a marinade, with a hint of garlic, lemon juice and plenty of olive oil and freshly ground black pepper.

Down in the south of France, fennel stalks are dried and tied into bundles, to be used with gamy fish such as red mullet. Travel on right down to Sicily and you come to some of the most inspired and fervent use of fennel – once again with fish, and in particular with sardines, on pasta or a dish of sardines boned and rolled up around a filling of fennel, pine nuts and currants. I once attempted what was supposed to be a Sicilian recipe calling for a staggering 225 g (8 oz) fennel herb. I stripped two end-of-season fennel plants bare and still had only half the quantity. The results were disastrous, like eating bottomless heaps of liquorice hay. I doubt that even the most figure-conscious of Roman lovelies could have waded her way through it. Nor did it strike me as the kind of thing that food-loving Sicilians of whatever girth or sex would have taken to.

Fennel's history is not confined to continental Europe, though one might be forgiven for thinking so these days. Back in the Dark Ages, Anglo-Saxons numbered its feathery fronds amongst the nine sacred herbs that held the power to ward off evil. Later on country folk made sure that a bunch of fennel hung over their door, and that keyholes were blocked with fennel seed on St John's Eve or, in other words, Midsummer's Eve, to keep them safe from the witches and ghosts that roamed so freely upon that night. On the food front, it was again with fish that it scored its greatest successes. Shakespeare's Falstaff talks of eating conger cooked with fennel. Gooseberry or rhubarb and fennel sauce with mackerel must surely be one of our most stupidly neglected national classics. If you've never tried it, just stew gooseberries or rhubarb with a drop of sugar, a little chopped fennel leaf and a knob of butter until very tender. Sieve or not as the fancy takes you and serve up forthwith with grilled or roast mackerel. Now there's a dish to convince any doubting foreigner that British food is worth eating.

Not that you should confine fennel to fish alone, magic though the partnership is. Freshly chopped, it is very pleasant on buttered new potatoes and other root vegetables. Bruise the leaves, or blanch them for a few seconds in boiling water to soften them a little and release their flavour, then add them, finely chopped, to a mayonnaise to serve with poached or smoked chicken, or a platter of grilled summer vegetables. It also goes very well indeed with shellfish and crustacea of all sorts, though that brings us back, once again, to the fruits of the sea. You just can't keep fennel away from them.

Fennel is not a herb that you come across frequently in supermarkets and greengrocer's, so it really is worth growing it yourself if you have any liking for seafood. It is a highly decorative plant, perfect for the back of a border, where it will rise majestically up to a height of 2 metres (6 feet). For greater impact, mix bronze-leaved and green-leaved plants, but don't confuse fennel the herb with Florence fennel, which is the vegetable version and has swollen basal stems and comparatively mean helpings of feathery leaf. For continuous luxuriant growth, cut down regularly and don't let it flower. Actually, I always do quite the opposite, because I love the look of the big yellow flowers, and after all, there's only so much fennel you can use up in one household in one season. A final word of warning: keep your fennel plant well away from dill, with which it will engage in amorous fashion, cross-pollinating willy-nilly. It is also supposed to put a bit of a damper on coriander. Keep a good distance between the two if you want to avoid verdant skirmishes.

Grilled Sardines with Warm Red Pepper and Fennel Vinaigrette

Storage and Preservation

The leaves are best used fresh but they don't have tremendous staying power. Store in a plastic bag or airtight container in the bottom of the fridge for a day or two, but be prepared for wilt to set in swiftly. The leaves can be chopped and frozen in ice-cube trays, covered with water. Unlike the leaves, the stems dry very well, preserving plenty of flavour. Hang up in bunches in a dry, airy place. Once absolutely dry as tinder, store in an airtight container. Use them as a bed for baking fish, lubricated with plenty of olive oil.

An easy dish for an easy summer barbecue, when sardines are plump and fresh, peppers ripe and plentiful and the fennel is tall and handsome. And if the rain buckets down, as it so often does, move the feastlet back indoors and heat up that grill.

Serves 4

8–12 sardines depending on size, scaled and cleaned
8–12 small sprigs of fennel
a little olive oil
coarse salt

For the vinaigrette
1½ tablespoons good-quality red wine vinegar
1 teaspoon Dijon mustard
5 tablespoons olive oil
3 tablespoons chopped fennel
1 small red pepper, grilled, skinned, deseeded and finely
    diced
salt and lots of freshly ground pepper

Pre-heat the grill or get the barbecue going well in advance. Rinse the sardines and pat dry. Tuck a sprig of fennel in the stomach cavity of each fish. Either grill or barbecue the fish brushed lightly with oil, seasoning with coarse sea salt as you turn, until just cooked through – 3–5 minutes on each side depending on the size of the fish and the strength of the heat.

Meanwhile, whisk the vinegar with the mustard, salt and loads of pepper in a small saucepan. Whisk in the olive oil and then stir in the fennel and red pepper. Heat through without boiling.

Lay the sardines on plates and spoon over some of the vinaigrette. Serve immediately.

Potato Gnocchi with **Fennel** and **Sun-dried Tomato Butter**

I love potato gnocchi, those light little dumplings that the Italians make so well. At least they should be light, though all too often they can be leaden. Not so long ago I was lucky enough to spend a day with that wonderful chef Franco Taruschio, who showed me how to achieve perfect gnocchi. It is very simple, but you have to acquire the knack. I'll try to explain the method to you, and all I can say is that it is worth persevering until you get a good result. If you are in a hurry, you can always use bought gnocchi, available from the fresh pasta section of most good supermarkets these days, though they are on the heavy side compared with home-made.

Either way, they make a grand first course or main course, dressed as they are here with butter scented with aniseedy fennel, crisp garlic flakes, salty olives and sun-dried tomatoes.

Serves 4–6

for the gnocchi
1.5 kg (3½ lb) floury potatoes, boiled in their skins
1 egg
250 g (9 oz) plain flour, sifted, plus extra for trays
freshly grated nutmeg
salt and pepper
fine shavings of pecorino or Parmesan cheese, to serve

For the butter
150 g (5 oz) unsalted butter
4 garlic cloves, thinly sliced
60 g (2 oz) sun-dried tomatoes in olive oil, very finely shredded
60 g (2 oz) black olives, pitted and sliced
3 tablespoons chopped fennel

To make the gnocchi, peel the potatoes while they are still hot, then rub them through a potato ricer, a mouli-légumes or a sieve while they are warm. Weigh out exactly 1 kg (2 lb 4 oz) of the potato purée and put it in a bowl. Make a well in the centre and add the egg, flour, nutmeg, salt and pepper. Work together thoroughly to make a soft, warm dough. Cover with a tea towel.

Flour 3 baking trays generously. Break off tennis-ball-sized knobs of the dough and roll out to form long sausages about the thickness of your thumb. Cut into pieces 2.5 cm (1 inch) long. Now they have to be shaped, and this is what helps to make them light and luscious, so ignore it at your peril. Take a fork and hold it with the tip of the tines down on the work surface, their outer curve facing upwards. With the tip of a finger, lightly press a piece of the dough against the tines, right at the bottom. Now in one swift movement roll and flip the dough up and off the fork, so that one side is ridged from the tines, while the other has an indentation from the tip of your finger. You don't need to take the piece of dough far up the tines – we're talking just enough to imprint the ridges on one side only. It gets easier as you get the hang of it, and soon you'll be flipping away merrily and snappily. As you make them, spread the gnocchi out on the floured trays. Once made, cover with a clean tea towel until needed.

Put a large pan of salted water on to boil. Now turn to the sauce. Melt the butter in a medium-sized frying pan and add the garlic. Fry gently for a few minutes until it just begins to colour. Add all the remaining ingredients and stir over a low flame for about 2 minutes, then draw off the heat.

When the pan of water reaches a rolling boil, carefully drop the gnocchi into it, not too many at a time (a quarter to a third of the entire batch will be quite enough). When they bob back to the surface, check one to make sure it is cooked, then quickly lift the rest out with a perforated spoon. Place in a warm dish and keep warm while you cook the remaining gnocchi. Reheat the sauce and then spoon it over the gnocchi. Scatter with shavings of pecorino or Parmesan and serve.

lovage
Levisticum officinale

Lovage, like rocket and purslane, is one of those forgotten British herbs that were once the toast of the realm. And not just this realm – right across Europe, going way back in time. For centuries there was no getting away from it. But now…now it's a bit of a herb fancier's secret, though one that is just beginning to be exposed to the shopping world at large; to my considerable surprise and delight, I spotted packs of lovage in a supermarket not so long ago.

But to begin at the beginning: lovage is native to continental Europe, and the ancient Greeks and Romans were more than passing keen on it. In AD 795, Louis the Pious (son of Charlemagne) included lovage in the long list of fragrant plants, flowers and vegetables that were to be planted on his estates in Aquitaine. I don't think there is any imperative connection between lovage and piety but it was also regularly planted in the gardens of many a medieval monastery. Travelling on post haste, the Tudors and Stuarts were partial to lovage in their salads and soups, and wallowed in baths perfumed with its glossy green leaves; Thomas Tusser, in the sixteenth century, was in no doubt that it was among the most 'Necessary Herbs to grow in the Garden of Physic', for it was considered a herb to dampen pain – the pain of gripes, poisons and infections, of flatulence and agues, and it can, it is said, even sort out the odd boil.

Once you get hold of a bunch or two of lovage leaves it is extremely easy to understand its longstanding pan-European popularity. What is harder to fathom is why it then fell from grace. I can offer no answers. It seems like sheer madness to abandon such a useful, well-flavoured, prolific herb. Lovage tastes something like celery but much more interesting. It is spicier, aromatic, and underscored with the scent of lemon and orange zests. Sounds pretty good, doesn't it? And it is, too.

The two things I use my lovage most frequently for are, firstly flavouring stock and, secondly, making lovage soup. When it comes to stock, a few leaves of lovage, snapped off the plant in the garden, means I have no need for a lone stalk of celery, snapped from a whole head which then languishes, semi-eaten, in the back of the fridge until it is as limp as an old dish-cloth. The lovage provides that particular celeryish taste and more, making for a rounder, fuller stock, excellent for sauces and soups, which brings me straight to number two. Lovage soup is absolutely the classic thing to make with lovage, and it is one of the most delicious, comforting and tantalizingly scented of vegetable soups. On a cool April day, when the early lovage is still tinged with bronze, lovage soup is as soothing a dish as you could ask for.

That is just the beginning. Lovage leaves, torn small, are good in a salad, but then most tender-leaved herbs are. I often add it to bouquets garnis for meat and fish dishes, or to flavour a tomato sauce or a soup of some other sort. Lovage and smoked fish partner well; lovage and cream cheese, too. Lovage, smoked salmon and cream cheese, all together on a bagel or in thin brown bread, makes the utmost best of both combinations. In fact, it does a brilliant job wherever celery might be used as a flavouring with some small degree of success. For instance, in a pan of lentils or cannellini beans, or tucked in with a nice ham hock, or under lamb shanks that are being braised long and slow. You can blanch the tender leaf stalks and young stems and eat them like rather more interesting celery, dripping with melted butter. The young stems make rather a good, if unusual, sweetmeat, candied as you would angelica (see p. 146).

Since it is still rare in supermarkets, I would urge you wholeheartedly to head off to a plant nursery and buy yourself a small pot of lovage for the garden. Be warned, however, this is a big plant, growing lustily up as high as a man in optimum conditions, with need of very little encouragement. It is not going to be suited to the average windowbox. Put it in a place where its grandeur can be displayed to good effect, in a nice, sunny position, its roots deep in well-drained, rich soil. Cut it back once or twice in the summer to encourage new growth, or be prepared to stake it up as it grows too big for its roots.

Lovage, Potato and Carrot Soup

Storage and Preservation

Once cut, the leaves and stems of the lovage plant can be stored in a plastic bag in the bottom of the fridge. The leaves will last for three or four days but the leaf-stalks will keep fresh for a few days longer, which means that it might be an idea to store them separately. The leaves can be dried and, it is said, retain their scent fairly well, though I have no personal experience of this. Dried or fresh, lovage leaves make a warming infusion.

It is worth growing lovage for soup alone (though there's plenty more to be made of it than that). It's thick and warming and nicely spiced with the celery taste of lovage. I like it just as it is, eaten with a hunk of bread, but for a thinner, more elegant version, use stock rather than water, diluting it with a little extra at the end. Float a spoonful of whipped cream speckled with more chopped lovage or chives on each bowl of soup as it is served and it will look pretty and stylish.

Serves 4–6

1 onion, chopped
4 large carrots, chopped
2 large potatoes, chopped
4 garlic cloves, chopped
zest, pared in strips, and juice of ½ lemon
4 tablespoons roughly chopped lovage leaf
30 g (1 oz) butter
1.2–1.75 litres (2–3 pints) chicken stock, vegetable stock or water
1 tomato, skinned, deseeded and chopped
salt and pepper

Sweat the onion, carrots, potatoes, garlic, lemon zest and lovage in the butter in a covered pan for about 15 minutes, stirring once or twice. Add the lower quantity of stock or water, plus the tomato and some salt and pepper. Bring up to the boil and simmer for about 20–30 minutes, until all the vegetables are very tender. Liquidize in batches, adding extra stock if you want a thinner soup, then stir in the lemon juice. Taste and adjust the seasoning and serve.

Opposite
**Lovage,
Potato and
Carrot Soup**

Blue Cheese and Lovage Dipping Sauce with Deep-fried Potato Skins

Crisp baked or deep-fried potato skins were a brilliantly economical move on the part of restaurateurs keen to make the most of their leftovers. What a tour de force – you could charge a fair old whack for a starter made principally from something you would normally have thrown out. Masterly, and an idea that we can well borrow in our own homes. Whenever you make mashed potatoes, bake or microwave the potatoes (you'll get a better, fluffier mash that way, anyway) and save the skins. Next day, you can either bake or deep-fry them to make a very moreish pile of crisp skins served with a blue cheese dipping sauce. If you can't get lovage, then try it with chives or coriander instead.

Serves 4

skins from about 1 kg (2 lb 4 oz) baked potatoes
sunflower oil
salt

For the dipping sauce
85–110 g (3–4 oz) mild to medium-strong blue cheese, such as dolcelatte, Danish blue or gorgonzola
about 6 tablespoons thick soured cream
2–3 tablespoons chopped lovage leaf
1 tablespoon lemon juice
salt and pepper

Make the dipping sauce first. Mash the blue cheese with a little of the soured cream until smooth, then gradually beat in the remaining cream. Stir in the lovage, lemon juice, salt and pepper. Taste and adjust the seasoning.

Cut the potato skins up into largish pieces (the exact size is neither here nor there – aim roughly for triangles or rectangles, around 4–5 cm (1½–2 inches) across). To bake them, toss in oil, working it over the skins with your fingers so that they are evenly coated, then spread out on a baking tray and bake at 220°C/425°F/Gas Mark 7 for about 8–12 minutes, until browned and crisp. Sprinkle with salt and serve immediately with the blue cheese dipping sauce.

To deep-fry, heat the oil to 180°C/360°F (to test, drop a cube of bread or a small piece of potato skin into the oil – if it immediately starts to fizz cheerfully and begins to brown within about 15 seconds, then the heat is right) and fry the skins until golden brown, turning once or twice so that they are evenly cooked. Don't fry too many at a time or you will lower the temperature of the oil too far and end up with greasy results. Scoop out with a slotted spoon and drain briefly on kitchen paper, sprinkle with salt, then serve piping hot with the dipping sauce.

lovage

tarragon
Artemisia dracunculus

Tarragon and I became acquainted in the early years of my life. When I was two, my parents decamped for a month to a troglodyte village near the Loire valley. We returned a year later, and a year after that my mother, seduced by the village, the people and the living, laid out the princely sum of £500 to buy a hole in the rock. No electricity, no running water, no drains and not even a well to compensate. But the view was fantastic.

Somewhere in those early years I must have been introduced to tarragon, the noble herb that the French have made their own. *Poulet à l'estragon* (tarragon chicken) is a dish as firmly rooted in my childhood as that cave and that village. All three remain essential to my well being to this day.

From my mother, I inherited the hole in the rock (updated eventually with modest mod cons). With it came an overgrown herb garden. As I cleared away the jungle of weed I discovered a baleful straggle of tarragon, thrusting forth valiantly. Lump-in-the-throat time. The scent of the lost plant took me straight back to Sunday lunches on the terrace with my parents. I vowed to regenerate the tradition and now, every summer, we sit down at least once to a fine dish of roast free-range chicken from the local farm, gilded with a creamy tarragon sauce. The essence, I always think, of all that is good about French bourgeois cooking.

Tarragon itself is not of French origin. It is native to southern Europe and Asia and is naturalized in parts of America to the west of the Mississippi river, I am told. However, it is not to be confused with so-called Russian tarragon, which comes from the icy wastes of Siberia and is worthless in culinary terms. A trace of bitterness creeps into my voice here, for I have been caught out on this one. When I came into possession of my very first garden, supplies of tarragon were at best irregular in local shops. I determined to grow it for myself, rushed to buy a plant, rushed home to plant it, perplexed by the absence of the glorious aniseed scent. Perhaps it developed as

the plant matured, I comforted myself. It didn't and I learned the error of my ways with a summer thwarted by lack of true French tarragon.

Both plants are forms of *Artemisia dracunculus* (for French add *Sativa* but the distinguishing tag for Russian is the well-chosen *Inodora*). *Dracunculus* means much what it sounds like – a little dragon – and from the same root, possibly via the Arabic, come all the European names for the herb – *estragon* in French, our tarragon, and the charming Italian *dragoncello*. I always imagine that this is because the pointed, slender green leaves resemble the jagged crest running down a dragon's back, but no. Every reference book insists that it is more to do with its supposed power to cure bites and stings from poisonous animals and insects, including mad dogs – let's hope Noel Coward's Englishmen took bouquets of tarragon with them when they stepped out in the midday sun. More prosaically, a simple infusion of tarragon aids digestion, soothes hiccups and dispels flatulence.

Some people describe tarragon as a delicate herb. This is nonsense. Fresh from the garden it is powerful stuff, with a marvellous, aniseedy, green taste. When used with discretion and love it is as beguiling as a herb can get. The key to cooking with tarragon is to treat it with respect and not to get carried away. Regular tasting is vital, since it will vary in intensity from plant to plant, month to month, location to location. If you do grow your own you will be well aware of its strength. One lusty clump is more than enough for most households, with plenty there to make your own tarragon vinegar. This is an easy task, worth undertaking with bought tarragon as well. Just push a handful of long sprigs of tarragon into a bottle and fill with high-quality white wine vinegar. Seal tightly and store for three weeks before using. This aromatic brew is one of the French cook's secret weapons. It injects subtle but unmistakable delight into salad dressings and sauces, particularly the famous sauce béarnaise (tarragon hollandaise, see p. 196) and the true tartare sauce.

Salade Cauchoise

Tarragon partners eggs, chicken and seafood uncommonly well and, as if that weren't enough, I urge you to try it with tiny new potatoes – just drop a sprig into the pan as they cook, or dress them with melted butter speckled with chopped tarragon leaves. *Quelle plaisir*!

Storage and Preservation

Tarragon has tender leaves on a tough stalk. Store fresh sprigs in a plastic bag or box in the lower part of the fridge. Excess tarragon can be dried but during the drying process some of its anise flavour is lost and the flavour is coarsened. For all that, I find dried tarragon a welcome addition to winter dishes. If you keep an orderly freezer, you may be better served by freezing the leaves, chopped first, then crammed into ice-cube trays or small pots.

From the chalky hills and valleys of the Pays de Caux in Northern France comes this salad of ham, potatoes and celery, traditionally bound together with crème fraîche, though mayonnaise can take its place. It would usually be served as a first course but is sturdy enough to stand as a main course for a light lunch or summer supper, or as part of a buffet.

Serves 4

500 g (1 lb 2 oz) waxy salad potatoes or new potatoes
1 tablespoon tarragon wine vinegar or plain white wine vinegar
5 celery sticks, thinly sliced (reserve a few of the leaves, if available, to garnish)
125 g (4 oz) high-quality cooked ham, cut into small strips
8 tablespoons crème fraîche or 6–7 tablespoons mayonnaise
2 tablespoons chopped tarragon leaves
salt and pepper

Cook the potatoes in their skins until just tender. Drain, cool slightly, then peel as well as you can and slice. Place them in a bowl while still warm and drizzle over the vinegar. Season with salt and pepper, then turn the potatoes gently to mix. Leave to cool.

Add the celery and ham to the potatoes, then carefully stir in the crème fraîche or mayonnaise and the tarragon. Taste and adjust the seasonings, then pile up in a shallow dish and garnish with the reserved celery leaves, or an extra sprig of tarragon.

Opposite
Omelette Tourangelle
(page 116)

Omelette Tourangelle

A big fluffy omelette flavoured with *fines herbes* (tarragon, parsley, chervil, chives), filled with soft goat's cheese and served with a roast tomato sauce. If you can't get chervil, then substitute a small amount of dill weed, fennel leaves or sweet cicely.

Serves 2 generously

5 eggs
3 tablespoons chopped *fines herbes* (a mixture of tarragon, parsley, chervil and chives)
a generous knob of butter
60g (2 oz) young soft goat's cheese or crumbled, derinded, semi-soft goat's cheese
salt and pepper

For the roast tomato sauce
8 plum tomatoes, halved
3 whole garlic cloves (unpeeled)
1 sprig of thyme
1 sprig of rosemary
½ teaspoon caster sugar
2 tablespoons olive oil

Pre-heat the oven to 200°C/400°F/Gas Mark 6.
To make the sauce, place the halved tomatoes cut-side up in an oiled, shallow ovenproof dish in a single layer. Tuck the garlic cloves, thyme and rosemary among them. Sprinkle with the sugar, season with salt and pepper and drizzle over the olive oil. Place in the oven and roast uncovered for 40–50 minutes, until the tomatoes are patched with brown. Remove the thyme and rosemary twigs, then tip the entire contents of the dish into a food processor. Process until fairly smooth, then sieve. Taste and adjust the seasoning, and reheat when needed.

Beat the eggs energetically with some salt and pepper, then stir in the herbs. Heat half the butter in a wide frying pan until it foams. Add half the eggs and make an omelette in the usual way. When it is just about cooked through, but still slightly damp and runny on top dot half the cheese down the middle. Flip the sides over to cover and slide it out of the pan on to a warm plate. Repeat with the remaining eggs and cheese. Serve the omelettes with the roast tomato sauce.

Roast Chicken Breasts with Tarragon Cream Sauce

A quick version of the classic French dish of roast chicken with tarragon sauce. Here I use chicken breasts instead of the whole bird, but it still retains all the essential flavours of the original. New potatoes are almost mandatory as an accompaniment or, failing that, noodles, tossed with a little butter and lots of finely chopped parsley. Add some lightly cooked spinach or roast carrots and the plate is complete.

Serves 4

a little oil
4 chicken breasts, with skin on
1 tablespoon honey
salt and pepper

For the sauce
75 ml (2½ fl oz) Noilly Prat or medium-dry white wine
150 ml (¼ pint) chicken stock
1 generous sprig of tarragon
150 ml (¼ pint) crème fraîche or double cream
2 tablespoons chopped tarragon

Pre-heat the oven to 200°C/400°F/Gas Mark 6. Place a small roasting tin, or other flameproof, ovenproof dish, on the hob and heat just enough oil in it to cover the base. Place the chicken breasts skin-side down in the tin and leave until golden brown. Season the upper side. Turn over and brush the skin side with the honey, then season with salt and pepper. Roast in the oven for 20 minutes, until done to a turn. Lift the chicken breasts out on to a warm plate and keep warm while you make the sauce.

Pour excess fat from the tin, then set it over a moderate flame. Pour in the Noilly Prat or wine and bring up to the boil, scraping in the residues from the chicken. Boil hard until reduced to no more than a tablespoon or two. Now add the stock and sprig of tarragon. Boil hard until reduced by one third. Stir in the cream, bring back to the boil, then boil until reduced to a light coating consistency. Remove the tarragon sprig and stir in the chopped tarragon. Season to taste.

Slice each chicken breast and fan out on individual plates. Spoon some of the sauce over and serve the remainder in a small jug.

chervil

Anthriscus cerefolium

The eighteenth-century French philosopher Voltaire was partial to scrambled eggs with chervil stirred into them. At least, that's what my neighbour François told me one warm February day in the small village I visit in France. 'How do you know?' I asked suspiciously. He rang his sister that night to check. She asked her husband and he said that he thought he'd once read something like that – or maybe it was just that he, too, loved the mild aniseed taste of chervil with buttery, creamy scrambled egg. I asked my other neighbour if she knew anything about Voltaire and chervil. 'No,' replied Solange, 'but I do know that it grows wild all over the bank near your gate, and further up the hill too. I'll bring you some tomorrow.' Sure enough, the very next day when I returned from market there was a posy of tender-leaved chervil tucked into the door handle. I may never know for sure whether Voltaire had a pash for chervil-scented eggs (a pretty sublime combination, so it wouldn't surprise me one iota) but at least I've discovered a vast resource right on my doorstep and, whenever I use it, I think of him, and François and Solange.

Chervil is the most subtle of the aniseed-scented herbs, with a slightly nutty flavour and small, fine, lacy leaves, so tender and downy. Its gentle presence is a delight, particularly with eggs but also with delicate white fish, or with chicken and guinea fowl. It adds a light scent to a lemony cream sauce. The French are especially fond of chervil; it is one of the essential foursome that makes up the classic *fines herbes*, along with chives, parsley and tarragon. An *omelette aux fines herbes* – the finely chopped herbs stirred into the eggs, which should really be free range, fried in sweet butter until the underneath is set but the surface remains *baveuse* (slightly runny and creamy) – is one of the great triumphs of the French kitchen. Together with a little lemon zest and juice, chervil can be blended generously into butter to serve with grilled or baked fish and, if you have enough to hand and can use it with some abandon, it will also flavour a potato soup very well indeed (add it when the soup is cooked but before liquidizing it).

Keep your eyes peeled and you will occasionally come across packs of chervil in the supermarket (it is sometimes included in herb mixes for fish) but the only way to ensure a reliable source is to grow it yourself. If, by any lucky chance, you do come across a patch of chervil that's run wild, as it does near me in France, do check rigorously for that unmistakable aniseed scent that wafts out when the leaves are rubbed. There is another plant that thrives in much the same terrain and looks very similar, but smells of very little. Don't get the two of them muddled up.

Storage and Preservation

Chervil is not a herb that keeps well. Wrapped in dampened kitchen paper, it will last a few days in the vegetable drawer of the fridge, but being so fine and delicate it wilts quickly, and soon begins to lose its worth. No doubt you could freeze it, finely chopped, or whizzed up into a purée with a little olive oil or whatever, but somehow that seems all wrong to me. Apart from the fact that chervil demands butter rather than oil, it is a herb that courts freshness. It is a spring and summer herb, with the kind of light, green flavour that suits those seasons. Don't even think of drying it either. Chervil was never meant for the winter months.

Carrot and Rice Soup

Chervil is a great friend to the natural sweet earthiness of carrots, and in this soup they come together elegantly. Settle for a mug of the soup on a cold spring evening, or offer it as a more elegant first course for a dinner party.

Serves 4

550 g (1 lb 4 oz) carrots, thickly sliced
white of 1 large leek, thickly sliced
1 celery stick, thickly sliced
1 onion, chopped
2 garlic cloves, chopped
45 g (1½ oz) butter
2 sprigs of thyme
2 sprigs of parsley
1 bay leaf
60 g (2 oz) pudding rice
1–1.2 litres (1¾–2 pints) chicken or vegetable stock
3 tablespoons chopped chervil, plus extra to garnish
lemon juice
4 tablespoons yoghurt, crème fraîche or whipped cream
salt and pepper

Put the carrots, leek, celery, onion and garlic into a pan with the butter. Tie the thyme, parsley and bay leaf together with string to make a bouquet garni and add it to the pan. Sweat, covered, over a low heat for 10 minutes, stirring occasionally. Add the rice, stirring to coat with the pan juices. Pour in 1 litre (1¾ pints) of the stock. Season with salt and pepper, then bring to the boil and simmer gently for 15–20 minutes, until the vegetables and the rice are tender. Stir in the chervil. Cool slightly and discard the bouquet garni. Process until smooth, adding extra stock if the soup is too thick for your liking. To finish, stir in a squeeze or two of lemon juice to heighten the flavour, then adjust the seasoning. Reheat, without boiling, if necessary. Spoon into bowls. Top each one with a tablespoon of yoghurt, crème fraîche or whipped cream (the cream is prettiest as it floats perfectly, melting gently). Scatter with chopped chervil and serve straight away.

Chervil, Cream and Lemon Sauce

A sauce to go with fish – we enjoyed it recently in France, spooned over a John Dory, roasted over an open fire in a cave house. A meal of spectacular simplicity, quality and deliciousness in fact. With the fish we ate salsify and tiny Chinese artichokes or *crosnes* as they are known in France. They look something like Michelin-man maggots but if you ever come across them don't let that put you off – they have a melting, sweet, haunting flavour that more than makes up for deficiencies in their appearance. To follow, a perfect Tarte Tatin (upside-down caramelized apple tart).

This sauce, made by my friend François, is a fundamental of good French cooking, and the ideal adjunct to sparklingly fresh fish of distinction: try it with turbot, Dover sole or brill, baked in a hot oven in buttered foil, or grilled or fried.

Serves 4–6

250 ml (9 fl oz) crème fraîche
2 tablespoons chopped chervil
2 egg yolks
1 tablespoon lemon juice
salt

Put the cream into a saucepan with half the chervil and some salt. Heat up until bubbling. Meanwhile, mix the egg yolks with the lemon juice. Draw the saucepan off the heat and stir a tablespoonful of the cream into the yolk mixture, then another and then a third. Now stir it back into the cream in the saucepan, along with the remaining chervil. Stir over a low heat for a few minutes, just until the sauce thickens slightly, without ever letting it boil. If it does boil the egg yolk will curdle and all you can do is sieve the sauce to get rid of nasty little lumps of coagulated yolk. Taste and adjust the seasoning – it should be on the sharp side but not too sharp, and with a gentle waft of aniseed from the chervil.

Stoved Jerusalem Artichokes with Chervil and Prosciutto

When they are cooked slowly and gently, the full nutty sweet flavour of Jerusalem artichokes is brought out at its best. Stoving them means that you lose not one iota of taste since none of the meagre dose of water is thrown away. Instead what you end up with is a thin film of buttery liquid packed with deliciousness, coating the artichokes. Add salt in the form of cured ham – prosciutto – and a hint of fresh aniseed with a scattering of chervil and there's a dish to conjure with. Very good with roast game birds or seared chicken.

If you have the time and the patience, peel the Jerusalem artichokes. It's not absolutely necessary, though they do look a little prettier in the end. They can be cooked in advance, then reheated with a tiny splash of water, but don't add the chervil until just before serving.

Serves 5–6

30 g (1 oz) butter
650 g (1½ lb) Jerusalem artichokes, halved (or quartered if very large)
45 g (1½ oz) prosciutto or pancetta, cut into fine strips
150 ml (¼ pint) water
2–3 tablespoons chopped chervil
coarse salt and pepper

Melt the butter in a frying pan large enough to take the Jerusalem artichokes in a single layer. Add the artichokes and prosciutto or pancetta and fry for about 3 minutes. Now add the water and season with coarse salt and pepper. Cover tightly and cook over a low heat for 30–45 minutes, shaking the pan every now and then to turn the artichokes. Check once or twice to make sure that they haven't boiled dry, adding a little more water if absolutely necessary. By the end of the cooking time there should be just a thin film of buttery liquid left on the base, while the artichokes are perfectly tender. If there is more water than that, uncover and boil away the juices before serving.

Sprinkle over the chervil, then turn the artichokes to coat them in the pan juices and chervil. Serve immediately, or when warm.

chervil

Raymond Blanc's Potage Maman Blanc
(Vegetable Soup with Chervil)

The herb and vegetable garden at Raymond Blanc's magnificent Manoir aux Quat' Saison is a sight to gladden the most jaded eye. It stretches on and on, in neat verdant rows, promising the most perfectly fresh vegetables at your every whim. There are four long rows of chervil, bushy and proud, regularly picked over by the great French chef himself. As he talked to me of chervil, the herb of his homeland, one of the almost omnipresent flavours of his childhood, he remembered the simple vegetable soup that his mother used to make, and his eyes lit up. He had been on the verge of cooking something more involved and complicated for me, but the plan changed and we settled, very happily, for soup.

The key to this soup lies in the freshness of the vegetables (it's really a gardener's soup) and abundant handfuls of fresh chervil. The rest is simple – a knob of butter, salt, pepper and lemon juice. A touch of cream does not go amiss, but it is by no means essential.

When choosing vegetables for a soup like this, pick what looks most beautiful and vibrant, and don't be bound by the list given below. Raymond suggested that you might add some potato or celeriac (which may need a touch more cooking, but not much), diced tomato, or young, sweet turnips. The trick is to cut the vegetables that take longest to cook into the smallest pieces so that in the end, they all cook in the same, remarkably short time.

Serves 4

2 shallots, halved lengthways, then sliced
15 g (½ oz) unsalted butter
60 g (2 oz) young, podded broad beans
4 ribs and leaves of Swiss chard, sliced thickly
2 or 3 ribs and leaves of red Swiss chard, if available, or more ordinary Swiss chard, sliced thickly
2 medium-sized carrots, diced small
1 medium courgette, quartered lengthways and sliced thickly
2 baby leeks, thinly sliced
salt and pepper
2 handfuls of roughly chopped chervil
a squeeze or two of lemon juice
2 tablespoons double cream, or an extra 30 g (1 oz) butter, chilled and diced

Melt the butter in a wide pan and sweat the shallots until translucent, without browning. Add all the remaining vegetables and 1 litre (1¾ pints) water. Bring to the boil, then season with salt and a little pepper. Simmer for about 4 minutes until all the vegetables are just cooked. Add the chervil, then draw off the heat. Stir in the lemon juice and cream, if using, or whisk in the cubes of butter, if using. Taste and adjust seasoning. Serve immediately.

curry leaf
Murraya koenigii

Let me come clean straight away. I am a relative newcomer to curry leaves, swayed to try them again, years after a not very successful encounter, by the passionate enthusiasm of two women I've met recently. A few months ago my tepid response to them was challenged by Sarah Kozak, a very keen cook and, as it happens, the producer of a television series I'm working on. 'But they are wonderful,' she cried, and proceeded to reel off a list of very tempting dishes that she regularly cooks with them. A few weeks later I met another keen cook, born in Bombay and brought up in southern India and Boston. I asked Manisha Gambhir Harkins about curry leaves and a smile broke out on her face. The scent of curry leaves sizzling in hot oil, she explained, was the scent of her childhood. It is the smell of southern India, the foundation that so many of its extraordinary, vibrant dishes stand upon. In a few short sentences she finally convinced me that curry leaves were something truly special. A third curry leaf *aficionado*, in the form of the renowned chef, Peter Gordon, came to complete my education, with an extraordinarily delicious Westernized dish featuring curry leaves in a big way. Armed with recipes from Sarah, Manisha and Peter, I tackled the leaves again, tracking down both fresh and dried varieties in good Indian grocers. And now, you know, I begin to see how very addictive they can be, for I'm well and truly hooked. If only I had a sure source nearer to my home, I'd probably use them frequently. As it is, I shall grab a bag of them whenever the chance arises.

Curry leaves are small, almond-shaped and elegantly twinned on long thin sprigs (if you come across the term a sprig of curry leaves, read it as some 6–10 fresh leaves), though they are often sold off the stem, loosely tumbled into plastic bags. Look out for the words *karipattar* or *meetha neem* and similar in Indian shops, or *daun kari* in Malaysian stores. In their uncooked, fresh state they smell curiously like a mixture of sliced green peppers, a hint of cumin and two-day-old mown grass. Their taste when cooked is warm and slightly bitter, redolent of toasted spices and tea. If fresh curry leaves are not to be found, dried leaves can replace them (you will need at least twice as many to achieve the same

Opposite
**Clockwise from top left: curry leaves; Thai basil; lemon grass; laksa leaves
Centre above: kaffir lime leaves
Centre below: holy basil**

Sarah's Aloo Aloo

intensity), though much of the essential character will have evaporated away. Dried or dry toasted curry leaves are essential for some spice blends and curry powders.

The taste of the curry leaf is usually brought out by frying it very briefly (it burns easily) in hot oil, as part of the process known as 'tempering' or making a *tarka*. The *tarka* is usually prepared by heating oil until it smokes, then adding mustard seeds, curry leaves, asafoetida, cumin seeds, or dried chillies, or other spices and herbs and sizzling them very briefly. The *tarka* may come right at the beginning of a recipe, with other ingredients then being added to the pan to soak up the flavours, or it may be poured over the cooked ingredients (such as lentils, potatoes, vegetables, meats, fish and practically anything you care to mention) right at the end of cooking, then stirred in to add extra richness and bring the dish to life. Ground up in their raw state, fresh curry leaves are also an essential ingredient in fresh coconut chutney.

If you are dropping fresh curry leaves into hot oil, take great care, as they spit and sizzle vehemently. Dried leaves are far tamer. Curry leaves are used primarily to flavour food, and some people may prefer to pick them out rather than eat them. I'm not one of them. I love their taste when they are crisp and fragrant. Dried leaves inevitably crumble and disappear, so there's absolutely no point in trying to pick them out.

Storage and Preservation

If your curry leaves are good and fresh, they will last, in their plastic bag in the vegetable drawer of the fridge, for up to two weeks. They freeze well, but they have a tendency to blacken. The flavour remains pretty good, however, so if you do come across a fine batch of fresh curry leaves, it is well worth laying down stocks in the freezer. You can also dry your own by leaving them on a rack in a very low oven until brittle, or try toasting them on a hot, flat, cast-iron griddle.

This recipe for an aromatic, rich stew of potatoes, chickpeas and tomatoes, scented with curry leaves, comes from Sarah Kozak, who restored my interest in curry leaves. It is an excellent dish for vegetarians that will win over meat eaters easily. Serve it with warm naan bread to scoop up the sauce and wipe the plate clean.

Serves 4–6

2 garlic cloves, roughly chopped
2.5 cm (1 inch) fresh root ginger, roughly chopped
3 tablespoons ghee, vegetable oil or sunflower oil
2 teaspoons black mustard seeds
2 teaspoons cumin seeds
1 teaspoon coarsely crushed coriander seeds
2 x 2.5 cm (1 inch) pieces of cinnamon stick
a good handful of fresh curry leaves (around 20–30)
2 red onions, finely chopped
400 g (14 oz) cooked chickpeas, drained if tinned
3 medium tomatoes, skinned, deseeded and roughly chopped
200 g (7 oz) small new potatoes, halved unless they are really tiddly
1 teaspoon ground turmeric
2 level teaspoons salt
400 ml (14 fl oz) coconut milk
a handful of roughly chopped coriander leaves

Either grind the garlic and ginger with 2 tablespoons of water in a small electric grinder, or in a cup with a hand-held processor wand, or pound to a paste in a mortar with a little salt, then work in the water.

Heat the ghee or oil in a wok or deep frying pan over a moderate-high heat. Add the mustard seeds, cumin seeds, coriander seeds and cinnamon stick. Stir for a few seconds until the mustard seeds begin to pop. Now add the curry leaves at arm's length and stir for a further 30 seconds or so. Tip in the onions, chickpeas, tomatoes and potatoes and stir briskly for about 2 minutes. Next scrape in the garlic and ginger paste and cook for another 3 minutes or so, stirring frequently. Now add the turmeric and salt and stir for another minute. Add the coconut milk, bring up to the boil, then simmer until the potatoes are just cooked through, adding a little water if needed. By the time the potatoes are done, the sauce should be fairly thick and clingy rather than runny. Serve hot, scattered with the coriander and accompanied by warm naan bread.

Peter Gordon's Roast Halibut
with **Curry Leaf** and **Lemon Roasted
Potatoes** and **Mango-ginger Dressing**

Peter Gordon shot to fame a few years ago, as one of our brightest and most exciting young chefs. Well, 'our' is perhaps a bit much: his restaurant, The Sugar Club, is in London but he comes from New Zealand, via large chunks of Asia. Extensive backpacking introduced him to all kinds of thrilling flavours, often thrown into food that was cooked on street stalls as he waited. What makes his 'Fusion' food stand out is that it works. Peter knows instinctively when to marry unusual flavours and when to leave well alone. The dishes that he conjures up are guaranteed to excite all but the most conservative diner.

Peter took me to the shop where he buys so many of the unusual ingredients that he loves to use, Food World, in north London, to show me fresh curry leaves at their best, still clinging on to long branches. Then he cooked this dish for me. It has become one of my favourite recipes in this book.

If you can't get halibut you could substitute cod or other firm, flaky white fish fillet. The curry leaves, however, are not negotiable! The cooking method for the fish is rather remarkable, creating a phenomenal amount of smoke and a kind of mini stove-top oven. I wouldn't advise using your very best, pride-and-joy, sparklingly clean new pan, but a good solid heavy pan that can take a bit of scrubbing afterwards will do the trick nicely, as long as you have some sort of lid for it.

Serves 4

4 x 200–250g (7–9 oz) chunks of halibut fillet
2–3 tablespoons roughly chopped curry leaves
60 ml (2 fl oz) extra virgin olive oil
16 sprigs of coriander, to serve
salt and pepper

For the potatoes
800 g (1 lb 12 oz) waxy potatoes or middling-sized new
    potatoes (e.g. Charlotte), scrubbed, then cut in half
    lengthways
60ml (2 fl oz) extra virgin olive oil
1 lemon
a good handful of fresh curry leaves or 2 handfuls of dried
    curry leaves
150 ml (¼ pint) boiling water

For the dressing
100 ml (3½ fl oz) salad oil, e.g. sunflower or grapeseed oil
30 ml (1 fl oz) lime juice
4 cm (1½ inch) fresh root ginger, chopped
1 large ripe mango, peeled, stoned and cut into large chunks
2 teaspoons Thai fish sauce (nam pla)

Pre-heat the oven to 220°C/425°F/Gas Mark 7. Put the potatoes into a roasting dish or tin into which they fit snugly, without gaping holes between them – slightly piled up is fine as they will shrink when they cook. Pour over the olive oil. Pare the zest off the lemon with a vegetable peeler and drop it in amongst the potatoes. Squeeze the juice and drizzle it over them. Add the curry leaves and some salt and pepper, then pour on the boiling water. Turn to mix, then cover with foil and roast for about 45 minutes. Remove the foil, give the potatoes a stir and return them to the oven for 15–20 minutes, give or take, until the water has evaporated and the potatoes are patched with brown.

Sprinkle the chopped curry leaves over the fish, season with salt, and then drizzle over the olive oil. Turn the pieces over in the marinade so that they are evenly coated, then cover with clingfilm and set aside.

Put the dressing ingredients into a liquidizer, starting with the oil, followed by the lime juice, then the ginger, mango and finally the fish sauce. Blend until smooth, then taste and add a little more fish sauce if needed. Set aside until required.

When your potatoes are busy on their final stage in the oven, and when you are about 10 minutes away from sitting down to eat, put a heavy-based pan over a high heat with a lid on it (but nothing in it) and leave for about 5 minutes, until incredibly hot. Lay the fish in it, and don't be too taken aback by the billows of smoke that rise up from the pan. Clamp the lid back on and cook for 30 seconds. Remove the lid, turn the fish over, then cover again and cook for a further 30 seconds. Turn the fish again and reduce the heat to moderate. Cover and leave to cook for a further minute on each side, until just barely cooked through.

To serve, lay some potatoes on each plate and sit a piece of fish on top. Drizzle with the mango-ginger dressing and finish with a few sprigs of coriander. Divine.

Manisha's Carrot and Watercress Salad

laksa leaf
Polygonum odoratum

This recipe, given to me by Manisha Gambhir Harkins, was what clinched my newfound love of curry leaves. She often ate this salad as a child – it is very common in southern India, served usually in small quantities as part of a *thali*, alongside another salad and more substantial dishes. The American in her has added the watercress, and now she often serves it as a starter before a heavy meal. It is addictively good, with a marvellous vivid, fresh taste that leaves you feeling incredibly healthy.

Serves 2–3

3 small or 2 medium carrots, grated
a good handful of watercress, trimmed of tougher stems
a pinch of salt
1½–2 tablespoons groundnut or sunflower oil
a small handful of curry leaves, preferably fresh, though dried
    will do
1 teaspoon black mustard seeds
½ teaspoon cumin seeds
a couple of squeezes of lime juice (optional)

Mix the carrots, watercress and salt in a small heatproof bowl. Heat the oil in a small pan or a wok. Add the curry leaves and mustard seeds. As soon as the mustard seeds begin to pop, draw the pan off the heat and add the cumin seeds. Return the pan to the heat, cover and let the seeds pop for about 10 more seconds. Remove from the heat and pour straight over the salad. Add the lime juice if using, then mix well and serve.

Opposite
Laksa Lemak
(page 128)

What a beguiling, totally unexpected taste these leaves have. They go by a legion of names – *rao ram*, Vietnamese mint, Vietnamese coriander and even Vietnamese basil, amongst others. The last three can all be justified to some extent but laksa leaves bear only a glancing resemblance to any of them. The leaves themselves are what is called lanceolate, i.e. oval, elongated, tapering to a point at the tip, and are around 5 cm (2 inches) long. The colour is a fairly ordinary green, with slight purplish markings. All in all, nothing too unusual in appearance, so you are lulled into a false sense of familiarity which is ripped to shreds when you begin to chew. The first hit is of the cool menthol of mint, then follows a hint of coriander and a trace of the anise scent of Thai basil. But what comes to dominate in the mouth is a strange, tingling pepperiness, which resembles not so much ordinary black pepper but the sensation you get from Szechwan pepper.

The big stumbling block to laksa leaf appreciation is that they are hard to track down. To find them, you will have to go to a good South-east Asian grocery, where they stock fresh greenery flown in from overseas. Outside the South-east Asian community they are very little known. Give it ten years or so, and I think they may catch on. If you do come across laksa leaves, substitute them for coriander in Thai, Vietnamese and Malaysian cookery, adding them to salads or stirring them into dishes just before serving to preserve their flavour. Though they can take a brief spurt of heat they do not take kindly to prolonged cooking.

Storage and Preservation

Store laksa leaves, wrapped in slightly dampened kitchen paper, in a plastic bag in the vegetable drawer of the fridge. Quite how long they will last depends on the state they were in when you bought them. If they were fresh off the plane, you can probably expect them to be useable for another four or five days. If the leaves are already beginning to show signs of deterioration, pick off the damaged ones and use the rest up quickly. This is not a herb to dry, though it may be suitable for freezing. Unfortunately, I can't say for sure, since I've never yet had enough to risk it in the freezer.

Laksa Lemak

Laksa Lemak, from Singapore, is one of my all-time favourite South-east Asian dishes. In fact it is possibly one of my all-time favourite dishes full-stop. A *laksa* is a spicy soup and there are many variations. The Singaporean *laksa* is rich with coconut milk and a-swim with rice noodles, prawns and occasionally other seafood. A true *laksa* will be flavoured with laksa leaf but if you can't find any, coriander will have to do instead.

It is not a quick dish to make, though the broth can be made in advance, then all you need do is reheat it and finish by adding the more substantial ingredients that take only a few minutes to cook. For a special occasion, it really is worth taking the trouble.

Serves 6

6 large scallops
250 g (9 oz) raw prawns in their shells
1 tablespoon groundnut, vegetable or sunflower oil
500 g (1 lb 2 oz) mussels
400 ml (14 fl oz) coconut milk
1–2 tablespoons fish sauce
400 g (14 oz) fresh flat rice noodles
3 kaffir lime leaves, very finely shredded, or 2 wide strips of
    lime zest
125 g (4 oz) beansprouts
a handful of laksa leaves or coriander leaves, roughly chopped
lime wedges, to serve

For the spice paste
3 lemon grass stems
3 red chillies, deseeded and chopped
2 garlic cloves, chopped
2.5 cm (1 inch) fresh galangal or root ginger, chopped
4 shallots, thinly sliced
1 tablespoon anchovy essence or anchovy paste
3 tablespoons groundnut, sunflower or vegetable oil
1 teaspoon ground turmeric
1 tablespoon ground coriander

Remove the dark vein that is sometimes left on the scallops. Separate the corals and the whites, then cut each white into 2–3 discs, according to size. Peel the prawns, saving the shells and heads. If necessary, make a little slit with the tip of a sharp knife down the back of each prawn, then remove the fine black gut that sometimes lies just below the surface. Set the prawns

aside. Fry the shells and heads in the oil until pink. Add about 1.75 litres (3 pints) of water, bring up to the boil and simmer for 30 minutes. Strain and discard the shells. Boil the stock down until reduced to 1.2 litres (2 pints).

While the stock is simmering, rinse the mussels thoroughly, scrape off any barnacles and cut away the beards. Rinse again. Discard any mussels that will not close when rapped firmly on the work surface. Pour 300 ml (½ pint) of water into a saucepan large enough to take the mussels. Bring up to the boil, add the mussels, cover tightly and shake over a high heat until opened – this should take no more than a few minutes. Any mussels that refuse point-blank to open must be discarded. Lift the mussels out, then strain the cooking juices to remove grit. Reserve the juices. Take about two-thirds of the mussels out of their shells and set aside.

For the spice paste, slice off and discard the upper half of the lemon grass stems, leaving just the lower 7.5–10 cm (3–4 inches). Slice thinly into little rounds and put into a food processor with the chillies, garlic, galangal or ginger, shallots, anchovy essence or paste and about 2 tablespoons of water. Process to a paste, adding a touch more water if necessary to lubricate. Heat the oil in a heavy pan and add the paste. Fry, stirring continuously and scraping the bottom of the pan to prevent burning, until browned – allow about 15 minutes. Now add the turmeric and coriander and fry for a further minute or so. Next add the prawn stock and the liquor from cooking the mussels. Bring up to the boil and simmer for 10 minutes. (You can prepare to this point in advance but do make sure that the seafood is kept well chilled in the fridge. Bring the stock back to the boil again before proceeding.)

Add the coconut milk and fish sauce, bring back to the boil, then push in the noodles. Once softened, add the kaffir lime leaves and simmer for 2 minutes. Tip in the prawns and simmer for 2 more minutes. Add the scallops, stir just once or twice, then add the reserved mussels and the beansprouts. Give everything one final stir.

To serve, spoon into big, deep bowls and perch the mussels in their shells on top. Scatter with laksa leaves or coriander and tuck a lime wedge neatly on top, to be squeezed over just before slurping it all down.

kaffir lime leaf
Citrus hystrix

Away from the big, crowded cities of Thailand, you will find kaffir lime trees growing in almost every garden and yard. One single tree is of inestimable value to a household, providing both the leaves and fruit for cooking, as well as the countless other uses that they have. The trees are big enough but not massive, growing some 3–6 metres high (which for us older generation is easier to imagine when translated to 9–18 feet), and the branches are heavy with the glossy, double green leaves and bear plenty of the gnarled lime fruit. The leaves themselves are most unusual, shaped like a stretched figure of eight, effectively a pair of leaflets growing on a single 'petiole' or central rib. When a recipe calls for one kaffir lime leaf, it means, usually, just a lone leaflet rather than the twinned pair. Like bay leaves, they are glossy and thick and strong, but the scent is something totally different. It has a clear, sharp but perfumed citrus zest aroma, most similar perhaps to our European lemon verbena, which can be used as a substitute though it is probably harder to find these days than kaffir lime leaves themselves. At a pinch you can replace kaffir lime leaves with strips of zest pared from ordinary limes but it really isn't the same.

The leaves are often used whole, very much like bay leaves, in soups and curries, where they can swish around to their heart's content. For salads, stir-fries and garnishes they are likely to be very finely shredded. The easiest way to do this is to pile up three or four leaves, then roll them up tightly like a mini cigar. With a sharp knife, slice them across slightly diagonally into narrow threads. They will still exercise the jaw but they have a texture that the enthusiast comes to appreciate. As you bite on them they release more of their inestimable flavour.

For cooking it is the zest of the lime rather than the juice that is used. The juice, however, comes into its own as a natural bleach, used in washing, and is also said to work wonders for the gums. Rind and juice are infused together to rinse hair, leaving it fragrant, glossy and clean and, even more imperative, warding off evil spirits and even lice. A whole lime left sitting in a fruit bowl and occasionally scratched when you are passing will see off bad smells into the bargain.

If you can lay your hands on a kaffir lime tree, they will, apparently grow quite nicely in the UK, in a container in a sunny room, or conservatory, like any other citrus plant. Frequent pruning encourages lush growth, so the more Thai dishes you cook, the perkier your tree should be.

Failing that, you will have to settle for buying lime leaves from Thai and other South-east Asian food shops, or from some of the larger supermarkets, where they swing on racks along with more familiar herbs. Sometimes they are packed on their own but you may also be able to salvage a few leaves from mixed packs of Thai herbs. The fresh leaves are so very much more exciting to use and taste than the dried, which have lost much of their immediate sprightly vigour. Still, they are better than nothing, and better than most substitutes. Whole dried leaves can be added straight to soups and sauces, where they will rehydrate as they simmer. Wherever shredded kaffir lime leaves are called for, you will have to soak the leaves first in a little warm water until they become soft and pliable, before cutting.

Storage and Preservation

Impressive things that they are, kaffir lime leaves will keep for weeks in an airtight container in the vegetable drawer of the fridge. I've used them after they've languished there for three weeks and found almost no deterioration in flavour. If you have difficulty finding kaffir lime leaves near you, then take advantage of visits to large centres where they are easier to find, by buying them in generous amounts and then popping them straight into the freezer in a sealed plastic bag when you get home. Frozen, they keep their spirit for a year, maybe longer.

Lime Leaf Beurre Blanc

Beurre blanc, or butter sauce, is one of the great sauces for fish, invented near Nantes at the mouth of the Loire river. Variations abound but this one, with the vivid aromatic vigour of kaffir lime leaves, is a brilliant way to dress up practically any white-fleshed fish or salmon. For a really luxurious meal, partner it with turbot, sea bass or brill, but use it, too, with cod, whiting, lemon sole and other lesser fish.

Beurre blanc has a bit of a reputation as a tricky customer but in reality it is not at all difficult to make. The key to success is getting the temperature right when the butter is being whisked in. It should be kept low, but not so low that the butter won't melt in. I usually find that drawing the pan off the heat frequently, so that it has a chance to sit for a few seconds without heat, keeps it from curdling.

Serves 6

2 shallots, very finely chopped
250 g (9 oz) unsalted butter, diced and chilled
2 tablespoons white wine vinegar
100 ml (3½ fl oz) white wine
100 ml (3½ fl oz) fish or chicken stock
4 kaffir lime leaves, bruised and then very finely shredded
a little sugar, if needed
1–2 tablespoons cream, if needed
salt and pepper

Sweat the shallots in 30 g (1 oz) of the butter in a small saucepan. When they are tender, add the vinegar, wine, stock and kaffir lime leaves. Boil hard until reduced to about 2 tablespoons with a good syrupy consistency. You can do this in advance, then heat it through gently again when you want to finish the sauce.

Whisking continuously with a wire whisk, gradually add the butter a few cubes at a time, whisking each batch in before adding the next. As the butter is incorporated, the sauce becomes thick, pale and creamy. When all the butter is mixed in, draw the sauce off the heat and season with salt and pepper. If it is a little on the sharp side, you can soften it with a little more butter, or a pinch of sugar or a tablespoon or two of cream.

Disaster strikes: if, as you are busy whisking, you notice that your sauce is beginning to look oily rather than thick and creamy, take the pan straight off the heat and plunge it into a bowl of icy-cold water (it's not a bad idea to have one standing by before you start on the sauce, just in case) to cool it down. As it cools off, the sauce should thicken to a cream. Take it back to the stove and start whisking in the remaining butter, taking enormous care not to overheat it again. With any luck, it should turn out all right.

Opposite
**Chicken and
Pineapple
Red Curry
with Kaffir
Lime Leaves**
(page 132)

Chicken and **Pineapple Red Curry**
with **Kaffir Lime Leaves**

Jars of ready-made Thai curry paste are a godsend, even though they are nowhere near as fragrant as the real thing, chopped and pounded and worked in the privacy of your own home. Here I've used it to conjure up a fairly quick dish of chicken and pineapple in an aromatic coconut sauce. Serve it on a bed of Thai fragrant rice, scented with a short length of pandanus leaf (see p. 154) if you can get it, or even plain long grain rice with a spike or two of lavender slipped into the pan as it cooks.

Serves 4

3 tablespoons sunflower or vegetable oil
1 red onion, thinly sliced
3 tablespoons Thai red curry paste
4 fresh or dried kaffir lime leaves
either 3 skinned chicken breasts or 6 boned, skinned chicken
    thighs, cut roughly into 2 cm (¾ inch) pieces
2 x 100 ml (3½ fl oz) cartons of coconut cream
1–2 tablespoons fish sauce
juice of ½–1 lime
340 g (12 oz) peeled and cored fresh pineapple (around ½ a
    medium–large one), diced into 1.5 cm (½ inch) cubes
2 tablespoons roughly chopped coriander

Heat the oil in a roomy frying pan until very hot. Add the onion and fry briskly until lightly browned. Scoop out and drain off most of the fat. Add the curry paste and lime leaves to the pan. Stir about over a moderate heat for 2 minutes. Now add the chicken cubes and stir, then cook for about 2 minutes. Return the onions to the pan with all the remaining ingredients except the pineapple and coriander and add barely enough water to cover. Leave to simmer, uncovered, for 10 minutes. Now add the pineapple and simmer for a further 2–3 minutes, by which time the chicken will be cooked and the sauce should have a good consistency and an even better taste. There's meant to be a fair amount of it, so that it moistens the rice admirably, but if it seems too watery, simmer it down for a couple of minutes longer. Taste and adjust the seasoning, adding a little more fish sauce if it needs more salt, then scatter with the coriander and serve over boiled rice.

lemon grass
Cymbopogon citratus

Queen Victoria liked lemon grass. Honest, it is perfectly true…she was partial to a cup of lemon grass tea every now and then. This wasn't quite as remarkable as it sounds. Victorian ladies may not have been familiar with the aromatic stir-fries of Thailand, and indeed would probably have thought them far too pungent and coarse for their tastes, but lemon grass… now that was something else altogether. It grew easily in the greenhouses that the gentry prided themselves upon and, infused in boiling water, with perhaps a little hint of sugar to sweeten it, it was very soothing on an upset or over-indulged tummy and equally reviving if ma'am was feeling a mite fatigued.

Perhaps they had picked up the idea in India, lemon grass's native territory. It is used principally by Gujeratis and Parsees there, though with little of the grand exuberance of Southeast Asians. It is reserved mainly for fortifying soups and, yes, lemon grass tea. Down in Sri Lanka it gets a little more of a look in, but is still a very minor bit-part player.

What a different approach in Thailand, Vietnam, Malaysia, Indonesia. In their warm, moist climate, lemon grass grows and multiplies like nobody's business, and to my mind is the defining flavour of the food, together with ample helpings of coriander. Its lemon zest perfume is irreplaceable and instantly recognizable, stirred, pounded, braised or bruised into the thrilling dishes of this part of the world. It grows in sizeable clumps, with its tight, many-layered, pale green-yellow stems crowding up, opening at the top to put forth long, grass-like blades of green. At its finest it can grow up to 3 metres (9 feet) tall.

Don't expect it to perform in quite such spectacular fashion back here, but don't imagine that it will reject the poor British climate lock, stock and barrel. Stick a stem of lemon grass in a jar of water on a sunny windowsill, or dip it into rooting powder and plant in a pot of compost, and with any luck it will soon send out tentative roots. Provide a bit of T.L.C., warmth and water, and you will soon be the proud owner of a small clump of prime, fresh lemon grass. As with most herbs, extreme conditions magnify the flavour, so your cosseted plant is unlikely to match the lemon

Lemon Grass and Kaffir Lime Leaf Kebabs with Coconut and Coriander Sauce

grass grown in the climate of South-east Asia, but what is lost in intensity is gained in freshness and smug pride.

Inside the tough, tight, bulbous base of the stems are secreted thousands of minuscule oil sacs which contain the magic aroma of the lemon grass. The aim is to release their contents into whatever is cooking. The lower part of the stem – say 12.5–15 cms (5–6 inches) up from the bulbous base – is where the oil sacs are most concentrated, and so where the cook should concentrate his or her efforts. The first step is to peel off one or two of the toughest outer layers. The next move depends on what you are cooking. For soups and any dish where you might want to remove the lemon grass before serving, it is enough to bash the stem with a meat mallet or something similar, squashing it down flat and bursting oil sacs left, right and centre. For curry pastes, a slightly lighter bruising, with the back of a wooden spoon, say, is a good start, then the lemon grass is sliced. For salads and stir-fries, where the lemon grass will be left in exactly the same state at beginning and end of the process, bruise it first, then slice incredibly thinly to diminish the fibrousness that can lead to jaw ache. The upper portion of the stem, while less laden with oil sacs, does tend to be more tender, and so in salads the faint-hearted can settle for that.

Lemon grass slips very nicely into Western dishes. I love it in puddings, infused first in a sugar syrup for easy distribution of flavour, and in cool summer drinks, too. It goes particularly well with fish and shellfish, bruised, chopped and added perhaps to a marinade or used in a bouquet garni. Try adding lemon grass to the beurre blanc on p. 130, with or without the lime leaves.

Storage and Preservation

Lemon grass is remarkably well tempered. In a plastic bag or airtight container, it will keep for two or three weeks in the fridge with little loss of flavour. Pop it into the freezer and it will last for some two to three months. Dried lemon grass is quite widely sold these days but it doesn't really compare with fresh. If you do have to resort to it, soak in warm water for an hour before using. Powdered dried lemon grass and lemon grass purées are probably best avoided.

In most recipes it is the lower, fatter part of the lemon grass stem that you really need, but not here. This is a way to make the most of the upper portion, using it essentially as a form of brochette or skewer to hold a sausage of minced pork, spiced with kaffir lime leaves and chilli. They also go very well with the sweet chilli sauce on p. 157.

Serves 3–4

4–8 long lemon grass stems
500 g (1 lb 2 oz) minced pork
3 fresh kaffir lime leaves, very finely chopped
1–2 red chillies, very finely chopped
1½ tablespoons fish sauce
a little sesame oil
lime wedges, to serve

For the coconut and coriander sauce
1 bunch of coriander,
2 garlic cloves, chopped
2 shallots, chopped
2.5 cm (1 inch) fresh root ginger, finely chopped
1 small green chilli, deseeded and chopped (optional)
1 tablespoon sunflower oil
3 tablespoons thick coconut milk (see p.134) or
    coconut cream
juice of 1 lime
2 teaspoons brown sugar
1 tablespoon fish sauce

To make the sauce, cut the leaves and upper couple of inches of stalk off the bunch of coriander and reserve. Discard the lower stalks. Fry the garlic, shallots, ginger and chilli in the oil until tender and lightly browned. Cool slightly, then scrape into a food processor. Add all the remaining ingredients, including the coriander leaves, and process until smooth. If it seems a little on the thick side, stir in a splash of water to give a thick, creamy sauce. Taste and adjust the seasonings.

Now turn to the kebabs. You only need the upper ends of the lemon grass stems, so save the lower, fatter base (about 7.5 cm/3 inches) of it, to use in some other dish. If what you have left is very long (at least 25 cm/10 inches) then you will need only 4 stems. Any shorter than that and you will need 8. If they are long, cut them in half. Set aside.

Mix the pork with the kaffir lime leaves, chilli and fish sauce, kneading with your fingers so that it holds together well. Divide into 8 portions. Roll each portion into a sausage shape, then flatten on the palm of your hand. Lay a lemon grass stalk down the centre, then bring the pork mixture up and round to enclose it, as if it were a skewer stuck through the length of a sausage. Mould the meat firmly so that it hugs the stem, then give it a little roll to even it out. Set aside until needed.

Pre-heat the grill and line the grill pan with silver foil. Brush the kebabs with sesame oil, then grill, turning once, for about 4 minutes on each side. Serve immediately, with the coconut sauce, lime wedges and pan juices.

An easy way to get thick coconut milk is to put a tin of coconut milk in the fridge for an hour or so. When you open it, the thick coconut milk will have risen to the top and can be scooped off.

This sauce came about by accident last December. Amongst the throng gathering for Christmas lunch was one lone vegetarian and I wanted to give him as much of a treat as the rest of us were getting. To go with the rather sumptuous version of a nut loaf I was preparing, I wanted a tomato-based sauce that would stand out from the crowd, without clashing. This was what I came up with, based largely on what I had in the fridge. It is very easy to make, with a startlingly good flavour. It goes well with all kinds of things – not only nut loaf but also more fleshy options such as grilled tuna, or chicken perhaps, griddled scallops, or maybe a nice peppered piece of fillet steak.

Lemon olive oil is available from some of the major supermarkets and many good delicatessens. It is made by pressing whole lemons with the olives so that the oils from both intermingle. Marvellous stuff. However, if you can't get any the sauce will still taste fine without it.

Serves 6

1 kg (2 lb 4 oz) tomatoes, halved
2 red onions, each cut into 8 wedges
1 large red pepper, deseeded and cut into large chunks
4 whole garlic cloves, unpeeled
3 tablespoons olive oil
2 tablespoons lemon olive oil
1 sprig of thyme
2 lemon grass stems, bruised and sliced
2.5 cm (1 inch) fresh root ginger, sliced
2 kaffir lime leaves
1 red chilli, deseeded and halved
1 tablespoon caster sugar
coarse salt and pepper

Pre-heat the oven to 220°C/425°F/Gas Mark 7. Put all the ingredients into a large, shallow roasting tin, turning so that all the vegetables are coated in oil. Roast, uncovered, for about 45–55 minutes, turning once or

Opposite
**Lemon Grass
and Kaffir
Lime Leaf
Kebabs with
Coconut and
Coriander
Sauce**

Lemon Grass and Ginger Syrup

twice, until all the vegetables are very tender and patched with brown. Cool for a couple of minutes, then fish out and discard the kaffir lime leaves. Spoon the remaining contents of the roasting tin into a food processor, including all the juices and herbs and scraping in any nice caramelized bits and bobs stuck to the side of the tin. Process until more or less smooth, then rub through a sieve to get rid of all the dross. Taste the puréed sauce and adjust the seasoning. If it is a little on the thick side, thin down with a splash of water or vegetable or chicken stock. If it is too thin, then it can be boiled down to a better consistency. Either way, reheat the sauce when needed.

This is a multi-purpose syrup, scented with lemon grass and ginger. You can use it as the basis for a jug of aromatic lemonade, or for a gin cocktail (add gin, ice cubes and mineral water), as a simple sauce to transform scoops of vanilla ice-cream into something rather exotic (add slices of mango, pineapple or lychees for even more exoticism) or whisk it up with cream to make a classic syllabub with a new perfume (see p. 137). If you have a little more time to spare and want to create a spectacular pudding for a party, then take the syllabub and add it to a pavlova, along with mango and passion fruit, for a truly sumptuous creation (see p. 138).

Makes about 200 ml (7 fl oz)

4 lemon grass stems, bruised heavily and finely sliced
20g (¾ oz) fresh root ginger, chopped
125g (4 oz) caster sugar
200 ml (7 fl oz) water

Put all the ingredients in a saucepan and stir over a moderate heat until the sugar has dissolved. Bring up to the boil and simmer for 10 minutes. Leave to cool, then strain. The scented syrup can be stored in the fridge in a sealed jar for a month or more.

Lemon Grass and **Ginger Lemonade**

Lemon Grass and **Ginger Syllabub**

Home-made lemonade, served in a glass beaded with icy condensation, is blissfully refreshing on a hot summer's day. There are lots of variations on the theme, but I particularly like this one, with the scent of lemon grass and the ticklish hint of ginger.

Serves 4–6

1 quantity of Lemon Grass and Ginger Syrup (see opposite)
juice of 2 lemons
600–900 ml (1–1½ pints) sparkling mineral water
ice cubes, a few slices of lemon, a few sprigs of mint, and a
  few borage flowers, if available, to serve

Mix the syrup with the lemon juice and mineral water to taste. Serve in tall glasses with plenty of ice, and a slice of lemon, a sprig of mint and a couple of borage flowers if you have them, afloat in each one.

With your lemon grass and ginger syrup stashed patiently in the fridge, you can conjure up this magical, luxurious, airy pudding within a matter of minutes. It is unashamedly rich, and unashamedly delicious. Serve it with crisp, almondy biscuits and, if you want to stretch the quantity a little more, with slices of fresh mango, or peaches in the summer.

Serves 6

1 quantity of Lemon Grass and Ginger Syrup (see opposite)
2 tablespoons lime or lemon juice
1 tablespoon brandy (optional)
300 ml (½ pint) chilled double cream
curls of lime zest or finely grated lime zest, to serve

Put all the ingredients except the lime zest into a bowl. Whisk until thick and virtually holding its shape but still slightly sloppy. Take care not to overdo it at this stage, especially in a hot kitchen – you don't want to end up with fragrant butter. Spoon into individual glasses, top with a little lime zest for colour and serve lightly chilled.

Mango, Passionfruit and Lemon Grass Syllabub Pavlova

The queen of pavlovas, the prima ballerina, the whatever other superlatives you care to throw at it, this is a showstopping way to end a dinner party. It is fundamentally a classic pavlova, but given a thorough up-lift with a deluge of lemon grass and ginger syllabub instead of plain cream, and finished with luscious mango (make sure they are very ripe and juicy) and sharply perfumed passion fruit. All the individual components can be made or prepared in advance, but don't assemble the finished pavlova until at most half an hour before serving.

Serves 6–8

4 egg whites
a pinch of salt
250 g (9 oz) caster sugar
2 teaspoons cornflour
1 teaspoon white wine vinegar
½ teaspoon vanilla extract

For the filling

4 passionfruit
½ tablespoon caster sugar
1 quantity of Lemon Grass and Ginger Syllabub (see p. 137)
    (you won't need quite all of it)
1 large, ripe mango, peeled, stoned and finely diced

Pre-heat the oven to 180°C/350°F/Gas mark 4. Make sure the egg whites are at room temperature before you begin on the pavlova. Line a baking sheet with non-stick baking parchment. Find a plate that is 20–23 cm (8–9 inches) in diameter and use as a template to draw a circle on the baking parchment. Turn the paper over so that the ink or pencil line is on the underneath.

Whisk the egg whites with the salt until they form shiny, soft peaks. Add a third of the sugar, whisk again until glossy, then repeat twice. Sift over the cornflour and add the vinegar and vanilla, then fold together. Spoon into the centre of the circle on your baking tray, then spread out with a spatula to fill the circle, levelling out the top and smoothing over the sides, to form a flat-topped, stubby pillar. Put it straight into the oven, then reduce the heat to 150°C/300°F/Gas Mark 2. Cook for 1–1¼ hours, then turn off the oven and leave the pavlova in it until completely cool. Invert on to a serving plate.

Scoop out the pulp of the passionfruit, and stir in the sugar. If you wish, rub through a sieve to remove the seeds, but it really isn't necessary. Shortly before serving, stir the syllabub then spoon enough over the pavlova to cover it fairly thickly. Scatter the mango on top, then drizzle the passionfruit pulp over the whole lot. Serve and enjoy.

the eastern basils:

Thai Basil, Holy Basil, Thai Lemon Basil
Ocimum basilicum 'Horapha', *Ocimum sanctum*
and *Ocimum canum*

We think of basil as the quintessential Mediterranean herb and yet it is used just as much, if not more, in South-east Asia. That's almost where its history begins, for the basil plant is native to Asia, and probably more specifically to India. Not surprising then, that there are umpteen different forms of basil grown throughout Asia. Three of them seize the culinary headlines, the three varieties beloved by Thai cooks: Thai basil, Holy basil and Thai lemon basil (or sweet balsam basil). Of these, the first two can be tracked down with relative ease in the UK in specialist shops. The third, the basil with the lemony scent, is one I have never yet come across, though perhaps I went looking at the wrong time, or merely failed to recognize it.

Thai basil, *bai horapa*, has a heady, sweet scent of pepper, fragrant basil and anise that is quite delicious. Thai cooks use it in generous quantities, almost as a vegetable or salad leaf rather than just a herb. Its dark green leaves are more elongated than our sweet basil and they grow on purplish stems topped with reddish-purple flowerbuds. It is added to curries (particularly those made with coconut milk), stir-fries, fragrant salads and soups. Mixed with our basil, or a little parsley, it also makes a great pesto, to swish into dishes of stir-fried noodles or straight Italian spaghetti. It is also widely used in the cooking of Vietnam, where it goes under the name *rau húng*. It adds a delicious fragrance to the Vietnamese answer to spring rolls (see p. 197), and is essential in the national dish, *phó*, a packed beef and noodle soup.

If you can get the seeds, it is easy enough to grow as long as it is kept warm. And if you bring a bunch of Thai basil home from a shopping spree, try leaving some of the finer stems in a glass of water on the windowsill, to encourage it to root. If you can't get hold of Thai basil, you can make an adequate replacement with a mixture of Mediterranean basil and tarragon.

In India, holy basil (*Ocimum sanctum*) which is known as *tulsi*, is sacred to the god Vishnu, who wears a garland of basil leaves. Basil plants are cherished in every Hindu household, playing an integral role in religious ceremonies both at home and in the temple. In Hindu weddings, the parents of the bride give their new son-in-law a basil leaf to symbolize that they are wholeheartedly giving their daughter to him. With all this religious significance attached to it, *tulsi* is almost never used in cooking, though it is occasionally infused with ginger to make an invigorating tea.

It couldn't be more different in Thailand and the other South-east Asian countries, where holy basil (known as *bai gkaprow* there) is thrown with gay abandon into the cooking pot. I remember a memorable meal taken in the market of Chiang Mai, when I tasted for the first time one of Thailand's favourite dishes, *gai pad gka-prow*, stir-fried chicken with holy basil (a recipe for which is in *Sophie Grigson's Meat Course*). In fact, it was more stir-fried basil with chicken, my bowl heaped up with the tender green leaves fried briefly with aromatics. The great thing about holy basil is that although the leaf is tender, heat really does bring out its flavour. For this reason you are less likely to find it in salads and other uncooked dishes.

The leaves have the fragrance of our European basil, blended with a little of the menthol of mint and plenty of pepper. There are two forms of holy basil: a light-green-leaved one and another, stronger type, with a purplish hue to the darker green leaves and the stems. The leaves are delicately serrated and less sturdy than those of Thai basil. When holy basil is not to be had for love nor money, substitute a mixture of European basil and spearmint or Bowles mint.

Thai lemon basil, *bai maeng-lak*, which is sometimes called sweet balsam basil (*Ocimum canum*) has, as the name suggests, a flavour that blends the peppery aroma of basil with lemon. It is used less than Thai and holy basil and is nearly always added at the end of cooking. It looks a bit like a form of mint, with moderately large, serrated, slightly hairy leaves.

Thai Fruit and Coconut Salsa

Storage and Preservation

To keep Thai basil perky, plunge the stems into a glass of cold water, cover the leaves with a plastic bag and stand it in the fridge if there is room enough. There never is in mine, so I go for the usual alternative of wrapping the greenery in moistened kitchen paper, then popping it into a plastic bag and storing it in the vegetable drawer of the fridge. Either way it should stay good enough to use for up to a week. The more fragile leaves of holy basil should be treated in the same way, but even so will only last for two or three days. As for the rare Thai lemon basil, I imagine it can take the same kind of handling, though I have no idea how long it will be before misery and wilt set in. If you do manage to lay your hands on it, use it up quickly before it gets a chance to lose its charms.

Holy basil can be dried, though much of the freshness and zip of the green herb is lost. I can't recommend it. You could try preserving any of the oriental basils in Italian fashion, either layered with salt in a jar and covered with oil (make it a neutral sort, such as sunflower, groundnut or safflower), or puréed olive oil and then stored in the fridge (see p. 61).

A fragrant, sweet and sharp hot salsa that goes very well with grilled chicken and other white meats. Coconut cream is sold in small cartons ready to use in liquid form. Don't confuse it with creamed coconut, which comes in hard blocks.

Serves 4

2 lemon grass stems
1 mango, peeled, stoned and finely diced
½ pineapple, peeled, cored and finely diced
100ml (3½ fl oz) coconut cream
1 tablespoon fish sauce
finely grated zest of 1 lime
juice of ½–1 lime
2 cm (¾ inch) fresh root ginger, finely chopped
6 spring onions, thinly sliced
1–2 red chillies, deseeded and very finely chopped
2 tablespoons chopped coriander
3 tablespoons shredded Thai basil
2 tablespoons shredded mint leaves

Cut off and discard the upper part of the lemon grass stems, leaving the lower 7.5–10 cm (3–4 inches). Bruise this with a rolling pin or a meat mallet, then remove the outer layer. Slice the inner stem very thinly. Mix with all the remaining ingredients except the basil and mint. Taste and adjust the seasoning. Just before serving, scatter over the shredded basil and mint, to be stirred in as people serve themselves.

eastern

Stir-Fried Noodles with **Holy Basil, Prawns** and **Shiitake Mushrooms**

I have a passion for stir-fried noodles spiced up with the vivid flavours of South-east Asia. I play around with all kinds of extra ingredients but this is a combination, with the scent of barely wilted holy basil, the sweetness of prawns and the meaty texture of shiitake mushrooms, that I particularly love. If you can get fresh egg oil noodles you will find that they are absolutely perfect for stir-frying, with a delicious slippery texture. As with all stir-frying, prepare and gather all the ingredients around you, combining the ones that go into the wok together in one bowl, before you start cooking. The going is too fast to have to rush off in search of some missing ingredient in mid-session.

Serves 3–4

450 g (1 lb) fresh egg oil noodles (from Chinese
    supermarkets) or 250 g (9 oz) dried egg thread noodles
    (from most ordinary supermarkets)
4 tablespoons groundnut, vegetable or sunflower oil, plus a
    little extra if using dried noodles
3 garlic cloves, chopped
2.5 cm (1 inch) fresh root ginger, finely chopped
½ red onion, finely chopped
1–2 red chillies, deseeded and finely chopped
125 g (4 oz) shiitake mushrooms, stems discarded, thickly
    sliced (or button mushrooms if you can't find shiitake)
125 g (4 oz) shelled raw prawns, roughly cut up if large
a good handful of holy basil leaves (about 30–40 g/1–1⅓ oz)
4 spring onions, finely chopped
2 tablespoons fish sauce
2 teaspoons sesame oil
½ tablespoon caster sugar
juice of 1 lime

To serve
3 tablespoons (about 45 g/1½ oz) roasted peanuts, finely
    chopped
fish sauce
chopped red chilli or chilli sauce
lime wedges

If using dried noodles, cook as directed on the packet. Drain thoroughly and, if not using immediately, toss with about ½ tablespoon of oil.

Put a roomy wok over the heat and leave until hazy. Now add the oil, leave for a few seconds to heat through, then add the garlic, ginger, onion and chilli. Stir-fry for 30 seconds or so, then add the mushrooms. Stir fry for 2–3 minutes, until beginning to soften. Next throw in the prawns and stir-fry until they are just pink. And now the noodles go in, and will need a minute or two of stir-frying to mix with all the other ingredients. Set aside a few of the basil leaves to garnish the dish, then add the rest to the pan with all the remaining ingredients. Stir-fry for a matter of 1–2 minutes, just long enough to wilt the basil but not to kill its peppery fragrance, and to mix everything nicely.

Turn out into bowls and scatter the finely chopped peanuts and reserved basil leaves over the top. Serve immediately, with extra fish sauce on the table, as well as chopped chilli or chilli sauce and lime wedges for those who want them.

scented geranium leaf
Pelargonium species

The scented geraniums are a group that comprises some of the most exquisite flavourings for puddings and desserts that you can imagine. An ice-cream, jelly or custard perfumed with Attar-of-rose geranium is impossibly wonderful; a sugar syrup infused with orange-scented leaves for macerating soft summer tree fruit is heavenly; and a cake with a light waft of lemon scented-geranium leaves curling up through its crumb is divine. Apparently there are some 200 different varieties of scented geranium but the three mentioned above are probably the most useful if you are thinking of setting up a small, scented pelargonium cook's corner. While you are down at the plant nursery, have a sniff at the leaves of any other scented pelargoniums to see whether they take your fancy.

These perfumed plants are all topsy-turvy, for while their leaves can hold their own (and frequently do) in any perfume factory in the world, the jolly little flowers are generally quite devoid of any smell worth mentioning. Not that they are to be sneered at, for they do a grand job of garnishing puddings, along with a few of the lacy leaves.

There are several ways of extracting the scent from the leaves. An old favourite is to line the base of a cake tin with a layer of leaves before pouring in the batter (see Rose Geranium and Almond Cake, p. 145). As the cake cooks, the scent gently permeates the crumb, working its way slowly upwards. To make scented sugar for puddings of all kinds, just plunge a couple of leaves into a jar of caster sugar, seal tightly and leave for a week or so. A quicker but more dangerous method is to put sugar and geranium leaves into a heavy pan and stir over a low heat until the leaves release their essential oils and the sugar sucks it up. Add them straight to a boiling syrup and they have a tendency to disintegrate – not the end of the world, as long as you remember to strain the syrup before using. Incidentally, a rose geranium-scented syrup, doctored with a shot or two of lemon or lime juice, then diluted with fizzy mineral water and ice makes a very refreshing summer drink.

Opposite
Clockwise from top left: sweet cicely; pandanus leaves; angelica (leaves and stems); scented geranium leaves; blackcurrant leaves

Rose Geranium Ice-cream

When trying to infuse the scent into jams or jellies, add the leaves only towards the end of the cooking time, to preserve their power. With jams this may mean putting up with the odd disintegrated speck of leaf scattered throughout but it is a small price to pay. The leaves hold together rather better in milk or cream, merely brought up to the boil, then drawn off the heat and left to infuse for a good half an hour or more. Use the scented cream or milk for custards, ice-creams and the like.

Recommended varieties are *Pelargonium* 'Attar of Roses' and *Pelargonium* 'Graveolens' for a scent of roses, *Pelargonium crispum* 'Variegata' for a lemon scent, *Pelargonium radens* for a rose-lemon fragrance and *Pelargonium crispum* 'Prince of Orange' for an orangey perfume.Use the *crispum* varieties sparingly.

Storage and Preservation

Being moderately thick and sturdy, the cut leaves and their more delicate flowers last remarkably well in sealed airtight boxes or plastic bags in the fridge, though some of their scent will dampen down a little after four or five days. The way to preserve their spirit is to seal it in a jar of sugar (see p. 142) or capture it in a clear jelly (see p. 145). The dried leaves retain much of their perfume, so are well-suited to pot pourri, but are too musty for cooking with.

I can't imagine many nicer ways to end a meal than with this fragrant, rich ice-cream, scooped on to plates with a few slices of ripe peach or melon, or some sweet raspberries and sliced strawberries. I like it made with single cream but for a lighter version you could replace the single cream with full-cream milk.

Serves 4–6

300 ml (½ pint) single cream
12 rose geranium leaves, lightly bruised to release their perfume
4 egg yolks
60 g (2 oz) caster sugar
300 ml (½ pint) whipping cream
the petals of 12 rose geranium flowers (optional)

Put the single cream into a pan with the rose geranium leaves. Bring gently up to the boil, then draw off the heat, cover and leave to infuse for 30–60 minutes.

Put the egg yolks in a bowl with the caster sugar and whisk until pale and thick. Gradually whisk in the perfumed cream (still with the leaves in it), then set the bowl over a pan of gently simmering water, making sure that the base of the bowl does not come into contact with the water. Stir until the custard thickens just enough to coat the back of a wooden spoon. Lift the bowl off the pan and leave until tepid, then strain.

Whisk the whipping cream lightly and fold into the custard, together with the rose geranium petals, if using. Churn in an ice-cream machine if you have one. If not, pour the mixture into a shallow container and leave in the freezer, turned to its coldest setting. When the mixture has set around the sides but is still runny in the centre, take it out of the freezer, break up the sides and push them into the centre. Return to the freezer. Repeat if you have time. Then leave in the freezer until the mixture is just about set but not yet rock solid. Scrape quickly into a food processor or a bowl and either process or beat hard to smooth out the jagged ice crystals. Return to the container and then to the freezer to finish freezing.

Transfer from the freezer to the fridge about 45 minutes before serving to soften.

Rose Geranium Jelly

Well, what a divine concoction this is. A clear, light-amber jelly, slightly tart from the juice of the lemons and with a heavenly, heady fragrance that wafts you straight to fantasies of elegant Edwardian teas on the lawn.

Serve the jelly with scones and clotted cream, spooned over rich fromage frais, on toast, or in sandwiches with cream cheese. Add a pitcher of home-made lemonade and a few cucumber sandwiches and dive back into rose-tinted summers past.

Fills about 5 jam jars

2 kg (4 lb 8 oz) cooking apples
1.2 litres (2 pints) water
juice of 2 lemons
preserving sugar (not with added pectin) or granulated sugar
2 handfuls (around 20–30g/¾–1 oz) of rose geranium leaves, or other scented geranium leaves

Cut the apples up roughly without bothering to peel or core them, discarding any bruised or damaged parts which would upset the finished jelly's longevity. Put the prepared apple into a large saucepan with the water and lemon juice. Bring up to a gentle simmer, then reduce the heat and simmer slowly for about 45 minutes, until very soft and pulpy, stirring occasionally. Spoon into a jelly bag suspended over a large bowl and leave to drain overnight, without pressing down on the pulp at all (you'll end up with a cloudy jelly if you do).

The next day, measure out the amount of juice and weigh out 450g (1 lb) sugar for every 600 ml (1 pint). Put the sugar in a very low oven, or the airing cupboard if it is on the hot side, to warm through. Pour the juice into a large saucepan, bring up to the boil and add the geranium leaves. Simmer for 5 minutes, then add the sugar. Stir constantly until it has dissolved, without letting the mixture boil. Once the syrup is quite clear, bring up to the boil and boil hard, without stirring, until setting point is reached, which may be as soon as a minute or so or up to 10–15 minutes. Skim off any scum, then strain the juice through a fine sieve into a warmed bowl to remove disintegrating leaves.

Ladle the hot jelly into hot sterilized jars (see p. 150). Seal quickly, label, then store in a cool, dark place.

Rose Geranium and Almond Cake served with a Compote of Summer Fruits

This is an idea I've adapted from old cookery books – fragrant leaves, such as scented geranium or blackcurrant, were used to line a cake tin before baking. It works just as well with elderflowers; as the cake bakes the scent works its way up into the crumb, leaving a delicate but distinctive presence. Try it, too, with heads of lavender flowers, fresh or dried.

Serves 8

rose geranium sugar (see method) to taste
enough scented geranium leaves to cover the base of a
    17.5 cm (7in) cake tin
125 g (4 oz) self-raising flour
a pinch of salt
2 eggs
125 g (4 oz) caster sugar
60 g (2 oz) butter, melted and cooled
60 g (2 oz) ground almonds

For the fruit compote
250 g (9 oz) strawberries, halved
250 g (9 oz) blueberries
juice of ½ orange

Make the rose geranium sugar: bury a handful of rose geranium leaves in a jar of sugar and leave for 3 days.

Pre-heat the oven to 180°C/350°F/Gas Mark 4. Line a 7 inch (17.5 cm) cake tin with non-stick baking parchment, or butter and flour it generously.

Make sure the geranium leaves are clean and haven't been sprayed with anything undesirable. Snip enough leaves from the plant to cover the base of the tin and sit them upper side down.

Sift the flour with the salt. Beat the eggs with the sugar until pale and fluffy. Add the melted butter, then fold in the flour and ground almonds to give a smooth batter. Pour into the cake tin, gently trying not to disturb the leaves. Bake for 30 minutes or until firm to the touch. Once the cake is perfectly cooked, take it from the oven and remove the greaseproof paper. Peel off the leaves and leave the cake on a rack to cool. Serve the cake on its own or with the fruit compote.

Make the fruit compote: mix all the ingredients and leave to marinate for at least an hour.

angelica
Angelica archangelica

This has to be one of the great unsung wonders of the herb garden. Angelica is a heavenly herb, with a glorious fragrance and majestic form. Every garden should have at least one angelica plant, situated in a spot where it can be admired from afar as well as up close. At its zenith it stands as tall as a man, with a fine architectural form equalled only by that of lovage. Its Latin name, angel of the archangel, derives, according to one source, from a dream in which an angel announced that an infusion of angelica would halt the spread of plague. Another story links it to the Archangel Michael. The big white umbels come into flower in early summer, around 8 May, which is his feast day.

The fragrance of the leaves and hollow stems is very special: sweet, musky and warm. I like it every bit as much as vanilla, and use it in similar ways to flavour cream- or milk-based puddings and ice-creams, infusing the greenery in the liquid over a very low heat. Try it in a custard to pour over summery puddings. It is excellent in both pudding and preserve jellies and in jams (try it in rhubarb or strawberry jam), and sensational thrown into the bowl when making lemon curd or other fruit curds. Like sweet cicely, it also works as an acidity-dampener for stewed fruit – throw a few leaves and stems in with rhubarb, plums, blackberries or apples as they cook and you can reduce the amount of sugar by up to a quarter. Add the young stems, before they become stringy, to fruit tarts and pies, both for flavour and to reduce the need for sweetening. In fact, if the fancy takes you, you can boil or steam the young stems and eat them, lightly buttered, as a spring vegetable.

Many years ago I made a trip with my parents to the area around Niort in western France, where they make a sweet green angelica liqueur (you may also be able to detect its presence in the liqueur Chartreuse), but it is another French town, Clermont Ferrand, that is home to the most widespread cultivation of angelica, primarily for candying into those short, bright-green lengths that used to be sold at great expense for decorating cakes and the like. When I was young, we always used them to represent holly leaves on the lemon soufflé that my mother served as an alternative to Christmas pudding. These days, candied angelica is rarer than it used to be and you might have to turn to delicatessens to track it down, or make your own which, I can proudly say, is a darn sight more delicious, and mercifully free of green dye.

If you do grow your own angelica, which is about the only way you'll ever get a chance to try it fresh, it is worth noting that though it is technically a biennial, it will last for many years if you cut off the flower heads regularly. Flowers or longevity? A difficult choice, but it may be made easier when you know that the seed, if planted as soon as it is ripe, will quickly germinate and grow into a fine new plant by the following summer.

Storage and Preservation

Angelica stems will last for up to five days, wrapped in kitchen paper, then in a plastic bag, in the bottom of the fridge. The leaves are more short-lived, wilting quickly even in the fridge. Use them within 48 hours of picking. Angelica can be dried but don't bother, unless you fancy making tisanes from it. This is a herb to be used fresh in its proper season, or to be preserved by sweet means.

Candied Angelica

Cut tender, young angelica stems into 10 cm (2½ in) lengths. Make a brine with 8 g (¼ oz) salt to every 2.3 litres (4 pint) water. Bring to the boil and pour over the angelica. Leave for 15 minutes, then drain. Blanch the angelica in fresh boiling water for 5–10 minutes. Drain. Peel away any tough outer skin from the stems. Weigh the angelica and weigh out an equal quantity of sugar. Layer sugar and angelica in a saucepan. Cover and leave for 1–2 days until the sugar has turned to syrup. Add just enough water to cover the angelica. Bring gently to the boil and simmer quietly until the angelica is clear and the syrup is reduced to a clear goo. Leave the angelica to dry on a wire rack in the airing cupboard for a couple of days. Store in an airtight container.

Opposite
**Strawberry
and Fresh
Angelica Tart**
(page 148)

Strawberry and Fresh Angelica Tart

By infusing angelica in the milk for the *crème pâtissière*, the classic French strawberry tart is elevated into one of the most sublime desserts. Make it for a party, for your loved ones or just for the pleasure of eating it yourself.

If you can only find those awful enormous watery apologies for strawberries that seem to have taken over these days, then you will do better to replace them with raspberries, or even tiny alpine strawberries, though they will set you back a pretty penny.

Serves 8

about 1 kg (2 lb 4 oz) small strawberries
icing sugar for dusting
angelica leaves, to garnish

For the pâte sablée
300 g (10 oz) plain flour
a pinch of salt
100 g (3½ oz) icing sugar
200 g (7 oz) unsalted butter
2 egg yolks

For the crème pâtissière
350 ml (12 fl oz) milk
1 vanilla pod
3 or 4 (depending on thickness) 7.5 cm (3 inch) lengths of
   fresh angelica stems
a pinch of salt
2 egg yolks
60 g (2 oz) caster sugar
45 g (1½ oz) plain flour

Both pâte sablée and *crème pâtissière* should be made in advance. For the pastry, sift the flour with the salt and icing sugar. Process with the butter and egg yolks to form a soft dough. Scrape up into a ball. Knead briefly to smooth out, then wrap in clingfilm and chill for at least 4 hours.

Pre-heat the oven to 180°C/350°F/Gas Mark 4. Roll out the pastry and use to line a 25 cm (10 inch) tart tin, gently easing it in – it will probably tear, but don't worry; just patch it up with the trimmings. Cover and chill for an hour. Prick the base with a fork. Line with greaseproof paper and weight down with baking beans. Bake blind for 20 minutes, then remove the beans and paper and return the pastry to the oven for another 15–20 minutes, until lightly browned and crisp. Cool on a rack.

To make the *crème pâtissière*, put the milk into a pan with the vanilla, angelica and salt. Bring gently to the boil, then turn down the heat very low, cover and leave for 30 minutes. (If you can't get a really low flame, just take the pan off the heat and set aside.) Whisk the egg yolks with the sugar until pale, then whisk in the flour. Gradually pour in the hot milk, whisking constantly. Pick out the angelica leaves and the vanilla and discard. Return the milk mixture to the pan and bring slowly to the boil, whisking to smooth out as many lumps as possible. Let it bubble for 1 minute, keeping the heat low and stirring to prevent catching. Draw off the heat and leave until tepid. If not using immediately, rub a knob of butter over the surface to prevent a skin forming. Reheat gently before using, so it spreads easily.

As near as possible to serving, spread the *crème pâtissière* in the pastry case. Hull the strawberries and halve them. Arrange them in concentric circles, covering the *crème pâtissière*. Dust with a little icing sugar and garnish with fresh angelica leaves.

Joyce Molyneux's Rhubarb and Angelica Jam

blackcurrant leaf
Ribes nigrum

Many years ago I had the great pleasure of working with the kindest, gentlest chef I've ever met – Joyce Molyneux of the Carved Angel in Dartmouth – on a book of her recipes. Her style of cooking had an enormous influence on me, bringing in, as it did, all kinds of unexpected ingredients in a quiet and unassuming way without any flashiness. This jam is one I have loved ever since and, like Joyce, I think it is marvellous over a bowl of good cream cheese, thick Greek yoghurt or fromage frais.

If you don't have any angelica, you can make an equally special and fragrant jam by replacing the angelica leaves with a handful of scented dark red rose petals.

Makes about 1.5 kg (3 lb)

900 g (2 lb) rhubarb, thickly sliced
900 g (2 lb) granulated sugar
5 largish segments of angelica leaf, chopped, or a small
    handful of angelica stems, sliced
juice of 1 lemon

Put the rhubarb in a bowl with the sugar and angelica stems, if using, mix, then cover with a tea towel and leave overnight at room temperature (unless the weather is sultry and hot, in which case it had better go in the fridge or a cool cellar).

Scrape the rhubarb and sugar into a large pan, then add the lemon juice and angelica leaf, if using. Stir over a medium heat until the sugar has completely dissolved, then increase the heat and boil for about 15 minutes until the mixture is thick, stirring occasionally to prevent catching. Test for setting point by dripping a little of the mixture on to a chilled saucer, drawing the pan off the heat meanwhile. Let it cool briefly, then nudge with your finger. If it wrinkles then the jam is ready to pot. If it is still runny, then cook for a little longer. Skim off any scum, then ladle into clean, hot, sterilized jam jars (see p. 150) and seal while still hot. Label, then store in a cool, dark place for at least a month before using.

What an unsung marvel. The blackcurrant leaf is blessed with a unique, elegant flavour that most of us never get to taste. It captures the dark, earthy scent of the blackcurrants themselves, replacing their fruity acidity with a clear, leafy undertone. And to think that I almost gave up on them altogether...I was sure that somewhere, some time in the past I had read about using blackcurrant leaves in recipes but could I find anything to guide me in my research, or even anything to reassure me that the leaves were not toxic? No, I could not. The best information I could come up with was that the entire plant, not just the berries themselves, is weighed down with copious quantities of vitamin C, that in Siberia they make a drink out of the leaves, and that goats are partial to them, but overall nothing much to report on the culinary front. I gave up and turned to other things.

Some weeks later, while flicking through one of my favourite tomes, *The Constance Spry Cookery Book* (first published in 1956), I found the confirmation that I'd been looking for: a recipe for a blackcurrant water ice and one for spiced plums with blackcurrants, which I give overleaf.

What made me particularly jubilant is that we have half a dozen blackcurrant bushes. Since lots of the currants go to waste during their short season, I was pleased to learn that at least the leaves can be put to good use at other times of the year. If you don't have your own blackcurrant bushes, ask around until you find someone who is willing to let you have a few handfuls of the leaves to flavour sweet syrups and creams, as well as ice-creams and sorbets. You could also try adding a few leaves to home-made strawberry, rhubarb or raspberry jam as it boils, or to compotes of fresh fruit cooked in light sugar syrup. You'll be delighted at the remarkable flavour.

Storage and Preservation
Like most things green and leafy, blackcurrant leaves will last for a few days in the fridge, sealed inside a plastic bag in the vegetable drawer, but I don't think there is much point drying them or trying to preserve them, other than as an integral part of a fruit-based preserve.

Melon in Blackcurrant Leaf Syrup

Constance Spry's Spiced Plums in Blackcurrant Leaves

The spirit of the blackcurrant leaf, caught in a sugar syrup, makes an excellent marinade for a dull melon, giving it life and energy; with truly fragrant melon it produces an exquisite light finale to a summer meal. Leave the melon to marinate in the syrup for a minimum of half an hour and, if time permits, up to 24 hours in the fridge, but bring back to room temperature before actually serving.

To make a blackcurrant leaf sorbet, make the syrup as below, doubling the quantity of leaves and stirring in the juice of about 2 lemons, tasting as you go. Freeze in the usual way. For an ice-cream, add the juice of just half a lemon and about an equal volume of double cream, lightly whipped, and then churn and freeze as you would any ice-cream.

Serves 4–6

1 canteloupe, Charentais or other melon
juice of 1 lime or ½ lemon
125 g (4 oz) raspberries, tayberries or loganberries

For the syrup
225 g (8 oz) caster or granulated sugar
300 ml (½ pint) water
2 strips of lemon zest
a good handful (about 10–15g/¼–½ oz) of blackcurrant leaves, plus a few extra to garnish

For the syrup, put the sugar in a saucepan with the water. Stir over a moderate heat until the sugar has dissolved. Add the lemon zest and bring up to the boil. Simmer for about 3 minutes, then add the blackcurrant leaves. Stir, then draw off the heat and leave to cool until tepid. Strain the syrup, pressing down on the leaves to push out the last drops of blackcurrant leaf scent.

Quarter and deseed the melon. Cut off the rind and cut the flesh into slices about 1 cm (½ inch) thick. Place in a bowl with what juice can be salvaged. Pour over the lime or lemon juice, then the syrup. Turn gently to mix, then cover and leave to marinate for at least half an hour. Shortly before serving, add the berries, stirring once to mix, and garnish with a few fresh blackcurrant leaves. Serve on its own, or with cream, if you want to add a touch of richness.

This is Constance Spry's lovely recipe for spiced plums, which gradually take on the earthy scent of the blackcurrant leaves. Serve them with duck or pork, or with cold ham. Either caster or granulated sugar can be used. When heating with the vinegar and salt, stir over a moderate heat until all the sugar has dissolved, then let the mixture come up to the boil. Use white wine vinegar, and seal the jars tightly with non-corrosive lids (if they are jam-jar lids, make sure that the interior is plastic coated).

To sterilize the jars, wash first in soapy water, then rinse in warm water. Without touching the insides, arrange them upside-down on a wire rack in an oven heated to 110°C/225°F/Gas Mark ½, and leave there for at least half an hour.

'**Choose good,** well-flavoured plums without blemish. Prick them all over with a wooden cocktail stick and pack them straight into (sterilized, but cold) wide-mouthed jars, with layers of blackcurrant leaves in between. Add a few cloves and 1 or 2 sticks of cinnamon to each jar. Allow 340 g (¾ lb) sugar to 600 ml (1 pint) vinegar and a level dessertspoon (2 level teaspoons) salt. Boil together and pour over the plums. Tie down tightly and leave about 6–8 weeks before opening.'

Opposite
Melon in Blackcurrant Leaf Syrup

sweet cicely
Myrrhis odorata

You really can't help but like sweet cicely. It is such a beautiful plant with a lovely name that suits it perfectly. The first leaves, soft and downy, poke up through the cold ground in February to keep company with early chives. Soon they multiply into a tuffet of lacy, tender, fern-like leaves, and before long the flower buds rise up and open to show clusters of creamy white, sweet anise-scented flowers, much beloved by bees.

The delicate leaves have a distinctive sweetness but the dominant note is that of anise, which gives rise to two of its several other names, anise chervil and anise fern. It is occasionally known as British myrrh, or myrrh fern, since the scent is supposedly similar to that of the incense myrrh, the resin of an unrelated bush. Sweet cicely's most interesting attribute, however, is its power to dampen acidity when cooked with sharp fruit such as rhubarb, plums or apples. Throw a small handful of sweet cicely into the saucepan and you will find that you can get away with less sugar in fruit compotes. It is worth pointing out, though, that long cooking does away with much of the light anise scent of the herb. If it is the scent that you are after, stir in more chopped cicely when the cooking is done.

Sweet cicely is excellent added to fruit salads but don't think that it has no place with savoury foods. The delicate nature of the leaves means that they are lovely in mixed green salads, or with cucumber, or scattered over soups or stews just before serving. I sometimes sprinkle them over omelettes, when they are just about cooked but still a touch runny in the centre, together with a few spoonfuls of young goat's cheese, or maybe some skinned broad beans and a spoonful of crème fraîche. The anise scent is perfect with shellfish, or stirred into a creamy sauce for fish or chicken. Indeed, the Prawn, Sweet Cicely and Tomato Risotto (see opposite) is one of the most successful and appetizing risottos I have ever made.

Every part of the plant can be used, not just the leaves. The flowers can be strewn over compotes and salads as a garnish or left on the plant to ripen first to delicious green seeds – again a welcome addition to salads but good, too, in omelettes, with cream cheese and in ice-cream. Left still longer on the plant, they will ripen and darken. They are supposed to develop a spicey aroma of clove, caraway and mace, but frankly I've found it hard to detect, and besides the seeds are extremely fibrous. As the flowers bloom and run to seed, the already light scent of the leaves diminishes. You will have to choose between one and the other.

The roots of the sweet cicely plant taste a little like celeriac powerfully laced with Pernod. You can eat them raw but I find them overwhelming. Cooking softens the flavour, and they can be served hot, buttered, or tossed in vinaigrette and left to cool for a salad. In his long-neglected book *Wild Foods of Britain*, published in 1939, Jason Hill writes also that: 'The roots, up to a finger thickness, taste, when boiled, like chestnuts flavoured with aniseed and we find them delicious candied... Sweet Cicely roots candied... Boil the roots till tender; drain and soak for an hour in syrup (1 lb [450 g] of sugar to 1½ pints [900 ml] of water and a little lemon juice), then boil gently until the sugar candies; drain off the syrup and dry the roots in a warm place.'

Storage and Preservation
Even when freshly picked, the leaves are soft and floppy, which doesn't give them much chance of survival. If you pop them swiftly into sealed plastic bags and store in the vegetable drawer of the fridge, they will last for a day or two, but no more than that, which is probably one of the reasons sweet cicely has not made it to the supermarket shelves. The leaves can also be frozen: chop finely, pack into ice-cube trays and top up with water, then pop into the freezer.

Prawn, Sweet Cicely and Tomato Risotto

This has to be one of the most heavenly risottos of all. I'm partial to a seafood risotto at the best of times but this one, made with big juicy prawns and the subtle aniseed softness of sweet cicely, is very special indeed. If you really can't lay your hands on any sweet cicely, then try it with chervil instead.

It is absolutely crucial that you use raw prawns (it doesn't matter so much if they have been frozen, as long as they have thawed before use) and they must be in their shells. Head-on prawns are even better than head-off. The shells are used to transform the stock into a shellfish stock, thus perfuming the rice right to the very core. Tiger or king prawns are just the ticket. You will not need any extra Parmesan for serving – too much will overwhelm the flavour of the prawns and sweet cicely.

Serves 4–6

550 g (1 lb 4 oz) head-on raw prawns in their shells, or 500 g (1 lb 2 oz) headless raw prawns in their shells
85 g (3 oz) unsalted butter
1.2 litres (2 pints) fish, vegetable or chicken stock
2 shallots, chopped
2 garlic cloves, chopped
300 g (10 oz) risotto rice, e.g. vialone nano, arborio or carnaroli
1 small sprig of rosemary (about 4 cm/1½ inches long)
1 bay leaf
250 g (9 oz) ripe tomatoes, skinned, deseeded and chopped
2 tablespoons chopped parsley
1 generous glass of dry white wine (around 200 ml/7 fl oz)
3 tablespoons chopped sweet cicely
30g (1 oz) Parmesan cheese, freshly grated
salt and pepper

Peel the prawns and reserve the flesh. Heat about 15 g (½ oz) of the butter in a pan large enough to take the stock with plenty of room to spare. When foaming, add the prawn shells and heads and stir about until they turn a pretty shellfish pink. Now pour in the stock and 600 ml (1 pint) of water and bring up to the boil. Simmer for 30 minutes to draw out the flavour of the prawns. Strain the shells out of the stock when it is done.

Meanwhile return to the prawns. If you can see a black line running down their backs, make a little slit with the tip of a sharp knife down the back, then remove the fine black gut that lies just below the surface. If they are tiger or king prawns, or other large prawns, chop each one in half or thirds.

Now down to business. Bring the stock back up to boiling point if necessary, then turn the heat down under the pan to a mere thread, so that the stock stays hot but does not boil away. Melt 45g (1½ oz) of the remaining butter in a wide pan. Fry the shallots and garlic very gently in the butter until translucent, without browning. Now add the rice, rosemary and bay leaf to the pan and stir about for around 1 minute, until the rice becomes translucent. Scrape in the tomatoes and parsley and pour in the wine. Season with salt and plenty of pepper, then bring up to a bare simmer. Stir continuously until all the liquid has been absorbed. Now add a generous ladleful of stock and keep stirring until that has all been absorbed. Repeat this process until the rice is just the right side of *al dente* – i.e. tender but with a slight firmness to it, though definitely not chalky. The consistency should be verging on soupy, as it still has a couple of minutes to go. The time taken for the liquid to be absorbed and the rice to be cooked should be about 20–25 minutes.

Stir in the prawns and sweet cicely and cook, stirring, for another 2–3 minutes, until the prawns have turned pink. Stir in the remaining butter and the Parmesan. Taste and adjust the seasoning, then serve.

Apple, Crème Fraîche and
Sweet Cicely Crumble

pandanus leaf
Pandanus latifolius, Pandanus amaryllifolius

What makes this different from an ordinary apple crumble is that it comes with its own in-built cream custard hidden beneath the layer of crumble. And, of course, there's a touch of sweet cicely, too, though it serves mainly to dampen acidity, since the long cooking mutes its flavour.

Serves 4–6

700 g (1 lb 9 oz) cooking apples
3 tablespoons roughly chopped sweet cicely
300 ml (½ pint) soured cream
2 egg yolks
1 egg
85 g (3 oz) vanilla sugar or plain caster sugar

For the crumble topping
200 g (7 oz) plain flour
a pinch of salt
100 g (3½ oz) caster sugar
85 g (3 oz) unsalted butter, diced

Pre-heat the oven to 190°C/375°F/Gas Mark 5.

To make the topping, sift the flour with the salt. Stir in the sugar, then rub in the butter until the mixture resembles coarse breadcrumbs. Set aside in the fridge until needed.

Peel and core the apples, then cut them roughly into chunks. Mix with all the remaining ingredients, then spoon into a baking dish to give a depth of about 2.5–4 cm (1–1½ inches). Spoon the crumble mixture over the top, smoothing it very lightly to even it out without pressing down. Bake for 50–60 minutes or so, until browned on top. Test with a skewer to make sure that the apple is tender. Serve hot or warm.

If you eat out in Thai or other South-east Asian restaurants, you might well have come across the pandanus leaf, either in bodily form or in spirit. It is sometimes referred to as the vanilla of the East, and it does indeed have some things in common with the West's most popular sweet spice. It is very widely used throughout South-east Asia and has that same remarkable quality of being able to shine in its own right or fade elegantly and unobtrusively into the background to support other flavourings. Its aroma, however, is quite different from vanilla – very fresh, with a waft of new-mown grass on a sunny morning, and a trace of jasmine into the bargain.

Pandanus leaves are long (and we are talking around a metre (3 feet) or so), mid-green, slender and elegant, rather like an iris leaf. You will find them at good Thai, Malaysian or Indonesian food shops, sold in big, strong bunches. They keep phenomenally well so if you do come across any, snap them up even if you can't use them straight away.

There are two principal ways of using the leaves. The first is as a wrapping, and this is how you will most likely have met them, wrapped around nuggets of chicken. As the little parcels are cooked, the scent of the pandanus seeps into the meat in a very pleasing way. In similar vein, I've made a bed of pandanus leaves, cut to size, in an ovenproof dish, laid whole flat fish, such as sole of either sort, brill or plaice, on top, then covered them again with pandanus, followed by a layer of foil, to bake in the oven. You might try adding some thinly sliced lemon grass, grated ginger or a little finely chopped garlic between the leaves. For lubrication, add a slug or two of olive or sunflower oil, a knob or two of butter, or a discreet measure of sesame oil.

Opposite
**Prawn,
Sweet Cicely
and Tomato
Risotto**
(page 153)

The second way of using pandanus is to slip short lengths of leaf into simmering dishes as they cook. In Asia a few inches of leaf will usually be added to the pot to give plain boiled rice that little something extra, or it may be added to stews and soupy noodles. I love it in puddings – not only rice puddings like the one here, but also infused into sugar syrups, juices for jellies, and milk and cream for custards, bavarois and ice-cream. And while you have a stock of pandanus leaf in the kitchen, pop a few pieces into a jar of sugar, then seal and stash it in the back of a cupboard for a few days or longer. The sugar captures the perfume and can bring it to cakes, meringues and any number of sweet dishes.

Storage and Preservation

Pandanus leaves are tough cookies and will keep in excellent condition for up to three weeks, maybe longer, in the vegetable drawer of the fridge. Since they come in sizeable bunches (you do need a fair amount if you are making something like the Pandanus-wrapped Chicken Parcels on p. 157), you may be tempted to try freezing some of the leaves; after all, you don't come across them that easily. Unfortunately, freezing is not ideal, since some of the flavour seems to be dispelled by the cold. Perhaps, after all, it is better to use them fresh on the rare occasions when you find them, and leave it at that.

This is nothing more nor less than a straight baked rice pudding, the usual vanilla pod replaced by a few strips of pandanus leaf. As a final crowning glory, the pudding is spread with a thin layer of lemon curd, echoing one of Asia's most delicious concoctions, *kaya*, a golden coconut curd scented with *kewra* water, made from the flowers of the pandanus plant.

Serves 4

a knob of butter
60 g (2 oz) pudding rice
600 ml (1 pint) milk
4 tablespoons double cream, plus extra to serve
15 cm (6 inch) length of pandanus leaf, cut in 3
2 strips of lemon zest
1 tablespoon caster sugar
a pinch of salt
3 tablespoons lemon curd

Pre-heat the oven to 150°C/300°F/Gas Mark 2.

Grease a 1½ litre (2½ pint) ovenproof dish with the butter. Put the pudding rice, milk, cream, pandanus leaf, lemon zest, caster sugar and salt into the dish and stir to mix. Bake, uncovered, for about 3 hours, stirring once after about an hour so that the buoyant pandanus is pushed down into the pudding. The pudding is ready when it is gorgeously browned on top and most of the milk has been absorbed by the rice. Spread the lemon curd on top and leave to cool until just warm. Eat with more cream drizzled over.

Pandanus-wrapped Chicken Parcels

You might have eaten something like this in South-east Asian restaurants but the home-made version is even more delicious. Once you've stocked up on the pandanus leaf the rest is pretty easy, though it does take a bit of time and patience to wrap all the little morsels of chicken. When you get the hang of it, however, the results are immensely attractive and pleasing. Serve them as a first course or a main course, and warn guests that they are not actually meant to eat the leaves. Unwrapping the parcels is half the fun!

Serves 6 as a first course, 3–4 as a main course

500 g (1 lb 2 oz) boneless chicken thigh fillets,
    each one cut in 4
18–20 pandanus leaves
oil for deep-frying (optional)

For the marinade
4 tablespoons roughly chopped coriander
2 garlic cloves, roughly chopped
6 black peppercorns, roughly crushed
3 tablespoons coconut milk
2 tablespoons fish sauce
juice of 1 lime
1 tablespoon light muscovado sugar
2.5 cm (1 inch) fresh root ginger, finely chopped
½ teaspoon salt

For the sweet chilli sauce
3 tablespoons caster sugar
2 tablespoons rice vinegar
2 tablespoons fish sauce
4 tablespoons water
2 red chillies, deseeded and finely chopped

Put all the marinade ingredients into a food processor and process until smoothly blended. Pour the marinade over the chicken pieces, cover and leave to marinate for at least 3 hours.

Pick the chicken pieces out of the marinade, then wrap each bit up in about half a pandanus leaf, winding it round to cover the meat entirely. There is a technique to this – the shape to aim for is a kind of pyramid, give or take, but don't get too obsessed with perfection. It doesn't matter if the chicken is not immaculately covered up. Secure the end of the leaf with a wooden cocktail stick.

To make the sauce, put all the ingredients except the chillies into a pan and bring up to the boil, stirring until the sugar has dissolved. Simmer for 2 minutes, then stir in the chillies. Draw off the heat and leave to cool.

The chicken parcels can be either deep-fried or grilled, which is what I prefer for the smokiness it imparts. To deep-fry, heat a wokful of oil (or use an electric deep-fryer) to 170°C/330°F (when a cube of bread is dropped into the oil it will fizz gently). Deep-fry half a dozen or so of the parcels for about 6 minutes. Don't fry too many at a time or you will lower the temperature of the oil too much. Once they are done, lift out with a slotted spoon and drain briefly on kitchen paper. Keep warm while you fry the remainder.

To grill, lay the parcels on the grill rack, positioned about 12.5 cm (5 inches) from a thoroughly pre-heated grill or barbecue, and cook for about 8 minutes, turning just once.

Either way, doublecheck that they are done by discreetly unwrapping one of the larger parcels to see that the meat is cooked right through. Then serve the little packages fully wrapped, so that each person can unwrap their own, passing the dipping sauce around to dip the undressed chicken into.

pandanus

marigold
Calendula officinalis and *Tagetes patula*

The marigold that goes to bed wi' the sun,
And with him rises weeping.
'A Winter's Tale', William Shakespeare

For its bright, cheery splashes of colour in the garden, the marigold is second to none. Pot marigolds (*Calendula officinalis*) are enormously popular throughout Europe and further afield, and have been much appreciated for centuries. They grow easily, with little need for attention, and if you leave some of the early flowers to run to seed they will self-seed merrily to create sunsplash drifts of flowers the following year. The fact that they are edible is a bonus, though this combination of colour and comestibility has sometimes led people astray. All too often the bargain saffron brought back gleefully from trips to Morocco, Tunisia, Turkey and elsewhere proves to be nothing but dried marigold petals (or worse, but let's not worry about that here). The colour is similar but the flavours are poles apart.

The gold of marigolds is a substance known as calendulin, and it will colour food to some degree, though not half as well as true saffron. The flavour is a relatively mild affair (stronger in the French marigold, *Tagetes patula*, than in pot marigolds) of sweetish, piney resin, with a touch of bitterness. In its own right it is quietly pleasing, though again not a match for that most costly of spices, saffron.

Despite this, marigolds have a long culinary history, and an even longer medicinal one. Way back in the Middle Ages, calendula concoctions were being used to treat problems inside and out, ranging from measles and intestinal disturbances to conjunctivitis and eczema. (I've found calendula cream fairly effective in controlling my toddler's eczema.) For cooking, the fresh petals and leaves are more interesting than all the potions and lotions, adding as they do merry streaks of gold and orange to foods of all kinds. That they look pretty in salads almost goes without saying, but if you soak the petals in warm milk (allow about two to three times as much milk as petals) they soon gild the milk a rich corn

Opposite
Clockwise
from top left:
borage;
marigolds;
nasturtiums;
lavender;
violets;
pansies;
roses;
elderflower

yellow. The dyed milk can be used in cakes, breads, puddings and batters to liven up the look of the crumb. Like saffron, marigolds may be cooked with rice, as long as it is the colour you are after rather than any major flavouring. As well as throwing them into the pan with the rice as it simmers, sprinkle fresh marigold petals over the rice when it is cooked – not only for their look but also because they retain more of their aroma. Petals stirred into creamy young cheeses (particularly nice with fromage frais or soft young goat's cheese), together with chopped green herbs such as mint, chives and tarragon, and maybe a hint of garlic, make a simple dish for a first course or cheese course.

The leaves tend to be a little more pungent than the petals, so they too can be thrown into dishes to good effect. Try a leaf or two with scrambled egg, or in a quick-cooking chicken or rabbit fricassée. On the island of Jersey, they use marigold leaves and petals in a warming chowder made with conger eel (there's a recipe for it in my book, *Fish*, written with my husband William Black) but even if conger eel is not your cup of tea a few marigold petals sprinkled over a bowl of steaming vegetable soup will cheer both heart and soul.

Marigolds open in the morning and close again in late afternoon, so to get them at their best pick them in mid-morning just as they are coming into full open bloom. To prolong the flowering season, pick flowers enthusiastically and cut any dying flowers before they fade quite away.

Storage and Preservation

A bunch of marigolds will last for a fair few days in a vase of water on the kitchen windowsill – you might as well enjoy them for as long as possible. If you have flowers only, keep them whole and stash them in the lower part of the fridge in an airtight container. To dry the petals, spread them out on a rack in the airing cupboard, or some dry, shady spot outside in good weather, as long as there is no wind to blow them away. Store in an airtight jar.

I would be lying if I said that I thought the marigold petals made an enormous difference to the taste of scrambled eggs with smoked salmon but you can, just, detect a little something if you try, and the streaks of orange against the yellow and pink look very attractive. If you are growing marigolds and fancy conjuring up a special breakfast for a loved one on a summer's morning, throw a few petals in with the eggs for fun.

Serves 2

4 eggs, preferably free range
the petals of 1 or 2 marigold flowers (the orange ones are more noticeable)
a small knob of butter
2 slices (about 60 g/2 oz) of smoked salmon, cut into narrow strips
2 slices of walnut bread, Granary bread, brioche or other good bread, or 2 halved bagels, toasted and lightly buttered
salt and pepper
a few marigold leaves or flowers, to garnish
lemon wedges, to serve

Whisk the eggs up with the marigold petals, a hint of salt (the smoked salmon will be salty so don't add too much) and pepper. For the quick but not quite so superlative version, melt the butter in a small heavy saucepan over a low heat, then add the eggs. Stir constantly until they have thickened to creamy curds. Draw off the heat, stir in the smoked salmon and pile on to the toast. Garnish with the marigold leaves or flowers and serve immediately, with lemon wedges.

The more luxurious but slower way to cook the eggs is to add the knob of butter to the bowl of eggs, then set it over a pan of gently simmering water, making sure that the base of the bowl does not come into contact with the water. Stir until the eggs thicken to form extra-creamy curds. There comes a point when you will feel very tempted to tip the whole lot into a pan and scramble them quickly. Don't – you will be almost there by then. Persevere and you will be rewarded with the most sublime and delicious scrambled eggs ever. Promise. Finish and serve as above.

Chicken, Red Pepper and Marigold Fajitas

Fajitas are just filled warmed tortillas and now that we can buy excellent wheat flour tortillas at most good supermarkets, we can conjure up our own fajitas with ease. These ones are filled with a mixture of spiced peppers and chicken, flecked with marigold leaves, and then with that comes a simple tomato salsa and dollops of either guacamole or soured cream (or both if you want to go right over the top). This is a meal for a relaxed party with family or friends, when formality is forgotten and easy fun is on the cards. Everything can be prepared in advance, then all you need do is warm up the chicken and peppers and the tortillas at the last minute.

When you want a quick supper, full of flavour, you'll find that the chicken and pepper mixture is delicious without all the extras – serve it with rice or noodles and a watercress or rocket salad.

Serves 4–6

1 tablespoon cumin seeds
1 tablespoon coriander seeds
1 teaspoon dried oregano
2 tablespoons olive oil
2 red peppers, deseeded and cut into strips
1 onion, sliced
2 garlic cloves, sliced
½ Scotch bonnet chilli (or 1 red jalapeño-type chilli), deseeded and cut into strips
4 skinned chicken breasts, cut into strips 1 cm (½ inch) thick
2 marigold leaves (optional)
juice of ½ lime
the petals of 3 marigold flowers
salt and pepper

For the salsa
450 g (1 lb) tomatoes, skinned, deseeded and finely diced
1 garlic clove, finely chopped
½ red onion, finely chopped
1–2 green chillies, deseeded and finely chopped
4 tablespoons finely chopped coriander
juice of ½ lime
1 level teaspoon of sugar (unless your tomatoes are spectacularly sweet)

To serve
8–12 large wheat flour tortillas
either guacamole (see p. 80) or a small pot of soured cream or crème fraîche (or both)
4–6 crisp lettuce leaves, finely shredded
a small bowl of pickled jalapeño chillies, or a bottle of chilli sauce

To make the filling, dry-fry the cumin and coriander seeds in a small heavy frying pan over a moderate heat until they give off a heady aroma. Tip them into a spice grinder or mortar, allow to cool for a couple of minutes, then add the oregano and grind to a powder. Put the oil into a wide frying pan and heat up over a moderate heat. Add the peppers, onion, garlic and chilli and stir for 2 minutes. Sprinkle over the spices, season with salt and pepper and stir again. Cover and reduce the heat to low, then leave to sweat for 10 minutes or until tender, stirring once or twice. Raise the heat up high and add the chicken and the marigold leaves, if using. Stir-fry for 4–5 minutes, until just cooked through, then stir in the lime juice and marigold petals. Taste and adjust the seasoning, and spoon into a warm serving bowl.

To make the salsa, mix all the ingredients together and leave to stand for at least half an hour. Stir again, then taste and adjust the seasonings just before serving.

Meanwhile, wrap the tortillas in foil or clingfilm and reheat in the oven or microwave, as instructed on the packet. Remove the foil or clingfilm and wrap in a cloth to keep warm. Put all the remaining accompaniments in bowls and arrange on the table, with the chicken mixture, tortillas and salsa. Let everyone make up their own fajitas, piling the chicken and peppers down the centre, adding dollops of guacamole or soured cream (or both), then salsa and finishing with some shredded lettuce. Those who like their food hot, hot, hot, can add extra pickled jalapeños or a shake of chilli sauce. Roll the whole lot up and bite into it.

Pilaff of Beetroot with **Marigold Leaves** and **Cool Mint** and **Garlic Yoghurt Relish**

The dark red of the beetroot coupled with the turmeric and marigold yellows transforms this into one of the most richly, vibrantly coloured rice dishes you are likely to come across – echoing the rich, deep hues of Moorish art. The taste, too, is rich and vibrant – a perfect dish for a vegetarian main course, or for a side dish with plainly cooked meats or grilled spicy sausages.

Serves 4–6

250 g (9 oz) basmati or long grain rice
30 g (1 oz) butter
1 tablespoon olive, sunflower or vegetable oil
1 onion, chopped
2 garlic cloves, chopped
½ tablespoon cumin seeds
2 cloves
1 cinnamon stick
1 level teaspoon ground turmeric
550 ml (19 fl oz) water
250 g (9 oz) beetroot, cooked (see p. 51), peeled and cut into
    1 cm (½ inch) dice
the petals of 2–3 marigold flowers
salt and pepper

For the yoghurt relish
2 garlic cloves, chopped
15 g (½ oz) butter
250 g (9 oz) Greek yoghurt
2 tablespoons chopped mint
1 tablespoon chopped chives (optional)

To make the pilaff, rinse the rice thoroughly, then leave to drain in a sieve. Melt the butter with the oil in a saucepan, then add the onion and fry gently, without browning, until translucent. Add the garlic, cumin seeds, cloves and cinnamon and fry gently for 1 minute. Now tip in the rice and stir for one further minute, until slightly translucent. Stir in the turmeric, then add the water and some salt and pepper and bring up to the boil. Reduce the heat to very low, cover tightly and leave to cook for 8 minutes. Stir in the beetroot, then cover again and leave, without stirring, for 5–8 minutes, until all the liquid has been absorbed and the rice is tender. Set aside a few of the marigold petals for decoration and stir the rest in. Taste and adjust the seasoning, then tip into a warmed serving dish, cover with foil and leave in a low oven (around 110°C/225°F/Gas Mark ½) for 10–30 minutes to dry in its own steam. Just before serving, sprinkle over the remaining marigold petals.

To make the yoghurt relish, fry the garlic in the butter until very lightly browned. Scoop out and stir into the yoghurt with the herbs and some salt to taste. Serve at room temperature, to spoon on to the pilaff.

Opposite
Pilaff of Beetroot with Marigold Leaves and Cool Mint and Garlic Yoghurt Relish

borage

Borago officinalis

The Pimm's flower. A real Pimm's, that most British, most refreshing, most quaffable of summer drinks, requires a handful of blue borage flowers for perfection. And a mini fruit salad floating around on the surface, including a slice or two of cucumber to match the cucumbery scent of the borage itself. That's the theory, anyway. Oddly enough, my most borage-ful Pimm's, about the only Pimm's that I ever make, come into being in France, where borage grows with unstoppable self-confidence all around the village, and particularly along the path below our gate. My French friends adore Pimm's; they love the Britishness (they are a very Anglophile bunch around those parts) and besides, the only time it ever occurs to me to buy a bottle of the stuff is in the duty-free on the way over. My French Pimm's is awash with borage flowers.

Borage has always been connected with drinks. Even Pliny wrote of steeping borage in wine to make men merry and joyful, then later Gerard, the herbalist, commented that the 'gallant blew floures', put into wine, drive 'away all sadnesse, dulnesse and melancholy'. Who am I to suggest that it might not be the borage but the booze itself that works this magic? Incidentally, and let's hope that you will never need to take advantage of this, he also avows that a 'syrrup made of the floures… quieteth the phreneticke or lunaticke person'. Presumably without the addition of any cheery hooch.

The leaves are also edible, though anyone who approaches a borage plant bare-handed cannot help but be aware of the stiff, prickly hairs that cover all the green parts. Ouch. One suggested derivation of the name borage is that it comes from the Latin *borra*, meaning rough hair. Only on the very young, newly formed leaves are the hairs soft enough to allow them to be enjoyed raw in salads. Once they've matured a little, they can be cooked like spinach, or added to dishes to impart that vague cucumberish touch.

The big question is, is there really any point to borage, other than its unquestionable prettiness? Well, a fairy's sigh of that cucumberiness is genuinely imparted to whatever the flowers or leaves recline in or upon. More than that, I am not prepared to commit to. The second question has to be, 'What does it matter, as long as they look so very delectable?' And there's only one response to that: 'Not a jot.' There's no enormous loss in ignoring the leaves but make the most of the flowers – in drinks, of course, and also scattered in salads, on rice, over puddings, and wherever else the fancy takes you.

If you don't have any borage growing in your garden, buy a couple of plants and let nature do the rest for you; they self-seed happily but are not so invasive that they become a burden. If you don't have a garden, you could easily grow borage in a windowbox, as a decorative addition, maybe, to a collection of herbs and other edible plants. There is also a white-flowered borage, but it is not half as attractive as the blue, with its occasional pink flower to tease the eye.

Storage and Preservation

Since the main point of borage is to enjoy its brilliant blue, five-petalled flowers, it seems a shame to hide them away in the fridge once picked. If you can't use them immediately, treat like any cut flowers: put them in a favourite small vase and stand it where everyone can see them. They should last for four or five days or so. As for preservation, you could try crystallizing them (see p. 166) if you have half an hour or so to spare, but there's absolutely no point in freezing or drying borage.

An Excellent Mixed Salad

Cucumber with Borage and Cream Sauce

In 1614 the exiled Italian Giacomo Castelvetro wrote *The Fruit, Herbs and Vegetables of Italy*, a marvellous account of the fresh horticultural produce that was eaten in Italy at that time, and which he so much missed in England. Way ahead of his time, he politely admonishes us for eating too much meat and indulging in too many sweet foods. His descriptions of the healthy, delicious ways of cooking fruit, vegetables and salads that were the norm in his homeland seem surprisingly modern as you read them today. It has taken almost 400 years for us Brits to recognize the value of what we now call the Mediterranean diet, which Castelvetro wrote about so enthusiastically and warmly. His book was finally translated into English by Gillian Riley and published by Viking in 1989, and it is well worth searching out a copy. Here is his description of his perfect spring salad. Gather together as many of the leaves as you can find and try it dressed with a simple wine vinegar and extra virgin olive oil vinaigrette.

'Of all the salads we eat in the spring, the mixed salad is the best and most wonderful of all. Take young leaves of mint, those of garden cress, basil, lemon balm, the tips of salad burnet, tarragon, the flowers and tenderest leaves of borage, the flowers of swine cress [use watercress], the young shoots of fennel, leaves of rocket, of sorrel, rosemary flowers, some sweet violets and the tenderest leaves or the hearts of lettuce. When these precious herbs have been picked clean and washed in several waters, and dried a little with a linen cloth, they are dressed as usual, with oil, salt and vinegar.'

Cucumber is so often restricted to salads but it makes a fine hot vegetable dish, stewed gently in a little butter in a covered pan without any added water, unless absolutely necessary, until tender. This is a double-helping version of that method, made with cucumber and borage leaves, transformed finally to a rich and unutterably gorgeous side dish with the help of a measure of cream. Add a scattering of borage flowers and it looks lovely, a joy with plainly cooked fish or white meats, and good enough to serve in ramekins, with squares of toast, as a first course.

Serves 4

1 large cucumber, peeled, then halved lengthways
30 g (1 oz) butter
a handful of young borage leaves, shredded
150 ml (¼ pint) double cream
a dash of lemon juice
a dozen borage flowers
salt

Scoop the seeds out of each cucumber half with an apple corer or a teaspoon and discard. Slice the halves into crescents, about 5 mm (¼ inch) thick. Melt the butter in a heavy saucepan and add the cucumber and a little salt. Turn the cucumber to coat it in the butter, then cover and leave to cook gently for 10 minutes. Uncover and raise the heat a little so that the juices begin to bubble away. Add the borage leaves and stir about. When there is only the tiniest amount of buttery juice left in the pan, pour in the cream. Stir, then boil down for a few minutes until thickened to a pleasing consistency. Stir in a dash of lemon juice, then taste and adjust the seasoning. Serve hot, with the borage flowers sprinkled prettily over the top.

Crystallized Borage Flowers

This is just a bit of fun for a weekend when the sun is shining and the garden is bright with flowers. Crystallizing flowers in a hot sugar syrup preserves their colour, even if their form is lost in the heat. A trace of their scent lingers on but that's barely the point. Borage flowers work particularly well, as do most of the smaller edible blooms, such as violets, cowslips and primroses (only to be picked from gardens and not from the wild), rosemary and sage flowers, the bright red bergamot, rose petals and even tender leaves of mint or lemon balm. Before dropping them into the boiling syrup, pull the tender coloured parts of the flowers away from the green (where practicable) which, though it can be crystallized, tends to be tough.

Use the crystallized flowers like small edible gems, to decorate cakes, buns and creamy puddings. My children adore them, preferring them to many commercial sweets.

borage flowers, pansies, violets, rose petals, etc.
450 g (1 lb) caster sugar
300 ml (½ pint) water

Rinse the flowers if absolutely necessary, then make sure they are quite dry.

Put the sugar and water in a saucepan and stir over a moderate heat, without letting it boil, until the sugar has completely dissolved. Bring up to the boil. If you have a sugar thermometer, stand it in a jug of hot water to warm it through. Once the syrup begins to boil, stand the thermometer in it. The syrup is ready to use once the temperature reaches 116°C/240°F, or soft-ball stage. Test the syrup manually, even if you are using a thermometer. To do this, have several glasses of icy water standing by. Drip a few drops of syrup into the water. If they sink to the bottom, forming soft balls that don't disintegrate but are still pliable and squidgy between your fingers, then it is ready. When you reach this point, turn the heat down to its lowest setting under the syrup.

Add about a dozen flowers to the syrup, stir lightly, then let them boil in the syrup for about 20 seconds. Lift out with a slotted spoon and lay them on baking trays lined with non-stick baking parchment, separating the flowers gently. Repeat with the remaining flowers. After 2 or 3 batches, your syrup will be getting too concentrated and the temperature will rise too high. Correct this by adding a few splashes of hot water.

Leave the crystallized flowers to dry, either in an airing cupboard (make sure the sheets don't fall on top of them!), in a very, very low oven or out on the kitchen work surface, if the weather is clement and the kitchen not too steamy. Once they are bone dry and tinkle like little pieces of coloured glass, they can be stored in airtight jars for several months.

Opposite
**An Excellent
Mixed Salad**
(page 165)

violets and pansies
Viola species

'To throw a perfume on a violet,
… Is wasteful and ridiculous excess.'
'King John', William Shakespeare

Who are the violets now
That strew the green lap of the new come spring?'
'Richard II', William Shakespeare

I love catching that first glimpse of a violet on an early-spring morning, out of the corner of my eye as I walk down the path to our gate. So small, so purple, so perfect and so sweetly scented. For too short a time I spot their nodding heads here and there, and then suddenly they are gone and I wish I had paid them more attention. I read recently that fields around Stratford-on-Avon, not far from our house, were once famous for their violets, cultivated for their scent. Sacks of the purple flowers (just think how many of those tiny dots it must take to fill even a small sack) were distilled to extract their oil and boiled up with sugar for syrup of violets. Perhaps that is why Shakespeare mentions violets so often in so many of his plays, but I think that those intoxicating fields however impressive, can hardly have been a match for a woodland bank spotted with white and purple violets and yellow primroses.

I've never ever thought of violets as raunchy – indeed, rather the opposite – but in his *Englishman's Flora*, my father wrote that 'scent suggested sex, so the violet was a flower of Aphrodite and also of her son Priapus', the goddess of love and her famously well endowed child. The ancient Greeks used them in love potions and drank violet wine. Hair of the dog-violet, perhaps, it was believed to be a most effective antidote to the after-effects of over-indulgence. All in all, it doesn't square with images of delicate Edwardian ladies dabbing violet water on their temples, does it?

Unless you happen to have a handy field of violets, old-fashioned delights such as syrup of violets are rather out of the question. You would have to pick an awful lot of flowers to make it worthwhile and, of course, you should not pick wild violets from the hedgerows, as their numbers are sadly on the decline. Stick with any violets growing in your garden and add to them if you can with new plants from a reputable nursery. If they are happy, they will spread as the years go by. Since small quantities are all you are likely to be dealing with, think of them in decorative terms above all else. A few shaken over a creamy, pale-pink forced rhubarb fool look lovely, or scattered in an early-spring salad of tender leaves, such as the one described by Giacomo Castelvetro on p. 165. Occasionally they are recommended for other savoury dishes but, by and large, I think them better suited to sweet things – on syrupy cakes, like the one opposite, over ice-cream, with poached fruit (especially pears) or maybe a rich, old-fashioned syllabub. They also crystallize well, harking back to equally old-fashioned Parma violets.

The long borders around half our vegetable and herb garden are lined with wild pansy plants (*Viola tricolor*). Cultivated wild pansies, to be sure, but still the same incredibly beautiful small, bright faces. When the plants were first settled in they looked so straggly and unkempt that I thought perhaps it had been a big mistake. A month or so later, when June days lengthened into lingering, warm evenings, the whole garden was transformed by them, bushy and lively and carpeted with flowers. Heartsease – really a much better name for them – have no scent but the million different patterns of purple, yellow and white make up for that. These three colours have earned them another name, the herb of trinity, possibly to distract from lustier titles – cuddle-me, kiss-her-in-the-buttery, love-a-li-do, tittle-my-fancy – merited by their

country reputation as potent aphrodisiacs. No proof of
that to be had, I'm sad to say. In culinary terms, they can
be used much like violets. The good news is that they
grow in such unfettered abundance; the bad is that they
smell and taste of precious little. Charming but trivial.

Old varieties of garden pansies are cultivated forms of
heartsease, while more modern ones are bred out of
hybrids of heartsease with the rarer mountain pansy.
They, too, are perfectly edible, and rather more interesting
to chew on than their wild forebears. Far more showy, but
even so, they are not enormously useful. Scatter them
over salads (green and leafy, or fruit), and puddings for
the fun of it, but don't expect much more of them.

Heartsease and pansies should not be consumed in any
great quantity.

Storage and Preservation

Violets will fade quickly. Stand them in a small glass of
water to keep them fresh for a day or so if you must, but
don't expect them to survive much longer. Heartsease is
a little hardier and may stay bright and lively for several
days in water, or stored in an airtight box in the vegetable
drawer of the fridge. Full-sized garden pansies will last for
up to a week in an airtight container in the vegetable
drawer of the fridge.

The best way to preserve a small haul of violets or
heartsease is to crystallize them (see p. 166). You can
crystallize garden pansies but they just look bedraggled
and miserable, and they don't last particularly well. Violets
can be infused in good white wine vinegar, but it seems a
bit of a waste, unless you have a considerable quantity at
your disposal.

This is really no more than a fanciful way to show off violas,
but the cake beneath them deserves a pretty finish. It is
a favourite of mine, based on a Tunisian recipe. In this
version the syrup that bathes the cake is perfumed with
lavender or rosewater, and lemon. Of course, if you did
have scented violets to spare, you could throw a handful
into the syrup to impart a rare perfume to the entire cake…

Serves 8

45 g (1½ oz) slightly stale breadcrumbs
200 g (7 oz) caster sugar
100 g (3½ oz) ground almonds
1½ teaspoons baking powder
200 ml (7 fl oz) sunflower oil
4 eggs
finely grated zest of 1 lemon
violets, heartsease, and/or garden pansies, to garnish

For the syrup
100 ml (3½ fl oz) water
juice of 1 small lemon
85 g (3 oz) caster sugar
8 fresh spikes of lavender flowers or 6 dried spikes, or
    1½ tablespoons of rosewater

Line the base of a 20 cm (8 inch) cake tin with non-stick
baking parchment, and grease the sides. Mix the
breadcrumbs with the sugar, almonds and baking
powder. Add the oil and eggs and beat well. Stir in the
lemon zest. Pour the mixture into the prepared cake tin.
Put into a cold oven and set the heat to 190°C/375°F/Gas
Mark 5. Bake for 40-50 minutes until the cake is a rich brown
and a skewer inserted into the centre comes out clean.
Cool for 5 minutes in the tin then turn out onto a plate

Make the syrup while the cake is cooking. Put all
ingredients into a pan, and bring gently to the boil, stirring
until the sugar has dissolved. Simmer for 3 minutes.
Remove the lavender flowers if you wish (I don't since
I think they look rather pretty scattered over the top of the
cake). Pierce holes in the cake with a skewer while it is
still warm and pour over the syrup. Leave to cool, spooning
excess syrup back over every now and then until it is all
soaked up. Decorate with flowers before serving. Serve
with crème fraîche, Greek yoghurt, whipped cream or
mascarpone, and some sliced fresh fruit on the side.

nasturtium
Tropaeolum majus

At last – a beautiful flower with a definite, clear, unmistakable savoury presence! No one could accuse it of being just some pretty frippery for dolling up sweet nothings. Oh no, sirree. Nasturtiums and their leaves are peppery and sassy. They don't just disappear into the general mêlée once their beauty has been admired. Nor are they simply a purveyor of perfume that detractors decry as reminiscent of the boudoir. The delicate, bright exterior masks a decidedly bold inner character, revealed only as your teeth sink in. If you are going to grow only one edible flower in your herb collection, be it in the garden or in the windowbox, then make it nasturtiums and make sure you have at least two varieties, one with a strikingly variegated leaf. They will earn their keep, if you don't forget all about them.

Once they've got going, nasturtiums spread and bloom unashamedly, creating splashes of their strong yellows, oranges and reds as they go. The good news is that every single part is edible. The flowers are the prize, the leaves as good as any other salad leaf (and rather more exciting than many), and both the buds and soft green seedheads can be pickled like peppery capers. How? First grow an awful lot of nasturtiums, then pick the buds or 'berries'. Soak for 24 hours in a heavy brine, then drain and pack into sterilized jars. Boil up white wine vinegar, with a few spices if you like, and sugar if you want a sweet pickle, then cool and pour over the seeds. Seal tightly and leave for at least 4 months before using.

It is the flowers and leaves that really count, though. Nasturtium flowers can simply be added to summer salads, and will bring enormous pleasure used in this way. I happen to be very partial to them in sandwiches, where they are strong enough to hold their own. Roughly shredded, they make a lovely addition to a risotto, stirred in right at the end of the cooking time; or stirred plentifully into soft, light, buttery mashed potato – again, just before serving. They are good with fish and chicken, in sauces or salsas to serve beside them. And don't forget to try them with soups – they add a neat pepperiness to a chilled gazpacho, a cold cucumber or Vichyssoise soup or a hot vegetable or chicken soup. Whatever you wish to incorporate them into, hot or cold, remember that they are very delicate, so should be added only at the very last minute.

Storage and Preservation
Nasturtiums wilt fairly swiftly. You would do almost as well to stand them in a jug of cold water on the windowsill as to store them in an airtight container in the vegetable drawer of the fridge. Either way, don't expect the flowers to last more than two or three days. The leaves on their own, stored in the fridge, have a longer lifespan – up to a week if newly picked. You can't dry either leaves or flowers but, to save a little of their particular flavour, try making a nasturtium vinegar: fill a container loosely with flowers, add a couple of strips of lemon or lime zest, then pour in enough white wine vinegar to cover. Seal and leave in a sunny spot for two weeks before straining and pouring into clean bottles.

Stir-Fried Duck with Aubergine and Nasturtiums

Until you perch the bright nasturtium flowers on top, this stir-fry looks rather depressingly brown but the taste soon makes up for any visual shortcomings, so don't worry! As long as they have only a few brief moments in the pan, nasturtium leaves take rather well to stir-frying, and cut a nice swathe through the fattiness of the duck.

Serves 4 generously with noodles or rice

1 small aubergine, cut into 2 cm (¾ inch) cubes
3 duck breasts, cut into slivers about 5 mm (¼ inch) thick
2 tablespoons sunflower, groundnut or vegetable oil
2.5 cm (1 inch) fresh root ginger, chopped
1 garlic clove, chopped
a handful of nasturtium leaves, cut into strips about 1 cm
    (½ inch) wide
a handful of nasturtium flowers
salt

For the marinade
2 tablespoons sweet sherry
1 tablespoon sesame oil
1 tablespoon soy sauce
1 teaspoon Chinese five-spice powder
¼ teaspoon chilli flakes

Spread the aubergine cubes out in a colander and sprinkle with salt. Set aside for half an hour to degorge. Rinse briefly, then pat dry on kitchen paper or a clean tea towel. Meanwhile, mix all the marinade ingredients together, then add the duck strips and turn to coat nicely. Leave for at least half an hour until ready to cook.

Shortly before cooking, drain the marinade from the duck and reserve meat and marinade separately. Line a plate with a couple of sheets of kitchen paper. Make sure all the ingredients are standing by, fully prepared, next to the stove. We swing into high gear from now on.

Heat a wok over a high heat until it smokes. Add the oil and let it heat through for about 20 seconds. Now add the ginger and garlic and swirl them around. Next add the aubergine and stir-fry for around 5 minutes, tossing and turning until patched with brown and just about tender – if necessary add a little extra oil but don't swamp the aubergine. Scoop out and drain on kitchen paper. Add the duck to the pan and stir-fry for about 1½ minutes. Return the aubergine to the pan and pour in the marinade. Stir, then let it simmer down for a few minutes until reduced by about half, stirring occasionally. Finally stir in the nasturtium leaves and stir-fry for about 30 seconds, until barely wilted. Serve immediately on noodles or rice, topped with a few brightly coloured nasturtium flowers.

Nasturtium, Pear and Parma Ham Sandwiches

A sandwich for smart tea parties or a light summer lunch. If you fancy a sweet sandwich instead, use nasturtium flowers but not the leaves, omit the Parma ham and add a drizzle of honey. Or replace the pear with slices of banana.

Makes 2

4 slices of good Granary bread
a little softened butter or cream cheese
½ ripe pear
a little lemon juice
4 slices of Parma ham
8 nasturtium flowers and/or leaves
freshly ground black pepper

Spread the bread with butter or cream cheese. Peel, core and thinly slice the pear, tossing it in a little lemon juice to prevent browning and to sharpen the sandwich a touch. Make a layer of pear on each sandwich, grind over a little pepper, then cover with the Parma ham and top with the nasturtium flowers and/or leaves. Add a little more pepper if you like, then clamp on the top slice of bread. Press down firmly, cut in half and eat.

roses
Rosa species

'The petals of my particular rose have fallen,
The carmine at their edges curling,
At one end crinkles into white,
They spill over a dead newspaper of this morning.
Don't look at them. Let's go.
Switch off the light.'
'Rose Disintegrating', Geoffrey Grigson

My father loved old roses and he loved their colours. Our farmhouse was painted a light but deep rose pink, the details on the old wooden doors of our kitchen cupboards were picked out in pink, against white, and our very best dinner service, brought out at Christmas and on birthdays, was that same pink again, with a plain white edging. I still have those old Worcester plates, and we still use them for celebrations. My father's roses were left to pleasure a new family when we sold the pink farmhouse but I can still remember so many of them, and how exactly they flowered, against what other foliage, in the month of June. Amongst two favourites were the striped *Rosa mundi*, with its golden eye, and the almost spherical cups of the 'Raubritter Macranther', a modern rose that masqueraded as old, though it could not disguise its perfumeless state. When I came down to breakfast on my birthday, in the middle of the month, there was always a vase of roses set at my place.

The rose sprang from the red, red blood of Adonis, so how could it fail to become one of the most beloved of flowers, and one of the most beautiful? The earliest roses, cultivated in Persia and passed eagerly along the roads that led to Greece and later Rome, were probably *Rosa gallica*, the Provins rose, and later the Apothecary's rose. The strong colours and marvellous scent of the various strains of *Rosa gallica*, have ensured that it has retained its admirers through the centuries. Together with damask roses (*Rosa damascena*), cabbage roses (*Rosa centifolia*) and tea roses (*Rosa indica*) they are still some of the most beautifully perfumed flowers in existence. The more powerful the scent, the more welcome they are in the garden and house and, for our purposes, most especially in the kitchen. Roses are not the stuff of everyday cookery, but if you have the time to take advantage of them, they are a joy to play with.

The red petals, pulled from the stem, hold their fragrance well, and serve as far more than mere garnish. Their flavour-fragrance is clear and distinguishable. Scattered over a simple green salad, together with some sprigs of chervil, they can transform it in one fell swoop. Roses and fruit are natural partners – macerate rose petals with strawberries or raspberries or, better still, succulent, sweet cherries, pitted so that their juice can ooze out. Sprinkle fruit and petals with a little sugar and a touch of lemon, orange or lime juice, stir, then leave alone for at least half an hour before serving. A dash of rosewater will heighten the scent of the roses.

Simmering the petals in sugar syrups for 5–10 minutes or so will draw out their fragrance – be generous with the petals – to use as a dressing for ice-creams and fruit salads or as the basis for a scented champagne cocktail. Or bury a handful of petals in a jar of sugar to make rose sugar. For a touch more drama, liquidize the petals with sugar, water and lemon juice (see the recipe for A Summer's Delight, p. 176) to make a startling rose sauce, or coulis, if you want to be fancy about it.

Many years ago, a small corner shop I used to frequent stocked a discreet hoard of pretty pink tins of rose petal jam, made in Pakistan. I bought a job lot and for a few months many of my friends were lucky recipients of one of the most exquisite preserves.

Before you start to use rose petals, there are two things you should undertake. The first is to give the rose a good shake before stripping off the petals, to dislodge any unwelcome wildlife. Check again after stripping, for some tiny creepy-crawlies may have clung tenaciously to the bitter end. Secondly, you ought really to nip off the small white heel at the base of the flower, which is slightly bitter. This is a tedious job, and to be honest, I usually skip it when the flowers are being added to salads and the like, and no one has ever been bothered by my laxity. For

something like a jam or syrup it is probably worth settling down comfortably to the lengthy task of 'heeling'. After all, it would be a crying shame to spoil them for want of a little patient application.

Be wary of buying roses for cooking with from a florist, as they may well have been sprayed with heaven knows what chemicals. If your own rose collection is too small, or non-existent, to provide sufficient, beg them from a rose-growing friend.

Dried rosebuds and petals are ground and used as a spice in Morocco and parts of the Middle East.

Storage and Preservation

Roses on their stems may as well be enjoyed if they are not going to be used immediately. Arrange them in a vase and put them where everyone can see and smell them. But don't leave them idling for too long. Their scent will weaken and that, after all, is what you want to catch. Rose petals dry well, spread out on a sheet of paper in a cool, shady place and covered with a length of muslin to stop them blowing away. The dried petals hold their scent well enough, and can be powdered to use as a spice or added whole to pot-pourri. Fresh petals can be crystallized in a sugar syrup (p. 166) or, for shorter-term preservation, brushed with lightly beaten egg white, then coated in caster sugar and left to dry on a sheet of non-stick baking parchment. They can be caught in a jam, or submerged in vinegar to make rose vinegar. For a simple rose liqueur, fill a jar two thirds full with rose petals, add about a quarter of their volume in sugar and then fill up with vodka or brandy. Seal tightly and give it a shake. Leave in a cool, dark place for at least three months, shaking every couple of days to dissolve the sugar. Strain and then bottle in pretty small bottles. A good brew for flambé-ing puddings, or just for sipping on a cold winter's night.

Rose, Orange and Chilli Vinegar

A glorious, almost shocking pink, fragrant vinegar, for summer salads and sauces.

Makes just under 500 ml (16 fl oz)

4–8 fully scented roses (see method)
zest 1 orange
1 or 2 dried bird chillies
up to 500 ml (16 fl oz) rice vinegar or white wine vinegar

Pull the petals off four of the roses and nip out their white heels.

Fill a half litre (16 fl oz) jar with them, tucking in the orange zest and chilli(es) and packing down well. Pour over the vinegar, seal tightly and shake once or twice. Place on a sunny windowsill and leave for three to five days. Strain. If you want a stronger perfume, then place the petals of another 4 flowers, heeled, in the jar and pour the strained vinegar over them. Leave, tightly sealed, on a sunny windowsill for a further 3–5 days. Strain again.

Bottle and seal tightly and store in a cool dark place.

Opposite
A Summer's Delight
(page 176)

Poached Chicken, Peach and Rose Salad

This is one of the prettiest of all summer salads, with flashes of pale orange, rose pink and bright green.

Serves 6

For the chicken
1 free range chicken
1 lemon
1 carrot, cut into four
1 onion, quartered
1 stick celery, quartered
1 bay leaf, 2 sprigs thyme or lemon thyme, 2 sprigs parsley, tied together with string to make a bouquet garni
salt and pepper

For the dressing
½ teaspoon caster sugar
1 ½ tablespoons Rose, Orange and Chilli Vinegar (see opposite) or tarragon vinegar or white wine vinegar
6 tablespoons single cream
salt and pepper

For the salad
2 little gem lettuces, shredded
2 ripe peaches, skinned and sliced
110 g (4 oz) freshly shelled peas (not frozen ones) or 200 g (7 oz) podded broad beans (which can be frozen and thawed, if necessary)
a small handful of mint leaves
the petals of one fully scented rose

Put the chicken into a large pan with all the remaining chicken ingredients and water to cover. Bring up to the boil, then simmer very gently for about 50–60 minutes until cooked through. Leave to cool in the poaching liquid. When cool, remove the skin and strip the meat from the bone. Tear about half of it into bite-sized pieces.

Make the dressing: whisk the sugar into the vinegar, then gradually whisk in the cream. Season lightly. If using peas, simmer for a couple of minutes in lightly salted water, then drain. If using broad beans, blanch in boiling water for one minute if fresh, then drain. Slit open the skins and slip out the beanlets inside. If using frozen broad beans, thaw then slice. Finish cooking the skinned beans in lightly salted water for 2–3 minutes. Drain.

Place the lettuce in a wide salad bowl. Top with the chicken, then scatter the remaining salad ingredients over the top. Drizzle the dressing over, and serve.

A Summer's Delight

Meringue, cream, strawberries and roses – the very essence of an English summer. Folded together and piled up high, with a deep red coulis of roses drizzled over the sides, this is a show-stopping pudding.

For the ultimate delight, make the meringues yourself (whisk egg whites until they hold their shape, whisk in 30 g (1 oz) sugar for every white until glossy, then fold in another 30 g (1 oz) sugar for every white; dollop on to trays lined with rice-paper or non-stick baking parchment and leave in a low oven until dried out right through) – but for a last-minute afterthought, cheat with high-quality bought ones.

Serves 5–6

500 g (1 lb 2 oz) ripe strawberries
50 g (scant 2 oz) vanilla sugar
1 tablespoon rosewater
300 ml (½ pint) whipping cream
60 g (2 oz) meringues, roughly crushed
petals of 1 fragrant dark red or deep pink rose
5–6 sprigs of mint

For the rose coulis
3 fragrant deep pink roses
60 g (2 oz) caster sugar
2 tablespoons orange juice
2 tablespoons lemon juice

Hull the strawberries and halve, or quarter if large. Mix in a bowl with the sugar and rosewater, then cover and leave for at least an hour and up to 4 hours, as long as the room is not too warm. In high summer, leave in the fridge so that they don't start to ferment!

To make the rose coulis, separate the rose petals, removing the white heels if you have the time and inclination, then liquidize with the sugar, orange juice and lemon juice until smooth.

Just before serving, whip the cream until it just holds its shape, then lightly fold in the strawberry mixture and the pieces of meringue. Pile into individual sundae glasses, drizzle over a little of the rose coulis, then decorate with a sprig of mint and 2 or 3 fresh rose petals.

Alternatively, pile into one large crystal bowl, drizzling rose coulis between dollops and letting the last of it trickle down the sides. Scatter with fresh rose petals and serve.

Rose Petal Sorbet

Clean and refreshing, this pale pink sorbet is one of the prettiest of puddings that can be made with rose petals. I'm not a great believer in using food colouring but here is one occasion when a drop or two really helps what might be a rather anaemic colour.

Serves 4–6

4 fragrant heads of roses
150 g (5 oz) caster sugar
300 ml (10 fl oz) water
juice of 1 lemon
1 tablespoon rosewater
a drop or two of red colouring (optional)

Shake any wildlife from the roses, then pick off the petals. If you have the time and patience, nip off the white heels, though this is not absolutely necessary. Put the sugar and water into a pan and bring up to the boil, stirring. Draw off the heat, add the rose petals, cover and leave to cool and infuse overnight. Strain, then stir in the lemon juice, rosewater and food colouring, if using.

Freeze in an ice-cream maker for best results. If you don't have an ice-cream maker, pour the mixture into a shallow container and slide into the freezer, set to its coldest setting. Leave until the sides are beginning to solidify, then break them up and push towards the centre. Return to the freezer and repeat once. Return to the freezer again and leave until just about set but not yet rock solid. Scrape out into a food processor and process briefly to smooth out jagged ice crystals. If you don't have a processor, you will just have to beat it hard with a wooden spoon until you have a smooth sludge – no long pauses to gain your breath, though, or it will melt. Either way, spoon back into the container and return to the freezer to finish freezing.

Transfer from the freezer to the fridge about 40–50 minutes before serving, to soften up.

Rose Junket

elderflower
Sambucus nigra

My mother occasionally made junket as a summer treat when I was a child. I adored the crust of thick cream on the surface, usually sprinkled with nutmeg if it was a plain junket, and the way the curd split as the spoon sank into it, separating and releasing the translucent whey. Best of all, I loved the way the cool curds slipped down the throat, light, milky and smooth.

Junket takes only a few minutes to make and when it is flavoured with rosewater and scattered with rose petals it is one of the most romantic of puddings. The cream makes it richer, but is by no means necessary. On hot days, the lightness of a pure milk junket may well be preferred. Either way, it is lovely served with raspberries or other soft summer fruit.

Serves 6

900 ml (1½ pints) full cream milk
1½ tablespoons caster sugar
2 tablespoons rosewater
½ tablespoon rennet
75g (2½ oz) clotted cream (optional)
fragrant rose petals, to serve

Warm the milk gently with the caster sugar, stirring until dissolved. When it is at about blood temperature (as a rough guide dip a clean finger into the milk; you should be able to keep it there comfortably for a slow count of ten before you have to take it out), stir in the rosewater, then pour the warm milk into a wide serving bowl (I always use a glass one, for no particularly good reason except that it seems to echo the purity of the junket). Stir in the rennet, then leave at room temperature without disturbing, until set. Junket begins to set almost immediately – it will be set, but not necessarily cold within half an hour at most. At this point you can move it carefully to the refrigerator.

Spoon the clotted cream, if using, into a bowl and beat lightly until runny. Drizzle it over the junket, then carefully spread it out to cover the surface and return to the fridge. Shortly before serving, scatter scarlet rose petals over the top.

Elderflowers are one of late May's small pleasures. Pretty, plentiful and free for the taking, they have a heady muscat scent that can be exploited in cooking as well as enjoyed for its own sake. It has to be said that the smell is not appreciated by everyone (it has been likened to cats' urine, but don't let that prejudice you) – most people are more than a little partial to its honeyed tones.

Elder trees are ubiquitous. They delineate hedgerows and borders in the countryside, they proliferate on wasteground and in gardens in towns and cities. You are never, ever, far from an elder. Not just here in Britain, either. They thrive right across the Continent, and have been known and appreciated for centuries. Even Pliny, writing in ancient Rome, stated that they were so very familiar to one and all that he hardly need describe them. Young Roman boys learned to recognize elders from their older brothers, who taught them how to trim the hollow stems to turn them into pop-guns and pea-shooters...a laddish habit that has persisted until this day, even if it is not quite so widespread as it once was.

Elder trees were once counted amongst the most valuable of medicinal plants, country cure-alls that could remedy anything from a cough or a wart to sciatica. Green elder could ward off witches and evil spirits, too. So revered was the elder in the seventeenth century that a Dr Martin Blockwich devoted an entire book, *The Anatomie of the Elder*, to praising its virtues. And in 1931, Mrs M. Grieve dedicated eleven pages to elder, one of the longest entries in her fascinating *Modern Herbal*.

I was brought up on elderflower fritters and elderflower and gooseberry fool, at least while the short season lasted each year. The fritters arrived as a treat at the end of kitchen suppers. Hot and crisp, straight out of the pan, my mother would slip them one by one on to our plates. A shake of sugar, a squeeze of lemon juice and they were ready for eating.

Even nicer, though usually reserved for special occasions, was the fool, a classic English pudding of the very best sort. In the south of the country, elderflowers come into bloom early and you're lucky if they coincide at all with the first gooseberries, so the season for combining them may be as short as a few days, if it exists at all. As you move northwards up the country, the seasons overlap in a much more reasonable manner, allowing plenty of time for fools and other pairings of gooseberry and elderflower. To flavour a fool, just add a couple of heads of elderflower to the gooseberries as they cook, hoicking them out once the gooseberry mush has cooled, before you fold in the cream or custard. Little almondy biscuits go particularly well with it.

Practically anything made with gooseberries is improved by the scent of elderflowers – gooseberry jam or jelly, gooseberry cakes, pies and crumbles, and I once made a memorable gooseberry and elderflower cheesecake.

Once picked, the power of the ivory flowers is short lived, so only go gathering on the day you intend to use them. Look for a bush or tree well away from roads and choose only the freshly opened flowers. The organic herb grower and edible flower devotee, Jekka McVikka pointed out to me that they should be picked before they have been pollinated. Once the bees and insects have done their work, the flowers no longer have any need for their scent and it quickly disappears. How to tell? Three pointers: the first is nasal – take a good sniff. The other two are visual: when they first open, the flowers are a pale cream colour. Once they've been pollinated, they turn snowy white. And finally, if a snow of petals tumbles down as you tug at the branch, leave the flower be for it is way past its best.

Once gathered, get the flowers home fast before they begin to droop, and shake or brush off any unwanted insect life. Don't wash the flowers or you'll lose much of their perfume. Arrange them in a jar of water, enjoy their prettiness for an hour or two, then use them up swiftly.

NB Elderflowers are distinctive but there are other plants with a passing resemblance, so do make sure you know what you are looking for before you go picking. Double-check leaves and flowers with a reference book, or a more knowledgeable friend, if you are in any doubt.

Storage and Preservation

Once picked, the flowers droop and fade speedily, whatever measures you take, and the essential scent evaporates into the ether. They can be dried, and sometimes you can even buy dried flowers in healthfood shops, but the best way to hold on to their fragrance is in elderflower vinegar or cordial. Recipes for both follow. The cordial can replace fresh flowers when their season is past and in some instances it is even more useful than the flowers themselves. It can be used as a basis for sorbets and ice-creams, or to drizzle over vanilla or fruit ice-creams, or to moisten cakes to serve with soft summer berries and whipped cream. Mixed with icing sugar, it makes a fantastic icing for plain cakes.

Elderflower Vinegar
To make elderflower vinegar, cram a preserving jar full of flowers, then cover completely with white wine vinegar. Leave on a sunny windowsill for a fortnight, then strain through muslin and bottle.

The vinegar is lovely in salads, and good for deglazing pans after frying chicken. Slug in a couple of spoonfuls of vinegar and bring up to the boil, scraping up the frying residues. Boil until slightly reduced, then draw off the heat and stir in double cream, salt and pepper. Warm through and serve.

Elderflower Bavarois

This airy, light, creamy mousse is sheer heaven. Serve it on its own, a pure dome of pale ivory, or accompany it with strawberries or, later on in the season, raspberries.

Leaf gelatine is sold in some of our better supermarkets and many delicatessens. It is so very much easier to use than the powdered stuff that I now refuse even to contemplate the hoo-ha of dissolving those irritating tiny granules. Keep a stash of leaf gelatine in a dry cupboard and you'll soon be making jellies at the drop of a hat.

Serves 8

3 heads of elderflower
450 ml (¾ pint) creamy milk
4 eggs, separated
125 g (4 oz) caster sugar
11 g (0.4 oz) leaf gelatine
150 ml (¼ pint) double cream

Bring the elderflowers and milk slowly up to the boil, then turn off the heat, cover and leave to infuse for 10 minutes. In a bowl large enough to take all the milk, whisk the egg yolks with 3 oz (85 g) of the caster sugar until thick, pale and creamy. Half fill a roasting tin with cold water and soak the gelatine leaves in it for at least 5 minutes, to soften.

Boil up the milk again, then strain through a fine sieve. Pour the hot milk on to the egg yolks in a steady, slow stream, whisking constantly. Place the bowl over a pan of simmering water, making sure the base of the bowl does not touch the water. Stir until the custard thickens enough to coat the back of the spoon, then lift off the heat. One by one, lift the gelatine leaves out of the water, shake off excess, and stir into the hot custard. Leave to cool until barely tepid and beginning to thicken.

Whisk the egg whites until soft peaks are formed. Sprinkle over the remaining sugar, then whisk until stiff and glossy. Fold into the custard. Leave in the fridge until beginning to set. Whip the cream and fold in. Rinse a 1.5 litre (2½ pint) mould out with cold water and shake out the excess. Pour the mixture into the mould, smooth down the top and cover with a lightly oiled sheet of greaseproof paper. Leave to set fully in the fridge (about 4–5 hours).

To unmould, remove the greaseproof paper and dip the mould into hot water for about 5–10 seconds if it is made of metal, 15–30 seconds if it is made of china. Run a knife around the edges to loosen, then invert on to a serving plate. Give it a firm shake and listen out for the satisfying plop as the bavarois drops out on to the plate. If no satisfying plop is to be had, you may need to dip the mould back in hot water for a few more seconds and repeat the whole process. Once it is out, lift off the mould and serve.

Elderflower and Lime Jellies

Elderflower Cordial

A light, refreshing dessert for a warm day – the spicy sourness of limes is a marvellous vehicle for the muscat fragrance of elderflowers.

Serves 5–6

3 limes
11 g (0.4 oz) leaf gelatine
125 g (4 oz) granulated or caster sugar
450 ml (¾ pint) water
4 large heads of elderflower
single cream, to serve

Pare the zest from 2 of the limes and cut into fine shreds. Blanch for 2 minutes in boiling water, then drain and cool. Squeeze the juice of all 3 limes.

Half fill a roasting tin with cold water and soak the gelatine leaves in it for 5 minutes. Place the sugar and water in a pan. Bring up to the boil, add the elderflowers and simmer for 5 minutes. Draw off the heat. One by one, lift the gelatine leaves out of their cold bath, shake off excess water, then stir them into the hot syrup. Stir in the lime juice, then strain the mixture. Taste and add more sugar if you think it needs it, while it is still warm. Don't make it too sweet, though. Pour into 5 or 6 glasses, then leave in the fridge to set.

Just before serving, pour a thin film of single cream over the surface of each jelly, then scatter over a little of the lime zest.

This recipe was given to my mother by a neighbour many years ago, and is quite the best way of preserving the evanescent scent of elderflowers. As long as the bottles are scrupulously clean, it will keep for several months in a dark cupboard. For longer-term storage, pour into plastic drinks bottles and freeze. Diluted with fizzy water or, better still, gin and fizzy water, it makes one of the most refreshing long summer drinks. It can also be spooned over ice-cream or added to fruit salads for extra zip.

Makes about 1.5 litres (2½ pints)

20 large heads of elderflower
1.8 kg (4 lb) granulated sugar
1.2 litres (2 pints) water
75 g (2½ oz) citric acid (available from chemists)
2 lemons

Put the elderflowers in a large bowl. Place the sugar and water in a pan and bring gently up to the boil, stirring until the sugar has dissolved. Pour the sugar syrup over the elderflowers and stir in the citric acid. Grate in the zest of the lemons, then slice the lemons and add the slices to the bowl, too. Cover and leave for 24 hours. Strain through double muslin, pour into scrupulously clean bottles, then seal and store in a cool, dark place.

Paul Rankin's Elderflower Fritters

I've always fried elderflower fritters in shallow fat, snipping off the stalks once the batter has set so that they can be turned over to brown on both sides, but Paul goes for the more dramatic option of deep-frying. Within split seconds of arriving in the hot oil the flowers burst out to form the perfect lacy fritter. Great fun to cook and watch. You can serve his fritters in a homely manner with lemon and sugar, or go one step further and dress them up with a dusting of icing sugar and a scoop of his rich elderflower mousse to make a very chic and stylish pudding.

Serves 4

sunflower oil for deep-frying
8–12 heads of elderflower, depending on size

For the batter
180g (6 oz) plain flour
1 tablespoon caster sugar
a pinch of salt
finely grated zest of 1 lemon
2 eggs
60 ml (2 fl oz) milk
60 ml (2 fl oz) dry white wine

To serve
wedges of lemon and icing sugar or extra caster sugar or Paul's Elderflower Mousse (see opposite) and icing sugar

To make the batter, sift the flour into a bowl with the sugar and salt. Add the lemon zest and eggs, then splash in about half the milk and half the wine. Begin whisking the liquids into the flour, gradually incorporating the rest of the milk and wine to make a smooth batter. Let it rest for at least half an hour before using.

Shortly before serving, heat the sunflower oil in a large, deep pan to 180°C/350°F/Gas Mark 4. To check the temperature, try frying a small cube of bread in it. It should start sizzling vigorously as soon as it meets the hot oil and brown within 30 seconds. One by one, take the flowers by their stems and dunk them into the batter. Lift out and let excess batter run off them, then slide into the oil. After a couple of minutes the underneath should have turned a delightful light golden brown. Turn the fritters and give them another minute to crisp the underside. Drain briefly on kitchen paper before serving.

Paul Rankin's Elderflower Mousse

This mousse, scented with a heartwarming slurp of elderflower cordial, can be made, quite literally, in less than 5 minutes. To my surprise, Paul uses half a tub of bought ready-made custard – the fancy sort, made with real eggs and cream, not the eggless substitutes – so once the cream is lightly whipped (so that it just holds its shape but is still slightly floppy), it is just a question of mixing everything together. Serve the mousse as an accompaniment to Elderflower Fritters (see opposite), or perhaps with a wedge of Elderflower and Almond Cake (see the method for Rose Geranium and Almond Cake, p. 145). I like it, too, served with a simple compote of gooseberries, or soft summer strawberries or raspberries. Since the mousse is scented with cordial, it can be made at any time of year, so in winter you might like to partner it with slices of fresh orange marinated in a little sugar syrup, with a hint of cordial in that, too.

Serves 4 or more

250 g (9 oz) mascarpone cheese
200 g (7 oz) bought custard
125–175 ml (4–6 fl oz) elderflower cordial
200 ml (7 fl oz) double cream, lightly whipped

Beat the mascarpone lightly to soften it, then add the custard and whisk until smooth. Whisk in the cordial and then finally the cream, taking great care at this juncture not to whisk more than is absolutely necessary – you don't want to end up with elderflower cordial butter! Taste and add a little more cordial if you think it needs it, then chill for at least half an hour before serving.

lavender
Lavandula species

Here's flowers for you;
Hot lavender, mints, savory, marjoram.
'A Winter's Tale', William Shakespeare

When you are stuck in a traffic jam in south London on a hot sweaty day, horns honking, petrol fumes and the stench of drains wafting in through the window, it's hard to imagine Battersea as a sweetly scented oasis strewn with fields of lavender, but that really is how Lavender Hill earned its name. The nearby village of Mitcham was even more famous for its vistas of purple lavender and the production of finest lavender oil. Which of the two seems more unlikely these days is difficult to gauge.

The sight and smell of a lavender field in full bloom is quite overwhelming in the most sensual of ways. The colour is startling, the scent glorious and heady, and if the sun is beating down as well you will soon be drawn into a state of delicious languid well being. Lovely if you have nothing much to do but no doubt a pain if you happen to have to work the fields. The centre for lavender growing in this country is now Norfolk but, for the ultimate experience, head off to Provence, where lavender fields shimmer in the heat. English writers always insist that our lavender is the better, with a headier scent, but they've got to admit that the summer weather is less dependable.

Lavender is native to the western Mediterranean, though it is now grown all over the world. The ancient Romans loved it – how could they not? – and threw it liberally into their bathing water. The very name comes from the Latin *lavare*, to wash – or at least that is the popular explanation, though *The Oxford English Dictionary* suggests that it is little more than wishful thinking. The Romans probably used what we now know as French lavender (*Lavandula stoechas*), with its merry, waving flags of purple poking up above the main flowerhead. It seems more than likely that they would have brought it with them when settlers came to colonize our savage islands, but it is fairly susceptible to frost so perhaps it failed to take root in our climate. Though lavender was known in Britain in medieval times, it didn't start to be widely cultivated until the late sixteenth century, and from then on enthusiasm was rampant.

It was, needless to say, one of the most revered of strewing plants, carpeted across floors to disguise the sour odours of the great unwashed. Furthermore, expensive though it may have been, lavender had the added advantage of being an insect repellent. In 1620 the Pilgrim Fathers took lavender plants with them to America. Only a few years later, Henrietta Maria, wife of Charles I, had large borders of white-flowered lavender planted in the gardens of her manor at Wimbledon.

Until relatively recently, lavender was grown principally for its medicinal qualities, though old recipes using lavender to scent food do exist. It is really only in the past decade that we have begun to discover a new taste for it, and the aromatic flowers have made ever-increasing incursions into fashionable kitchens – and indeed some of the less fashionable, like my very own. I can't pretend that I use lavender with tremendous regularity but every now and then the urge comes over me to capture something of its magic. I am invariably delighted with the results and then left wondering why I don't take greater advantage of the bushes of lavender that draw the bees so successfully to their flowers.

Both leaves and flowers can be used in cooking. The leaves have a milder, more herbal scent than the flowers but when young are rather pleasant chopped up and added to a salad. They work well in stews of rabbit and chicken, too, when the flowers have yet to bloom. Later on, a few heads of fresh lavender flowers can replace them to give a more scented dish. Rubbed over meat before roasting, the leaves or flowers impart a trace of a lavender scent. I rather like it with rice as well, in moderation – a couple of flowerheads in the pan gives a light fragrance that sits well with curries and South-east Asian dishes, especially if you are using one of the more nondescript long grain rices. Try it, too, perhaps increasing the quantity, in a rice pudding simmered on top of the stove. Infused in a jelly (see the recipe for Rose Geranium Jelly, p. 145) it makes a lovely preserve that goes as well on toast or scones as it does with roast game or lamb. You could also dip a few heads (tied like a bouquet garni so that they can be removed with ease) in strawberry, apricot or rhubarb jam as it boils. A lavender syrup is easy to concoct and, as long as it is not too strong, is excellent for poaching fruit (especially cherries, nectarines, plums and peaches) as the basis for a sorbet or to use as a flavouring for whipped cream. You can drizzle it over pound cake, turning it into a moist pudding to serve with soft fruit and whipped cream or mascarpone. If lavender cakes take your fancy, strew the flowers over the lined base of a cake tin before pouring in a sponge batter (see Rose Geranium and Almond Cake, p. 145). Infuse it in cream or milk for ice-creams, mousses, bavarois and other creamy cold summer puddings.

For the most reliable source of culinary lavender, choose one of the many varieties of English lavender, *Lavandula angustifolia*, to grow in your garden or in a capacious pot on a sunny balcony or terrace. The flowers are at their best shortly before they open up fully. If you buy lavender, you may have to make do with dried, which is stronger than the fresh, so use it cautiously until you have its measure. Check, too, that it has not been sprayed with heaven knows what horrible chemicals, and is safe to use in food.

Storage and Preservation

Once picked, lavender flowers should be used as quickly as possible but, if necessary, they can be stored for a few days in an airtight container in the bottom of the fridge. To dry lavender, pick the flowers just before they swell into full bloom, on a sunny morning after the dew has dried. Either spread them out on racks outdoors, covered loosely with muslin if the weather holds, or string up in bunches in an airy place. The individual flowers have a tendency to drop and scatter, so be prepared. If the flowers are to be used for cooking or to make lavender bags, then take the first opportunity to rub them off the stems so that they can be stored in airtight containers.

To make lavender vinegar, which I can highly recommend, push a generous handful of lavender flowers into a bottle and cover with the best white wine vinegar. Stopper tightly and leave on a sunny windowsill for at least a week and up to three weeks, before straining and rebottling. It is lovely in salads and cream or butter sauces and, with a spot of sugar, makes the basis of a very refreshing summer drink, diluted with plenty of fizzy mineral water.

Baked Goat's Cheese with Lavender

French friends tell me that lavender and goat's cheese is all the rage in France, so I gave it a whirl. You might not expect them to be good companions but, surprisingly enough, they are. Here the goat's cheese (use the semi-soft sort with a soft, bloomy, white rind) is first marinated, then baked with lavender to serve as a first course, with a salad dressed with walnut oil and lavender vinegar if you happen to have some lurking around on your shelves.

Toasted walnut bread is fabulous with goat's cheese. Many of the larger supermarkets now sell it, if you can't find it in local bakeries or delicatessens. Mathematics dictates that you will have one extra round of goat's cheese to dispose of – either make it the cook's perk or grill it along with the rest just in case anyone fancies a bit more than their allotted share, or save it for a sandwich later on.

Serves 4

3 small goat's cheeses (e.g. Capricorn)
8 thin slices of walnut bread, if available, or brioche
8 spikes of lavender flowers
about 85–125 g (3–4 oz) small salad leaves (such as rocket, lamb's lettuce, watercress, buckler leaf sorrel, salad burnet, claytonia, etc.)

For the marinade
4 sprigs of lavender leaves, roughly chopped
5 spikes of lavender flowers
3–5 tablespoons olive oil

For the dressing
½ tablespoon lavender vinegar or balsamic vinegar
a pinch of sugar
2 tablespoons walnut oil
salt and pepper

Carefully trim the rind off the bottom and top of the cheeses, then cut each one into 3 slices. To make the marinade, bruise the lavender leaves gently, then chop roughly. Pick the flowers off the spikes. Scatter half the leaves and flowers in an oiled dish large enough to take the goat's cheese in a single layer. Lay the goat's cheese on top, then sprinkle over the remaining lavender flowers and leaves and season generously with freshly ground black pepper. Drizzle over the olive oil. Cover and leave to marinate for at least an hour, turning the cheeses carefully once or twice.

Meanwhile, toast the bread lightly on both sides, then stamp out rounds a little larger than the goat's cheeses. To make the dressing, whisk the vinegar with the sugar, salt and pepper, then gradually whisk in the walnut oil. Taste and adjust the seasoning.

Pre-heat the grill. Shortly before sitting down to eat, carefully extract the slices of goat's cheese from the marinade, brush off the lavender and lay each one on a round of bread. Press a fresh spike of lavender flowers gently on to each one. Grill until sizzling and melted. As they grill, quickly toss the salad leaves in the dressing and divide between 4 plates. Lay 2 of the discs of toasted cheese on each plate and serve at once.

Lavender Shortbread

Nothing more than straight shortbread with some lavender flowers worked into the mixture. A simple device but one that adds a delicate lavender fragrance, which turns good shortbread into something even better. Enjoy the shortbread with a cup of coffee or tea, or serve it with fruit-based or creamy puddings. To measure the lavender, first pick the little flowerlets off the stems. If you use dried lavender, you will need less as it has a stronger flavour.

When shortbread is baked in a circle and cut into triangular wedges, they are known as petticoat tails.

Makes 12 petticoat tails

85 g (3 oz) plain flour
85 g (3 oz) cornflour
125 g (4 oz) unsalted or slightly salted butter, softened
60 g (2 oz) caster sugar
3–3½ teaspoons fresh lavender flowers or 2–2½ teaspoons dried lavender flowers

Pre-heat the oven to 150°C/300°F/Gas Mark 2. Sift the flour with the cornflour. Beat the butter with the sugar until light and creamy. Work in the flour and lavender to form a soft dough. Knead briefly to even out, then roll out (cover the dough with a sheet of greaseproof paper, then roll over that, so that the rolling pin doesn't stick) or press out with your hands on a baking sheet, to form a circle about 5 mm (¼ inch) thick. Prick all over with a fork, then bake for about 30 minutes, until a very pale biscuit colour. Remove from the oven and, while still warm, score the surface with a sharp knife to form 12 wedges. Leave to cool, then break into wedges (the petticoat tails) along the scored lines. Store in an airtight tin.

Lavender and Orange Ice-cream

The citrus tones of orange juice balance the toilet-water scent of lavender to produce a delicious ice-cream. Use more or fewer spikes of lavender depending on how strong a presence you fancy.

Serves 6–8

15–25 spikes of fresh lavender flowers or 10–15 dried lavender heads
zest of 1 orange, pared off in strips
300 ml (½ pint) single cream or milk
4 egg yolks
60 g (2 oz) caster sugar
300 ml (½ pint) whipping or double cream
juice of 1 orange

Put the lavender flowers and orange zest into a saucepan with the single cream or milk. Bring gently up to the boil, then draw off the heat, cover and leave to infuse for at least 45 minutes.

Whisk the egg yolks with the sugar until pale and thick. Bring the cream or milk back to the boil, then draw off the heat and pour into the egg mixture, stirring constantly. Set the bowl over a pan of lazily simmering water, making sure that the base of the bowl does not come into contact with the water. Stir until the custard thickens just enough to coat the back of a wooden spoon. Lift the bowl off the pan and leave to cool, then strain to remove eggy threads and the spent flowers and orange zest.

Whisk the cream until it holds its shape lightly and floppily. Fold into the cold custard with the orange juice. If you have an ice-cream machine, freeze it in that. If not, pour the mixture into a shallow container and leave in the freezer, turned to its coldest setting. When the mixture has set around the sides but is still runny in the centre, take out of the freezer, break up the sides and push them into the centre. Return to the freezer. Repeat if you have time. Then leave in the freezer until the mixture is just about set but not yet rock solid. Scrape quickly into a food processor or a bowl and either process or beat hard to smooth out the jagged ice crystals. Return to the container, then to the freezer to finish freezing.

Transfer from the freezer to the fridge about 45 minutes before serving to soften up.

lemon balm
Melissa officinalis

Don't plant lemon balm in your garden. Or at least, not straight in the ground, unless you are prepared for an onslaught of lemon balm marching through the flowerbeds. It's not that I don't like lemon balm. It's a beautiful plant, with tender, heart-shaped, saw-edged leaves and a strong sweet, lemon zest scent (not entirely dissimilar to air-freshener sprays, though certainly less chemical) but it is invasive. In my garden in France, which used to spend a large part of the year untended, lemon balm ran riot, colonizing the shadier parts in big unruly clumps. Concerted effort one summer eradicated a fair amount, but the roots are strong and lemon balm resurfaces time and again. Tempting though it may be to settle either the plain or variegated lemon balm in a choice site in the herb patch, resist unless you are prepared to cut it back hard before it flowers. Instead, plant it in pots or grow it in a windowbox, and try not to let it run to seed.

Though old herbals make no mention of the stress that unchecked lemon balm can bring they do all have plenty to say about it. Lemon balm is one of the blessed herbs that seem to have wondrous properties. A tisane of fresh leaves mixed with mint and sweetened, if needs be, with a little honey is a great way to soothe an over-active mind at the end of the day. And, apparently, a daily dose of lemon balm in tea form or in a glass of wine will 'renew youth, strengthen the brain, relieve languishing nature and prevent baldness' (*London Dispensary*, 1696).
To prove the point, the cases of a pair of notably long-lived lemon balm addicts are often cited: the thirteenth-century Llewellyn, Prince of Glamorgan, who lived until he was a riproaring 108, and a mysterious John Hussey of Sydenham, who beat him by eight years to the ripe old age of 116. Two examples, however remarkable, are hardly enough to prove the point but if you are feeling old beyond your years, a cup or two of lemon balm might be worth a try.

Opposite
Clockwise from top left: lemon balm; variegated lemon balm; lemon verbena; apple mint; flat-leafed parsley; curly parsley; bergamot; Bowles mint Centre: spearmint

Sautéed Fennel and **Carrots** with
Lemon Balm and **Lime**

The generic name, *Melissa*, comes from the Latin for a honey bee. A cluster of thrumming bees around the flowers makes it clear why, and old bee keepers' lore still has it that rubbing lemon balm inside the hive ensures that the swarm will never move on. Lemon balm honey is said to be very good indeed.

For the cook, the charms are pretty obvious. The lemony nature of the herb makes it a clear winner with fish or chicken, added to white sauces, butter sauces, herb butters, marinades or even summery raw salsas made with fruit, tomatoes or avocado. From salsas it is but a short step to salads, and a few leaves of lemon balm, roughly shredded or torn up, make an invigorating addition to a green salad, a tomato or cucumber salad or, for that matter, a fruit salad of practically any sort. Infused in cream or milk, it adds zest to custards, mousses, fools and ice-creams and, like so many of the sweetly fragrant herbs, it can be used to line the base of a cake tin before pouring in the batter (see p. 145), for a delicate trace of its fragrance.

Storage and Preservation

The leaves will keep well in an airtight box or plastic bag in the vegetable drawer of the fridge for up to five days. They can be chopped and packed into ice-cube trays, topped up with water and frozen. Dried lemon balm is a weakened echo of fresh but good for making tisanes or scenting sugar syrups. Tie the stems in bunches and hang up to dry in a dark, airy, place. When dry, crumble the leaves and stash in airtight jars. Use up within about six months at the outside.

I'm very partial to sautéed vegetables and I don't mean just potatoes, divinely good though they are, but all kinds of other vegetables, too. Carrots sauté extremely well, developing a deep caramel sweetness; globe artichokes and Jerusalem artichokes are good, too, and I love the sweet aniseed of sautéed fennel. Here I've partnered fennel with carrots, adding a final shot of freshness with lemon balm and lime. Very nice with chicken or lamb.

Serves 3–4

1 large head of fennel or 2 small ones, trimmed and cut into
    1 cm (½ inch) dice
340 g (12 oz) large carrots, cut into 1 cm (½ inch) dice
2 tablespoons sunflower oil
2 tablespoons chopped lemon balm
finely grated zest of ½ lime
2 squeezes of lime juice
salt and pepper

Mix the fennel and carrots. Heat the oil in a wide, heavy frying pan over a moderate heat. Add the vegetables and sauté for about 10–15 minutes, until tender and patched with brown. Draw off the heat and stir in all the remaining ingredients. Serve immediately.

One Fat Lady's Hake stuffed with **Prawns** and **Melissa** served with a **Villein Sauce**

Clarissa Dickson Wright has become internationally famous as one of the *Two Fat Ladies*, the dastardly duo that hi-jacked the cookery world with their forthright utterances and wonderfully down-to-earth recipes, celebrating our marvellous inheritance of good food that is so often neglected in favour of modern contrivances. I take some small credit for their meteoric rise to stardom, as I gave Clarissa her first television outing in an early series of mine, and introduced her to the producer who paired her with Jennifer Patterson.

She's harder to track down these days, but when I did make it to her doorstep in a small village just outside Edinburgh, she cooked this glorious, simple dish of hake, a much under-rated fish, with prawns and oodles of lemon balm, or *melissa*, as she prefers to call it. The sauce is based on a medieval herb sauce, an ancestor, I guess, of the fashionable Italian Salsa Verde (see p. 81) and Green Goddess mayonnaise.

Serves 4

1 hake, weighing around 1 kg (2¼ lb), cleaned
olive oil
salt and pepper
6 generous stems of lemon balm, complete with plenty
    of leaves

For the stuffing
4 shallots, chopped
1 tablespoon olive oil
45 g (1½ oz) butter
150 g (5 oz) shelled raw prawns, each one cut into 2 or 3
    pieces if large
a generous handful of lemon balm leaves
salt and pepper

For the sauce
2 shallots, finely chopped
4 tablespoons olive oil
30 g (1 oz) butter
a generous handful of lemon balm leaves
3 hard-boiled egg yolks
3 tablespoons chopped parsley
1 teaspoon Dijon mustard
1 tablespoon capers or caper berries, rinsed and soaked if
    salted, chopped
1 tablespoon red wine vinegar
salt and pepper

Preheat the oven to 220ºC/425ºF/Gas Mark 7.
Rub a few spoonfuls of olive oil over the hake and season with salt and pepper. Make a bed of the stems of lemon balm in a roasting tin or large ovenproof dish.

To make the stuffing, sauté the shallots in the oil and butter until tender and translucent. Add the prawns and sauté for a couple more minutes until just barely cooked through. Stir in the whole lemon balm leaves, cook for a few seconds longer until they are all wilted, then draw the pan off the heat. Season. Fill the cavity of the fish with the prawns, lemon balm and about half of the shallots. Transfer the fish carefully (you can seal up the cavity with a couple of wooden cocktail sticks, if you wish, to prevent the stuffing falling out) on to the bed of lemon balm stems. Spoon the remaining shallot and buttery juices from the pan over the hake. Roast for 20 minutes until just cooked through.

Meanwhile, make the sauce. Fry the shallots in 1 tablespoon of olive oil and all the butter until tender and translucent. Stir in the lemon balm, until it has just wilted. Draw off the heat and tip into a bowl. Pound the egg yolks with the parsley in a mortar, with a pestle (or use a sturdy bowl and the end of a rolling pin) until well mixed. Tip into the bowl with the cooked shallots and lemon balm. Stir in the mustard, capers, vinegar, and remaining oil, to make a creamy sauce. Season to taste, adjust the balance of flavourings, adding a dash more vinegar if needed, and then serve with the hake.

If you fancy a smoother sauce, you can drop the pounding and just put the cooked shallots and lemon balm into the processor with all the other ingredients and process until more or less smooth.

Citrus Salad with Warm Lemon Balm Sabayon Sauce

The rich, mousse-like sabayon sauce, scented with lemon balm, turns a rather pure salad of citrus fruit into a luxurious pudding. I like it best when the sabayon is still a little warm but that means a fair bit of last-minute whisking (an electric whisk is a big help) in the kitchen while your guests wait. If you want to avoid that, it can be made in advance but you'll have to settle for a cold sauce. Either way, serve the salad with crisp shortbread (see p. 185) or thin biscuits such as *langues de chat*.

To ring the changes you can replace the wine with orange juice or try different herbs instead of the lemon balm. You can make a lavender or angelica sabayon by sprinkling in a little fresh lavender or some chopped angelica leaves, or scented geranium sabayon by pounding the leaves with the sugar (see p. 211).

Serves 4

2 oranges
1 pink grapefruit
1 yellow grapefruit
1 lime
6 lemon balm leaves, roughly torn up
2 tablespoons honey
a pretty sprig of lemon balm, to garnish

For the sabayon sauce
2 egg yolks
30 g (1 oz) caster sugar
125 ml (4 fl oz) dry but fragrant white wine
6 lemon balm leaves, chopped
4 tablespoons double cream

Using a sharp knife, segment the citrus fruit in the following way: cut off all the peel, slicing just into the flesh, so that none of the white pith remains. Carefully slice down close to the membrane separating each segment on either side, so that the perfectly naked, skinned segments fall out. Place them in a dish with the torn lemon balm leaves, drizzle over the honey and turn carefully. Cover and set aside until needed.

To make the sabayon, put all the ingredients except the cream in a bowl and set it over a pan of simmering water, making sure that the base of the bowl does not touch the water. Whisk continuously with an electric whisk if possible (or a strong arm and a balloon whisk if you have to) until the mixture becomes quite pale and billows up to form a thick, mousse-like cream – this may take as much as 10 minutes or even a little longer. Draw off the heat and keep whisking for a couple of minutes. Add the cream and whisk for a further 20 seconds or so (make that a little longer if you are doing it by hand), then serve at once with the citrus salad, garnished with the lemon balm sprig.

If you want to avoid last-minute whisking, you can make the sabayon sauce in advance, but when you take it off the heat and before you add the cream set the bowl in a bowl full of ice cubes and keep whisking until it is cold. This will prevent it separating. Then add the cream and whisk again briefly. Store, covered, in the fridge, until it is needed.

Opposite
Citrus Salad with Warm Lemon Balm Sabayon Sauce

lemon verbena

Aloysia triphylla (syn. Lippia triphylla, Lippia citriodora, Verbena triphylla)

It amazes me that lemon verbena is not better known and more widely used. It has the most thrilling fresh lemon juice and lemon zest scent, which translates vividly into food and, what's more, it looks pretty into the bargain. For Europeans it is a relatively modern herb, brought back from its native South America by the Spaniards in the seventeenth century and grown initially for its perfumed oil. It eventually crossed the Channel in 1784. One would have thought that two or three hundred years was quite enough time for the word to spread but there is, as yet, no sign that it is going to claw its way on to the list of widely available cut herbs. If you want to try it you will probably have to grow it for yourself, or beg some from a green-fingered friend.

Being a half-hardy refugee from warmer climates, it appreciates a sheltered spot in the garden or, better still, a roomy container that can be lugged indoors in the winter months. Outside, it should just about survive, as long as the roots are protected with a snug blanket of straw or other warming mulch and the frosts are not too severe. The leaves tend to be tardy, so don't give up in despair at the sight of nude branches in the late spring. Leave it be until summer is well under way before deciding that it is past redemption.

Once you reap your first small harvest of lemon verbena you will be amply rewarded for all that cosseting. The rough, lance-shaped leaves will find a good home with almost anything that benefits from the tartness of lemon, bringing an extra aromatic scent with them. That means that they go well with an enormous number of foods: tuck sprigs inside chicken or fish before cooking; chop and add to sauces (a few minutes' simmering really brings out the citrus zip); simmer in a sweet syrup for summer fruit salads and autumnal compotes; add to stuffings for fatty meats like pork, duck or goose to cut the richness (actually, it is also well suited to a herb stuffing for chicken); pop a few spoonfuls of chopped leaves into terrines and pâtés; or thread on to skewers of meat or fish for the barbecue.

To scent sugar, throw a few leaves into a jam jar, then top up with sugar and leave in a sunny place for a week or so. When you haven't a week in hand, or if you fancy the idea of vivid green sugar for sprinkling over cakes and puddings, pound sugar cubes with the leaves as in the fool recipe opposite. Sweeten whipped cream with the scented sugar and serve with soft summer berries, finishing the dish with jaunty sprigs of greenery. At a pinch, lemon verbena can be used as a substitute for lemon grass in South-east Asian cooking. Infused in hot water, it is soothing and calming, a good after-dinner alternative to coffee for those who cannot take caffeine late at night. Lightly bruised leaves will also add a hint of sharpness to cool summer drinks, cocktails and punches.

For many of the older generation, the scent of lemon verbena brings back bitter-sweet memories of their 'privileged' childhood. The herb grower Alexander Gardiner records that around the turn of the century, in better-off households where children were raised largely in the nursery by nannies, mothers would often place a leaf of lemon verbena between their breasts when they dressed for a ball. 'When the rarely seen mother went to the nursery to kiss the children before leaving for the evening, the all-pervading scent filled the air long after her departure.'

Storage and Preservation

The fully grown leaves are moderately sturdy and will last for up to a week in an airtight plastic box or bag in the vegetable drawer of the fridge, though they are at their best and most vibrant when freshly picked. They can be chopped and packed into ice-cube trays with water to cover, then frozen. To dry, pick the leaves and flower buds just before they come into bloom. Hang up in bunches and leave to dry in an airy, shady place. Stored in an airtight container, the dried leaves will keep their scent for two or three years, maybe more. They are excellent for tisanes, but though they may be added to slow-cooked sauces and stews they lose much of their sprightly zest.

Roast Sea Bass with Lemon Verbena and Chive Dressing

Strawberry, Mascarpone and Lemon Verbena Fool

The lemony scent of verbena is a natural with fish. Here it adds zest and vigour to a simple oil-based dressing for roast sea bass. The one trouble with sea bass is that it has become horribly expensive, a special-occasion-only sort of a fish. For a cheaper and more everyday version of this recipe, replace the sea bass with mackerel (two large ones or four smaller ones) and reduce the oven time to 12–15 minutes.

Serves 4

1 generous sprig of lemon verbena
1 sea bass, weighing around 1.3 kg (2½ lb), cleaned
2 tablespoons extra virgin olive oil
1 tablespoon lemon juice
1 garlic clove, sliced
salt and pepper

For the dressing
5 tablespoons olive oil
1½ tablespoons roughly chopped lemon verbena
juice of ½ orange
1–2 tablespoons lemon juice
1 heaped tablespoon chopped chives
2 tomatoes, deseeded and finely diced

Pre-heat the oven to 220°C/425°F/Gas Mark 7.

Tuck the sprig of lemon verbena in the stomach cavity of the fish and season with salt and pepper. Place in a lightly oiled baking dish. Whisk the oil lightly with the lemon juice and garlic, then brush over the fish, pouring any excess over as well. Season well with salt and pepper, then roast for 20–25 minutes until the fish is just cooked through.

Meanwhile, put all the ingredients for the dressing except the chives and tomatoes into a saucepan, season with salt and pepper and bring slowly up to the boil, stirring frequently. Draw off the heat and leave to infuse for at least 10 minutes. Shortly before serving, reheat gently, add the chives and tomatoes and stir over a low heat for a few minutes to warm through. Serve in a small jug, to pour over the roast fish.

A summery pudding to die for, we decided, as we argued over how many it would serve and whether each one of us should taste it again, just to check that the balance of sugar to verbena to strawberries to mascarpone was about right. The conclusion: if necessary we could finish it off between the two of us but when we weren't being quite so greedy, and after a meal, then it would do quite generously for three people and, with a little more restraint, for four. Then we tasted it again...just to make absolutely sure.

Serves 3–4

a small handful of lemon verbena leaves, plus a few sprigs to garnish
45 g (1½ oz) sugar cubes
340 g (12 oz) strawberries, hulled
250 g (9 oz) mascarpone cheese

Put the lemon verbena leaves into a mortar or strong bowl with the sugar cubes. Pound together with a pestle or the end of a rolling pin until the sugar is completely crushed and the verbena leaves have disintegrated completely, colouring the sugar a rather beautiful green.

Now crush the strawberries with a fork (a food processor is too efficient, though not entirely out of the question). Gradually work them into the mascarpone with enough of the verbena sugar to sweeten to taste. Spoon into individual dishes and serve topped with a sprig of lemon verbena.

mint
Mentha species

*'The smell...rejoyceth the heart of man, for which cause
they use to strew it in chambers and places of recreation,
pleasure and repose, where feasts and banquets are made.'*
John Gerard's *Herball* (1597)

Bedlam. Mint is bedlam. There are, I've read, some
600 different sorts of mint, all of them rather morally
lax. One glimpse of a fair mentholated leaf and it longs to
cross stems and generate a new little hybrid all of its own.
Who cares if it confuses botanists and, worse, innocent
cooks? Cool mint has no scruples – a characteristic it
shares, curiously enough, with hot chillies. Like chillies,
too, the flavour of mint is heavily affected by climate and
terrain, but that is true of most herbs to a certain extent.

Broadly speaking, however, we cooks need not be too
exercised by the profligacy of the mint community. As far
as we are concerned there are two crucial kinds of mint
that earn their keep in the kitchen garden, with a handful
of secondary varieties that are useful and fun to tangle
with but far from essential. Number-one mint has to be
spearmint (*Mentha spicata*), also known simply as garden
mint. This is a smooth-leaved plant with the characteristic
bright green colour that we associate with mint and the
clean, crisp, slightly sweet, breezy flavour that echoes the
freshness of a perfect spring morning. No wonder we
love it so much with the first of the real new potatoes or
with tender young peas (if you grow your own you will
understand this alliance perfectly), or indeed in the form
of mint sauce, to go with young Easter lamb. If buying a
pot of spearmint for the garden, try to get Moroccan mint,
the most perfectly flavoured of all the varieties.

The second important form of mint is Bowles mint. The
name may not mean a great deal to you, but you have
probably met it none the less. It is a type of round-leaved
mint and these leaves are soft and hairy. Their fuzziness
may have dulled the appeal of Bowles mint, which is a
shame, for the flavour is truly excellent. When they are
finely chopped, one hardly notices the fuzziness anyway.
You may also come across some fine culinary mints that
are crosses between spearmint and Bowles mint.

Secondary mints include apple and pineapple mint,
which are also forms of round-leaved mint, particularly the
beautiful white and green variegated types. Apple mint
does indeed have a fruity scent to it, which makes it very
welcome in sweet dishes or with pork. Eau de cologne
mint (which may also be called lemon or bergamot mint)
is very pleasantly scented, and just the ticket in fruit
salads or some kind of fruit punch or, of course, in a
Pimm's. Incidentally, for the famous mint julep, use
spearmint or Bowles mint. You may also come across
ginger mint, basil mint, and more, all of which are a
pleasure to grow and smell, even if you never make any
use of them in cooking. Black peppermint makes a most
soothing infusion and adds a prime minty scent to a mug
of hot chocolate. Pennyroyal, on the other hand, which is
smaller and tough enough to plant between paving
stones, has such a strong presence that it is almost
unpalatable. It was once known as the pudding herb
because it was frequently added to savoury pudding
mixtures and also to stuffings.

Garden mint has long been a British favourite, though
used in a fairly restrained way. Its other monikers, lamb
mint and mackerel mint, come from its favoured alliances
with lamb and fat, oily mackerel (I like to add a little
shredded mint to a sharp gooseberry or rhubarb sauce to
serve with this most delectable of fish). We only have to
look to Italy, or a little further afield to the Middle East, to
discover more imaginative ways of using it. One of my
favourite Italian salads is made by frying courgettes in
plenty of olive oil with sliced garlic, until well browned,
then dressing them hot with red wine vinegar and oodles
of fresh mint. Much the same can be done with small
spring carrots, though lemon juice rather than vinegar is
the sharpener to use here. In the Middle East, mint is used
in great quantity with other herbs in salads, such as the
one on p. 208. All around that part of the world,
combinations of creamy yoghurt, with or without cucumber
(diced and salted first for a sauce or relish), crushed
garlic and generous amounts of chopped mint make
marvellous first courses (in particular the Greek *tzatziki*,
though it is not alone), sauces, relishes and even soups.

Mint Sauce

Wherever the recipe originates, I think it is true to say that mint does not benefit from long cooking. Above all it is the freshness that everyone loves and that disappears with prolonged heating. Stir or sprinkle freshly chopped or shredded mint in just before serving, so that the flavour is released but not dissipated. That menthol whiff is well known as a digestive (one of the justifications often cited for serving mint sauce with lamb, as if the fact that it tastes good wasn't enough on its own), and a handful of fresh mint makes the most marvellous after-dinner infusion, especially for those like me who cannot drink coffee in the evenings. All you have to do is cram sprigs of fresh mint (spearmint, Bowles mint, peppermint or even one of the more frolicsome varieties) into a teapot, pour on boiling water, stir once, then leave to infuse for a few minutes. You won't even need a tea strainer. To make a cold mint infusion, add a touch of sugar or honey (even if you don't much like sweet drinks, a little will improve the overall flavour) to the mint, and half or more of a lemon, sliced skin and all, before adding the boiling water. Leave to cool, then strain and chill.

Storage and Preservation

Being a plant that loves damp and water, mint has a tendency to wilt fairly speedily once picked. It doesn't take long in a warm kitchen for the leaves to lose their perky, fresh appearance and start to droop, although the flavour holds true for a little longer. Better to wrap the mint quickly in a couple of sheets of damp (but not soaking) kitchen paper, pop it into a plastic bag and store in the vegetable drawer of the fridge, where it will keep well enough for two or three days. Chopped, the leaves may be mixed with a little water and frozen in ice-cube trays. In fact, mint dries remarkably well for a tender-leaved plant and, of all the options for preservation, this is probably the best. During warm weather, tie it in bunches and hang up to dry in an airy, dry place. In less clement times, spread the stems out on a rack and place in a very low oven. When the leaves are dry, strip them off the stalks and store in an airtight container.

Mint sauce is one of the great simple gems of English cooking, the perfect idiosyncratic accompaniment to tender spring lamb. Bottled mint sauce can be vile, and bears little resemblance to the real thing. Since it takes only a few moments to make, there's not much point in wasting your money on the ready-made version, especially if you grow your own mint.

This is how my mother made mint sauce, and how I still like to make it. The important things, as she pointed out in her book *English Food*, are not to be mean with the mint, and to use boiling water to release its fragrance. Serve it with roast lamb, of course, in true English style, or spoon a little over steamed new potatoes or carrots. It will keep in the fridge for several days, though it is at its best when newly made.

Serves 6

a bunch of mint leaves
1 level tablespoon caster sugar
4 tablespoons boiling water
4 tablespoons white wine vinegar

Chop enough mint leaves to fill the measuring jug to the 150 ml (¼ pint) level – I love chopping herbs by hand, and it can be done fairly quickly with a mezzaluna, the Italian half-moon knife with two handles, but if you want to speed things up even more, chop the mint in a food processor, pulsing in brief bursts so that you don't reduce the leaves to a soggy paste. Put the mint into a jug with the sugar, spoon on the boiling water, stir quickly, then leave to infuse and cool. Stir in the vinegar, mix well, then adjust the seasonings to suit your taste, adding a little more sugar or a little more of the vinegar to get the right balance.

Sauce Paloise

Sauce paloise is basically a béarnaise sauce made with mint instead of tarragon. And a béarnaise sauce is basically a hollandaise sauce flavoured with tarragon. And there you have it, or so I thought until recently. In fact, there is a little more to the story than that. Sauce paloise has an even more precise position in classic French cuisine (the fancy restaurant sort rather than the domestic version). It is the sauce to accompany grilled meats à la paloise, which are also served with green beans bathed in cream and little melting browned noisette potatoes. Quite a plateful! In fact, sauce paloise does go very well indeed with grilled lamb chops, or even pork chops, and it's not bad with a steak if that takes your fancy. I like it even better with a perfect, juicy grilled fish steak (salmon, swordfish, halibut or cod) but I think I would rather save the rich, creamy green beans for another meal.

Whether it is a plain hollandaise, sauce paloise or sauce béarnaise, I like to use the speedy, more foolproof processor method. It yields up a marginally less unctuous sauce than the traditional method, though the result is still something to revel in with great delight. Try to make it at the last minute, just when it is needed (apart from the initial reduction, which can be done in advance). If absolutely necessary, you can keep it warm in a bowl set over a pan of very gently simmering water, as long as the base of the bowl comes nowhere near the water itself.

Serves 6

3 tablespoons dry white wine
3 tablespoons white wine vinegar
1 heaped tablespoon finely chopped shallots
2 sprigs of mint
3 egg yolks
175 g (6 oz) butter
3–4 tablespoons chopped mint
salt and pepper

Put the white wine, wine vinegar, shallot and sprigs of mint in a saucepan and boil hard until reduced to about 2 tablespoons. Strain, pressing down on the mint to squeeze out the last drops of flavour, then leave to cool.

Put the egg yolks into a food processor with the cooled mint reduction and a little salt and pepper. Whizz briefly to mix together. Melt the butter and draw off the heat when good and hot. Turn on the processor again and slowly trickle in the hot butter. Be cautious at first, as if you were making a mayonnaise. When about one-third of the butter is in you can afford to be more dashing, speeding up the flow of molten butter. Carry on until you reach the milky white sediment at the bottom of the pan. It doesn't matter if a little of it makes its way in but discard most of it.

Quickly put the chopped mint in a sieve and shower with boiling water to release the flavours. Drain well, then stir into the sauce. Taste and adjust the seasoning, and serve while still warm.

Sauce béarnaise

Make it in the same way as sauce paloise, substituting tarragon for the mint and using tarragon vinegar if you have some to hand. Particularly good with egg dishes, fish and grilled chicken.

Vietnamese-style Parcels of Pork with Fresh Herbs

This recipe is based on a Vietnamese dish but adapted to fit the limitations of my local shops (no Vietnamese rice paper round here, nor dried flower mushrooms) and my passion for Chinese hoisin sauce. The result, though not authentic, is none the less delicious and makes a great first course for a dinner party. The wrappers for the parcels are just leaves of iceberg lettuces but inside is a fragrant mixture of fried pork and wild mushrooms, mountains of fresh mint and coriander, a spike of spring onion and fresh red chilli and the sweet darkness of hoisin. Fresh-tasting and satisfying all in one.

All the cooking can be done in advance, leaving just the preparation of the main ingredients to be tackled a few hours before serving. Then it is just a question of putting everything out on the table and letting your guests put their own parcels together.

Serves 4–6

85 g (3 oz) (more or less) shallots, thinly sliced
vegetable or sunflower oil for deep-frying
1 small bunch of mint
1 small bunch holy basil or Thai basil or sweet
    basil (optional)
1 small bunch of coriander
6 spring onions, cut into 4 cm (1½ inch) lengths and
    finely shredded
2 red chillies, deseeded and cut into very thin rings
hoisin sauce
12 leaves of crisp lettuce, such as iceberg

For the pork filling

10–15 g (¼–½ oz) dried porcini or shiitake mushrooms
3 tablespoons mirin or sweet sherry
250 g (9 oz) minced pork
2 tablespoons fish sauce (*nam pla*)
2 garlic cloves, finely chopped
1 teaspoon finely grated fresh root ginger
freshly ground black pepper
2 tablespoons sunflower or vegetable oil
4 shallots, very finely chopped

Make the pork filling in advance. Soak the dried mushrooms in the mirin or sherry, adding just enough water to cover and no more. Leave for 30–45 minutes, then pick out the mushrooms and chop very finely, discarding the stalks if you used dried shiitake. Let the soaking liquid settle, then carefully drain off, leaving any grit behind in the bowl.

Meanwhile, mix the pork with the fish sauce, half the garlic, the ginger and plenty of freshly ground black pepper and leave for about half an hour. Then heat the oil in a wok or wide frying pan over a medium heat, add the shallots and the remaining garlic and sauté for a few minutes, until the shallots have softened. Now raise the heat to high, add the pork mixture and fry briskly for 5 minutes, breaking up any lumps, until lightly browned. Add the mushrooms and fry for 1 more minute, then add their soaking liquid and let it simmer down until more or less evaporated, leaving a fragrant, moist mixture of pork and mushrooms. Taste and adjust the seasoning, adding a little more fish sauce or a pinch of sugar if it needs it. Serve cold, or reheat just before serving.

Next fry the shallots: heat about 5 mm (¼ inch) depth of oil in a frying pan over a moderate heat. Add the shallots and fry fairly quickly until golden brown and crisp. Lift out with a slotted spoon and drain on kitchen paper. They can be fried several days in advance and stored in a well-sealed container in the fridge.

Shortly before serving, pick the leaves off the mint and basil stems and place in a bowl. Cut the lower part of the stalks from the coriander, leaving only 3 cm (1¼ inch) or so of stalk and all the leaves, then pile into a bowl. Put the fried shallots into a separate bowl and the spring onions and chillies into more bowls. Hoisin sauce goes into yet another bowl, and they all go in the centre of the table. Pile the lettuce leaves high in a bowl (don't worry if a few of them are torn in half – they'll just make slightly smaller parcels). Now you are ready to roll.

To make up a parcel, take a lettuce leaf. Put a spoonful of the fried pork in the centre and over that a sprinkling of fried shallot, a few whole mint leaves, basil leaves and coriander sprigs, a little spring onion, some chilli if it takes the fancy, and a crowning drizzle of hoisin sauce. The edges of the lettuce leaf are folded over as best you can, and then the whole is eaten with great relish.

Tomato Salad with Mint and Cream Dressing

Tomato and basil is the famous duo, but long before basil made it big over here tomato and mint were getting along famously. It's a happy combination, with a particular freshness that you don't get with peppery basil. You can dress the tomatoes with a straight vinaigrette but even nicer is this rich cream dressing.

Serves 4

450 g (1 lb) ripe, luscious tomatoes
a pinch or two of sugar if needed
salt and pepper
a small handful of mint leaves, roughly torn up

For the dressing
2 tablespoons red wine vinegar
4 tablespoons double cream

Slice the tomatoes and arrange on a plate. Season with a hint of sugar (unless they truly are sweet, slightly tart, richly flavoured Mediterranean-style tomatoes), a little salt and freshly ground pepper. To make the dressing, stir the vinegar into the cream and season very lightly with salt and pepper. Drizzle over the tomatoes, then scatter with mint leaves. Serve immediately.

Opposite
**Tomato Salad
with Mint
and Cream
Dressing**

Duck Breasts with Cherries and Mint

Duck with cherries is one of the classic combinations. The tart fruitiness of warmed cherries tones down the fattiness of the duck and a touch of mint brings even more benefits, with a light waft of coolness. Ordinary dark red cherries are fine for this dish but if you can get sour Morello cherries it will be even more delectable. Serve with peas or spinach and little roast new potatoes, or maybe a creamy dauphinois of potatoes and celeriac.

Serves 4

4 duck breasts
300 ml (½ pint) good red wine, e.g. Cabernet Sauvignon
300 ml (½ pint) duck or chicken stock
1½ tablespoons redcurrant jelly
225 g (8 oz) cherries, stalks removed, stoned if you are patient
1 generous tablespoon shredded mint leaves
salt and pepper
4 sprigs of mint, to garnish

Pre-heat the oven to 200°C/400°F/Gas Mark 6.

Season the skin of the duck breasts with salt and pepper and the cut sides with pepper only. Prick the skins all over with a fork. Heat a frying pan, just big enough to take the breasts in a single layer, over a gentle heat and lay the breasts in it skin-side down. As their fat begins to run, raise the heat so that they are frying briskly in their own fat. When the skin is nicely browned underneath, transfer the breasts, skin-side up, to a rack in a roasting tin and pop them into the oven for 9 minutes to keep them pink or about 10–12 minutes if you prefer them fairly well done (not too much longer or they will be as tough as old boots). When they are cooked, take them out of the oven and let them rest for 5–10 minutes before serving.

Pour the fat from the frying pan and add the wine. Bring up to the boil, stirring and scraping in the juices and browny bits from frying the duck breasts. Let the wine boil down until reduced to a thin glaze over the base of the pan. Now add the stock and bring back to the boil. Boil hard again until reduced by half. Add the redcurrant jelly and stir in until dissolved. Add the cherries and some salt and pepper and simmer for a few more minutes to give a lovely syrupy sauce. Stir in the shredded mint.

Slice each duck breast and fan out on a plate. Spoon over the sauce and garnish with a sprig of mint. Serve.

Ibizan Mint Cheesecake with Blueberry Coulis

An unusual cooked cheesecake based on an Ibizan recipe, where they use their own moist curd cheese and fresh mint. I like to make it in a puff pastry case, but if you prefer, line a 22 cm (9 in) tin with shortcrust pastry and bake blind before adding the filling.

Though it is nice on its own, this cheesecake is even better with the blueberry and mint coulis below, which has absolutely nothing to do with Ibiza or the rest of the Balearic islands.

Serves 8

250 g (9 oz) puff pastry
3 tablespoons honey
Blueberry and Mint Coulis, to serve

For the filling
11 mint leaves
450 g (1 lb) ricotta cheese
4 eggs, lightly beaten
1 tablespoon Pernod or other anise liqueur
125 g (4 oz) caster sugar

Roll out the pastry on a lightly floured board and cut out a 25 cm (10 inch) circle. Carefully cut a 21 cm (8½ inch) circle out of the centre of the larger circle, leaving a ring of pastry which will form the 'walls' of the tart. Lift the smaller circle out, then roll it out again evenly to recreate a 25 cm (10 inch) circle. Lift this on to a dampened baking tray. Brush the edges with a little of the beaten egg from the filling and carefully lay the ring of pastry on top, easing it to match the edges all the way round. With the back of a knife blade, knock up the pastry all the way round the edge to help it to rise. Prick the base all over with a fork. Chill the pastry case for half an hour while you make the filling.

Place a baking sheet in the oven and pre-heat to 230°C/450°F/Gas Mark 9.

To make the filling, chop 6 of the mint leaves very finely. Beat the ricotta cheese to soften it, then beat in the eggs, Pernod, chopped mint and sugar. Set aside.

Line the centre of the pastry case with a circle of baking parchment or greaseproof paper, making sure that the walls are not caught under the edges (the idea is that they should rise majestically). Weight down with a single layer of baking beans, then place on the hot baking sheet in the oven and bake for 8 minutes. Take out and remove the paper and beans. Reduce the temperature of the oven to 190°C/375°F/Gas Mark 5. Return the case to the oven for 4 minutes to dry out. Allow the pastry case to cool slightly, then fill with the ricotta mixture. Bake for about 20–30 minutes, until just set. When it is nearly done, warm the honey slightly.

Remove the cheesecake from the oven, brush the honey over the pastry edge and the centre of the cooked tart to glaze, then lay the remaining mint leaves on top in a decorative fashion. Serve warm or cold, accompanied by the coulis.

Blueberry and Mint Coulis

This sauce is fabulous with the Ibizan cheesecake above but that's not its sole purpose in life. It is sensational just spooned over scoops of vanilla or fruit ice-cream or drizzled around a moist, puddingy sort of a cake.

Serves 8

250 g (9 oz) blueberries
85 g (3 oz) caster sugar
1 tablespoon lemon juice
2 sprigs of mint

Put the blueberries, caster sugar, lemon juice, 1 sprig of mint and 4 tablespoons of water into a saucepan. Bring gently up to the boil, stirring until the sugar has dissolved. Simmer gently for about 10 minutes. Taste and adjust the sweetness to please your taste; if it seems a touch on the bland side, add a dash more lemon juice. Remove the sprig of mint. Chop or shred the leaves of the remaining mint sprig, stir into the sauce and it is ready to use – warm or cold, as the fancy takes you.

parsley
Petroselinum crispum and *Petroselinum crispum* 'Neapolitanum'

Parsley and onions have much in common. Together they are probably the most widely used flavourings for savoury dishes, in this country at any rate and throughout much of continental Europe, too. We use them heedlessly, automatically and, quite rightly day in, day out. Yet for all their popularity we ignore their individual charms, rarely according them any great status in their own right. Parsley is not a herb that sets our pulse racing or our mouth watering – not like basil, say, or coriander, nor even like rosemary or thyme, which are closer to home roots. And why is parsley taken so very much for granted? Quite simply because it is a herb of magnificent versatility and peerless quality. Its special flavour has that particular ability to enhance and harmonize with practically any other savoury ingredient without ever dominating.

This is not to say that it is dull or bland. Far from it. If you break the habit inherited from generations of cooks and allow parsley to take centre stage, you will find that it has more than enough vigour of its own to carry the limelight. I urge you to try the parsley salad on p. 208 – you may be surprised at how easily parsley assumes the lead.

Parsley has not always enjoyed such culinary ubiquity. The ancient Greeks were not at all keen on bringing parsley into the kitchen, for they associated it with gloom and doom and athletic prowess – an odd partnership, admittedly, but parsley was supposed to have sprouted from the spilt blood of the messenger of doom, Archemorus, and was twined to form the victor's crown at the games held in his name. And it doesn't stop there. More recent folklore connects parsley with the Devil. Its seed is notoriously slow to germinate because, legend has it, it has to make its way down to Lucifer and back a full seven times before the shoots can push their heads above ground to find the light. Who would have thought that squeaky-clean parsley had such dark depths?

For some time curly-leaved parsley, with its dark frilly leaves, has ruled the British roost, with flat-leaved parsley lagging so far behind that it was almost unknown. Then chefs and cooks discovered 'the Mediterranean', and

with the cooking of the Med came a new passion for the smooth, paler leaves that are preferred in the sunshine lands. Well, it's all a matter of taste, and not just in the mouth. The flavour of the two may differ marginally, though when they are chopped up finely I, for one, would hesitate to insist that I could tell the difference. There are a few recipes that indisputably work better with one or the other (flat-leaved for salads, curly-leaved for deep-frying), for practical reasons, but after that it comes down to individual preference and what is to hand. Personally, I like the look of flat-leaved parsley best, certainly for garnishing and scattering roughly chopped or torn up over a finished dish to provide a lively splash of green, not to mention an extra note of flavour. This visual preference, which I believe is why most fashionable chefs choose flat-leaf over curly, is a thoroughly modern notion. Nearly all of my older cookery books state firmly that curly-leaved parsley is far more attractive. Well, I suppose many people once thought flared trousers were flattering too, and although fashion pundits try again and again to restore them to favour, most of us have realized that they only suit those with legs right up to their armpits. Enough said.

Trying to list every dish that parsley fits well would take forever and would quickly become tedious in the extreme. Every cook knows that it appears more frequently in recipes than practically any other ingredient, except onions, salt and pepper. You will surely know, too, that it is the most constant herb to appear in a bouquet garni. And nothing perks up plain rice or flat noodles that are to be served as an accompaniment to European-style stews quicker than a generous knob of butter and plenty of finely chopped parsley.

Many of you will have given up long ago on parsley sauce, having been fed dire flour-paste versions flecked with dreaded, musty dried parsley at least once or twice during childhood. Believe me, with fresh parsley and attention to detail, it doesn't have to be like that. If you want a more vigorous, zippy parsley sauce, then turn to the recipe for Coriander Salsa Verde on p. 81 and substitute parsley for the coriander, throwing in a small handful of basil leaves as well for good measure, to make a proper Italian salsa verde to serve with fish or poached chicken.

You will probably also be aware that chewing a sprig of parsley dampens the whiff of garlic that lingers on your breath after a garlicky feast. It also happens to be blessed with generous helpings of iron and vitamins A and C and, last but not least, 'if parsley is thrown into fishponds it will heal the sick fishes therein', according to the sixteenth-century herbalist Turner, who took his theory straight from Pliny. I just wish I'd known that before we worked our way through three short-lived goldfish, the expensive and emotion-laden legacy of one funfair win and two children in love with their flickering friends.

Storage and Preservation

Store parsley, like most herbs, splashed with a little water and wrapped in a plastic bag, or wrapped in damp kitchen paper, in the vegetable drawer of the fridge, where it should keep for at least four or five days. It is also one of the herbs that can take being treated like a bouquet of flowers, stalks plunged into a glass of water on the windowsill, though it will begin to wilt visibly within a few days.

Preserving parsley...why would you want to preserve parsley anyway? If you grow your own, choose a flat-leaved variety that will survive winter frosts much more cheerily than curly-leaved parsley. The furls and frills of the latter harbour tiny puddles of water that freeze and damage the leaves. Otherwise, a supply of fresh parsley of one sort or the other is more or less guaranteed in even the meanest of supermarkets right through the year, not to mention from market stalls, good fishmongers and greengrocers. If you happen to live near Greek, Turkish or Middle Eastern food shops you will probably also be able to lay your hands on generous bunches of fresh flat-leaved parsley with no difficulty. I can see no point whatsoever in freezing parsley. If you do happen to have a huge quantity on your hands, then either make up a giant batch of parsley sauce or (and this is what I'd opt for) a small vat of salsa verde, (see above). Both freeze tolerably well.

Why anyone in their right mind ever considered that drying parsley was worth the effort is beyond me. I suppose someone, somewhere thought he could con people into handing over decent money for tubs of useless dusty, musty, dead-as-a-dodo flakes of nothingness. He was right, of course, and if you have ever been taken in by him, bin the evidence and don't let him diddle you again. Dried parsley is utterly pointless.

Persillade

This is a French mixture of finely chopped parsley and garlic or shallot that is stirred in or sprinkled over at the last minute to perk up all kinds of dishes. I like it fresh and raw but some cooks frizzle it briefly in a little butter or oil to take off the raw edge, or add it raw five minutes or so before the dish has finished cooking.

Gremolata

The Italian answer to persillade, this time a mixture of very finely chopped parsley, garlic and lemon zest. A heady mixture that can lift any dish straight out of the ordinary. It is most famously sprinkled over that lovely Milanese dish of osso buco, stewed veal shank, but in fact it is one clever trick that canny cooks keep up their sleeve for any number of concoctions, since it not only works miracles in the flavour department but also looks good, too. Sprinkle gremolata over a rather dull and dutiful stew – be it chicken, beef, lamb or vegetable – and wow! Suddenly it's leaping and dancing into favour. Even more exciting, of course, if the stew was good to begin with. I love it over fish, and anything with a tomatoey sauce, or even a tomato soup. If you don't much fancy a burst of raw garlic (gremolata, like persillade, is usually added right at the end of the cooking time), pop the gremolata-ed dish back in the oven for five minutes to soften the blow.

Opposite
Griddled or Barbecued Tuna, Sauce Vierge and Gremolata
(page 204)

Griddled or Barbecued Tuna, Sauce Vierge and Gremolata

Here I've sprinkled gremolata (see p. 202) over speedily cooked tuna steaks, moistened with sauce vierge, which is actually a fancy name for warmed, scented olive oil and only worth making with good extra virgin oil (*vierge* is the French for virgin, hence the name).

Serves 4

4 portions of tuna steak, cut about 2–2.5 cm (¾–1 inch) thick, weighing around 175–200 g (6–7 oz) each
a little extra virgin olive oil
salt and pepper
lemon wedges, to serve

For the sauce
½ teaspoon coriander seeds, lightly crushed
½ teaspoon black peppercorns, lightly crushed
75 ml (2½ fl oz) extra virgin olive oil
2 teaspoons good red wine vinegar or sherry vinegar
2 tomatoes, skinned, deseeded and finely diced

For the gremolata
2 tablespoons chopped parsley
grated zest of 1 lemon
1 garlic clove, chopped

Begin by seasoning the tuna steaks with salt and pepper. Set aside. To make the sauce, put the coriander seeds and peppercorns into a small heavy-based saucepan set over a moderate heat and dry-fry until they give off a tantalizing aroma. Now reduce the heat and add the olive oil. Heat for a few seconds, then stir in the vinegar. Draw off the heat and set aside while you prepare the rest of the dish.

Mix the ingredients for the gremolata on a board and chop them together until they are very finely chopped. Put into a small bowl, cover and set aside until needed.

To barbecue the tuna steaks, make sure that the embers are white hot and pack a powerful heat. Arrange the rack of the barbecue so that it is fairly close to the heat. Brush the tuna steaks lightly with oil and cook close to the heat for about 1½–2 minutes on each side, until browned on the outside, but still pink in the centre. To griddle the steaks, put a griddle pan over a high heat and leave for about 4 minutes. Brush the tuna steaks lightly with oil and lay them on the griddle pan. Cook for 1½–2 minutes on each side.

As they cook, stir the tomato dice into the sauce vierge and warm through if you wish (but do not let it boil). Lay the tuna on plates, spoon a little of the sauce vierge around and over them, then sprinkle with the gremolata and serve with wedges of lemon.

parsley

Gammon Steaks with Parsley Sauce

When it comes to parsley sauce, you can introduce the parsley in two distinct ways. The commonest is to stir it in when the sauce is made, having bathed it first in hot water to release the flavour, so that it retains a freshness. The second, and this is the method I use here, is to cook the parsley gently into the butter right at the beginning so that it begins to melt down and cooks right into the very core of the sauce, tinging the entire thing pale green. Either way, it is a lovely sauce, given half a chance, and deserves to be made properly, with diligence and affection. It goes famously well with fish but is as much at home with slices of hot boiled ham or gammon steaks.

Serves 4

4 gammon steaks
30 g (1 oz) butter
1 tablespoon sunflower oil

For the sauce
½ bunch of flat- or curly-leaved parsley (about 30 g/1 oz)
30 g (1 oz) butter
15 g (½ oz) plain flour
300 ml (½ pint) milk
4 tablespoons double cream
a dash of lemon juice
salt and pepper

To make the sauce, cut the parsley leaves from the stalks and chop roughly. Melt the butter over a gentle heat and add the parsley. Cook very gently, stirring occasionally, until the parsley begins to disintegrate into the butter, turning dark, dark green – about 20 minutes. Now continue just as if making an ordinary white sauce: stir in the flour and keep stirring for a minute or so. Draw off the heat and gradually stir in the milk. Add a small splosh first, stir in thoroughly, then another splosh, and stir, and carry on like this until you have a thick cream. Then you can add the milk more generously, again stirring it in well until smoothly amalgamated. If you do end up with a few lumps, don't panic. Whizz the whole lot up in a food processor when it is done and no one will be any the wiser.

Bring the sauce up to the boil, then reduce the heat and simmer gently for 5 minutes, stirring occasionally to prevent catching. By now the taste of raw flour should have disappeared, but if not, cook it a little longer, possibly raising the heat a touch. Stir in the cream and simmer for a few more minutes, until the sauce is of a pleasing pouring consistency. Stir in a good dash of lemon juice and some salt and pepper. Taste and adjust the seasoning. If not serving immediately (it reheats fine, but don't keep it hanging around too long), spear a knob of butter on the tines of a fork and rub it over the surface to prevent a skin forming, then reheat when needed.

For the gammon, place the steaks in a shallow dish and cover with boiling water. Leave to stand for 10 minutes, then drain and dry – this will dampen down excessive saltiness. Using a sharp knife, cut little nicks through the fat and skin around the edges, to prevent curling up in the pan. Heat the butter with the oil in one or two frying pans, depending on how big they are. Fry the gammon steaks over a moderate heat for about 3 minutes on each side, until patched lightly with brown and cooked through. Serve with the parsley sauce.

Chicken Stew with **Parsley** and **Cornmeal** Dumplings

This is a wonderful stew, made extra special by the star anise, and by the brilliant yellow, grainy dumplings flecked lavishly with green parsley. Good star anise comes whole, like a small flower of hard wooden petals, but if, as often happens, yours has broken up in the jar, you will need about 8 petals in all.

Serves 4

2 tablespoons olive or sunflower oil
1 red onion or ordinary onion, cut into 8 wedges
3 celery sticks, sliced
1 free-range chicken, cut into 8–10 pieces
2 garlic cloves, chopped
1 glass of red wine (around 125 ml/4 fl oz)
500 g (1 lb 2 oz) tomato passata
1 bouquet garni consisting of 2 sprigs of parsley, 1 sprig of
    thyme, 1 sprig of rosemary and 1 bay leaf
1 star anise
salt and pepper

For the dumplings
85 g (3 oz) quick-cooking polenta or fine cornmeal
85 g (3 oz) plain flour, sifted
2 teaspoons baking powder
60 g (2 oz) butter, melted
3 tablespoons finely chopped parsley
2 garlic cloves, finely chopped

To make the stew, heat the oil over a high heat in a roomy, heavy-based casserole. Add the onion wedges and leave undisturbed for a couple of minutes to brown and caramelize on their first side. Turn twice more to brown the other sides of the wedges, then scoop out and set aside. Now add the celery to the pan and sauté until patched with brown (this takes longer than you might imagine, as an awful lot of water in the celery has to sizzle away before it can begin to brown). Scoop out the celery and stash with the onion. Next add the chicken to the pan and brown on both sides. Drain off excess fat, then add the garlic and return the onion and celery to the pan. Add all the remaining ingredients and stir about. Cook down hard for 5 minutes, then add enough water just to cover the chicken. Bring up to the boil, then reduce the heat and simmer gently for about 40 minutes, until the chicken is cooked. If the sauce seems overly liquid and copious, boil down hard for another 5–10 minutes or so. Don't reduce it too much, though, as the dumplings will absorb some of the liquid. Taste and adjust the seasoning.

Meanwhile, make the dumplings. Mix the cornmeal, flour, baking powder and some salt, then mix in the melted butter, parsley, garlic and just enough water (you will need only a couple of splashes) to form a soft, slightly sticky dough. Roll into hazelnut-sized balls. Drop the dumplings into the stew, then cover with a lid and leave to simmer very gently for 15 minutes, until the dumplings have puffed up and you are confident they have cooked through. Serve immediately.

Opposite
**Chicken
Stew with
Parsley and
Cornmeal
Dumplings**

Parsley, Anchovy, Red Onion and
Tomato Salad

Middle Eastern Herb Salad with
Cracked Wheat, Saffron and **Chickpeas**

I love parsley salads. You don't want massive quantities but in small helpings they are unexpectedly delicious. Serve after a big main course, or as a first course with nice bread and butter and maybe even a little wedge of goat's cheese or fine Brie on each plate as well.

Serves 4

½ red onion, very thinly sliced
about 80 g (scant 3 oz) flat-leaved parsley
150 g (5 oz) cherry tomatoes, halved
12 marinated anchovy fillets or 8 tinned anchovy fillets, cut in half lengthwise

For the dressing
juice of ½ lemon
2 pinches of sugar
5 tablespoons olive oil
salt and pepper

Put the onion in a shallow dish and cover with boiling water. Leave for 10 minutes, then drain thoroughly and pat dry. Cut the thicker parts of the stalks from the parsley leaves. (You can save them to flavour stocks or soup, or simply discard them.)

In a salad bowl, whisk the lemon juice with the sugar, salt and pepper, then gradually whisk in the olive oil. Taste and adjust the seasoning. Cross the salad servers in the bowl and pile the parsley, onion and tomatoes over them, laying the anchovies over everything. Toss at the table.

This heavily herb-strewn salad is a more substantial version of the Middle Eastern tabbouleh, fleshed out with chickpeas. The cracked wheat, or bulgar, forms a relatively minor part – it is the herbs themselves, lots and lots of them, that take pride of place. Though it tastes just fine as soon as it is made, it improves vastly if left for a good few hours or, better still, overnight.

Serves 8

60 g (2 oz) cracked wheat (bulgar or burgul) or couscous
a large pinch of saffron strands
150 ml (¼ pint) hot water
1 bunch of parsley
1 small bunch of mint
1 small bunch of coriander
200 g (7 oz) dried chickpeas, soaked overnight and cooked, or a 400 g (14 oz) tin of cooked chickpeas, well drained
finely grated zest and juice of 1 lemon
½ red chilli, deseeded and finely chopped
250 g (9 oz) tomatoes, deseeded and finely diced
1 teaspoon ground cinnamon
6 tablespoons extra virgin olive oil
2 garlic cloves, crushed
salt and pepper

Put the cracked wheat or couscous into a bowl with the saffron and pour over the water. Stir, then leave for 20–30 minutes to swell and soften. Drain off any water that has not been absorbed. Chop the leaves of the parsley, mint and coriander finely. Mix into the cracked wheat or couscous with all the remaining ingredients, then cover and leave in the fridge for a few hours or, better still, overnight, to allow the flavours to mellow and blend and the leaves to soften. Stir again, then taste and adjust the seasoning. Serve as a first course with good bread, or as an accompaniment.

Deep-fried Parsley

bergamot
Monarda didyma

Most of the tender herbs can be deep-fried to a crisp, brittle greenness, which changes the flavour sometimes subtly, sometimes more dramatically. You can try it with basil, lovage (a great favourite of mine) and sage (lovely with pork chops or veal, but fry plenty as the flavour is considerably softened). These elegant, curled, brittle leaves are lovely sprinkled over salads or as a finishing touch for soups.

The best of all the fried herbs, though, is parsley, which sizzles to a brilliant green and a marvellous flavour reminiscent of the deep-fried 'seaweed' served in Chinese restaurants. It makes a classic accompaniment to fish and is an excellent finishing touch to pan-fried sole, brill, turbot or lowly plaice. Scatter it generously over fish that has been coated with a rich parsley sauce for the ultimate, all-out, give-parsley-the-limelight-it-deserves experience. Everyone loves deep-fried parsley, so make plenty of it – it hardly takes any time.

> sprigs of curly-leaved parsley
> sunflower or vegetable oil, or a blend of sunflower and olive
>   oil, for deep-frying

If the parsley has to be washed, rinse it thoroughly and then dry it even more thoroughly – water and hot oil are not safe companions. Use an electric deep-fryer, a wok or a frying pan for the frying. If you use a frying pan, you will need at least a 1 cm (½ inch) depth of oil in it. Heat the oil over a moderate heat until it reaches a temperature of around 180°C/350°F. Slide an experimental sprig of parsley into the oil; it should sizzle furiously. As soon as it stops sizzling (within a few seconds), scoop out with a slotted spoon and drain on kitchen paper. If it is brown rather than green, then it is overcooked and will have a bitter edge. Either take the next batch out before the sizzling stops or reduce the heat slightly. Once you have got the balance right you can get on with frying the rest of the parsley. Fry it in small handfuls (not too much at a time, mind you), scooping it out as above. Drain on kitchen paper. As it cools it will crisp up. Serve within half an hour. You can store it in an airtight container in the fridge for 2 or 3 days but to restore crispness spread it out on a baking tray and pop into a warm oven for a minute or two.

Bergamot, with its stunning pom-poms of bright red flowers (or pink, purple or white, depending on variety) that rise grandly above the dark green leaves, is so very theatrical and surprising that it almost seems unfair that it should also have a delicious fragrance. A plant that has it all. It comes originally from North America, where the Oswego tribe of Native Americans used it to make an infusion. From this it derives one of its common names, Oswego tea. The first account written of it by a European was in *Joyfull Newes out of the Newe Founde Worlde*, the earliest American herbal, written by the Spanish physician Nicholas Monardes in the sixteenth century, and it is from him that it derives its botanical name. If you have a garden that is not yet graced by bergamot, rush out and buy a plant of it as soon as the opportunity arises. It belongs to the same family as mint and, like mint, prefers to grow in a shady spot, in well-drained moist soil. Having said that, our two clumps of bergamot seem happy enough in direct sunshine – sometimes plants surprise the conscientious gardener.

Both the flowers and leaves have an unmissable citrus scent, tempered with the breeziness of mint and a drop of spice. In theory it is the herbal equivalent of the aroma of the bergamot orange, which is how it derives its commonest name. Personally I find the resemblance less striking than many other writers, but then it has been a long time since I passed a true bergamot orange near my nose. Following the same reasoning, a leaf or two of bergamot dropped into a mug of hot China tea is meant to replicate the taste of Earl Grey, which is scented with the oil of the bergamot orange. The leaf does make for a most refreshing cuppa but I wouldn't mistake it for a fine sip of Earl Grey.

Besides tea, the young leaves of bergamot, which oddly are more scented than older ones, and the bright flowers are rather good added to fruit salads, just as they are or infused in a syrup, but they also make a pleasing addition to savoury sauces for chicken and white fish and to stuffings for pork and duck. They are lovely in salsas and with sweet potatoes (stir some into soured cream or yoghurt to spoon over them). The flowers make a particularly attractive addition to summer salads, either clustered in pom-pom heads or pulled apart, and can be crystallized (see p.166).

Storage and Preservation

The young leaves, which have the better flavour, are very prone to drooping once they have been picked. Even in an airtight box in the lower part of the fridge they begin to wilt after only a day or two. The flowers are a little stronger but ideally both should be used and enjoyed soon after harvesting. Unless, that is, you intend to dry them for infusions or to add to pot-pourri (the flowers keep their colour remarkably well). Pick stems of young leaves or older stalks complete with flowers, tie in bunches and hang in an airy, dry place to dry.

A reprise of a classic gratin dauphinois, replacing ordinary potatoes with sweet ones and the nutmeg with the spicy freshness of bergamot. It is very rich and very moreish. Try it with roast game, lamb or beef.

You will need white-fleshed sweet potatoes, not the orange-fleshed ones, which are too cloying for a dish like this. Since retailers resolutely refuse to distinguish between the two when they mark up the labels (they look identical), you may have to scratch away a small area of skin to reveal the colour of the flesh. If the shop assistant dares to complain, politely suggest that they label them more clearly.

Serves 6–8

1 kg (2 lb 4 oz) white-fleshed sweet potatoes
30 g (1 oz) butter
2 garlic cloves, finely chopped
2–3 tablespoons chopped bergamot leaves and/or flowers
400 ml (14 fl oz) double cream
200 ml (7 fl oz) full cream milk
salt and pepper

Pre-heat the oven to 150°C/300°F/Gas Mark 2.

Peel the potatoes and slice them as thinly as a one-pound coin. Rub the butter generously all over an ovenproof dish. Layer the sweet potatoes in it neatly, seasoning well between the layers with salt and pepper, the chopped garlic and bergamot. Mix the cream and milk together and pour them over the gratin. The liquid should just reach to the upper level of the potatoes.

Bake for about 1½ hours, until the sweet potatoes are very tender, have absorbed most of the cream and milk and are nicely browned on top. Serve hot, warm or cold, with roast game, lamb or beef.

a mixed bunch

There are many recipes scattered throughout this book that can be read as blueprints for all sorts of variations, replacing the stipulated herb with any number of alternatives and thus producing something that tastes quite different. These recipes, often classic ways of using and preserving herbs, are good to know, especially if you grow your own herbs and need ways of making the most of them when they are in their prime.

Herb Vinegars and Oils

Recipes for these are scattered throughout the book (see pp. 33, 66 and 89, for instance). There are two basic methods for extracting the flavour of herbs into a long-keeping liquid. The first is simply to stuff a bottle full of your chosen herb (or a mixed bouquet of herbs, adding perhaps some chillies or cloves of garlic for extra entertainment), then fill it with either high-quality olive oil or vinegar (in most cases white wine or cider vinegar is the one to go for). With vinegar as your flavour-bearer, you should then leave the tightly stoppered bottle on a warm, sunny windowsill for at least three or four days and up to a week or more, to encourage the transfer of scent. Oil suffers more at the touch of sunshine, so a couple of days on the sill is quite adequate, and it may be a more sensible idea to opt for a slower exchange in the safety of a dark, cool cupboard. Alternatively, you can warm the herbs with the oil or vinegar over a gentle heat, then leave to infuse, covered, in a warm place for an hour or two. Either way, strain the perfumed oil or vinegar, then pour into clean bottles and add a fresh branch of the herb for visual prettiness. Use flavoured vinegars and oils not only in salad dressings but also for marinades and as flavourings to stir into soups, stews and sauces at the end of their cooking period.

Herb Sugars

Again two methods: you can either tuck a few sprigs of herbs or heads of scented flowers down into a jar of sugar, then leave for a week or more, tightly sealed, until the sugar has sucked up all the scent. Or, for a quicker result that will need to be used up swiftly, pound sugar cubes with herb leaves in a mortar, until the cubes have broken down to ordinary sugar and the leaves have disintegrated to colour and flavour the sugar (see pp. 18 and 142).

Herb Syrups

Throw herbs into sugar syrups, and simmer for 5–10 minutes to extract their flavour. Use the syrups to dress ice-creams or fruit salads, or as the basis for making sorbets and ice-creams. Sprinkle over moist cakes for an unusual pudding. For a wonderfully refreshing summer drink, dilute with fizzy mineral water and sharpen with a little lemon or lime juice (see pp. 136 and 137).

Ice-creams and Sorbets

See pp. 16, 65, 144 and 176 for methods.

Jellies and Jams

A simple apple jelly is rather a plain, ordinary affair, but add handfuls of herbs to the juice as you extract it and it comes vividly to life (see p.145). Mint, thyme and sage jellies make superb accompaniment to meats. Jellies flavoured with sweeter herbs are lovely spread on toast. Herbs can also add a delicious fragrance to jams – see the recipe on p. 149. Make a small bundle that can easily be removed and let it simmer with the fruit.

Herb Butters

These are one of the easiest ways to jazz up plainly cooked meat or fish (particularly when it has been grilled, barbecued or quickly fried), and they are also a quick, easy way to dress steamed or boiled vegetables of all sorts. Process lightly salted butter with a good handful of herbs, roughly torn up, and perhaps some garlic or lemon zest and a dash or two of lemon juice. If you don't have a food processor, chop the herbs and other flavourings finely and mash them into softened butter. Once mixed, pat the butter into a sausage shape, and roll up neatly in clingfilm or foil. Chill until needed, then slice as required. It will keep in the fridge for up to a week. Herb butters also freeze well (see p. 97).

herb gardens and growers/suppliers

Most good plant nurseries sell herb plants for gardens, while most supermarkets sell good ranges of cut herbs. But both are limited. The following places specialize in herbs, both plants and cut, so you may well be able to fill gaps and find rarities. Check that they are open to the public, and when, before turning up on the doorstep. Many of the specialists will send out plants by post.

Abotts Vegetable and Herb Garden
Thingwall
Birkenhead
Wirral
Tel: 0151 608 4566
Sells organic cut herbs

Arne Herbs
Limeburn Nurseries
Limeburn Hill
Chew Magna
Bristol BS40 8QW
Tel: 01275 333399
Wide selection of herbs, including many hard-to-find varieties

Cheshire Herbs
Fourfields
Forest Road
Nr Tarporley
Cheshire CW6 9ES
Tel: 01829 760578
Specializes in basils of all sorts

Elly Hill Herbs
Elly Hill House
Barmpton
Darlington
Co Durham DL1 3JF
Tel: 01325 464682
Open most days – ring first to check

Grange Cottage Herbs
4 Grange Cottages
Nailstone
Nuneaton
Coventry CV13 0QN
Tel: 01530 262072
Mail order. Organic herbs

Hambledon Herbs
Court Farm
Milverton
Somerset TA4 1NF
Tel: 01823 401205
Mail-order organic dried herbs

Hexham Herbs
Chesters Walled Garden
Chollerford
Hexham
Northumberland NE46 4BQ
Tel: 01434 681483
Beautiful walled gardens. Northern national collections of thyme and oreganum

Hill Farm Herbs
Park Walk
Brigstock
Northants NN14 8HH
Tel: 01536 373694

Hillside Herb Farm
Kimbolton
Leominster
Herefordshire HR6 0JA
Tel: 01568 613023
Organic herb plants and cut herbs

Hollington Nurseries
The Walled Garden
Woolton Hill
Newbury
Berkshire RG20 9XT
Tel: 01635 253908
Very pretty walled garden

Iden Croft Herbs
Frittenden Road
Staplehurst
Kent TN12 0DH
Tel: 01580 891432
National southern collections of mint and oreganum. Impressive wall of bay. A most beautiful garden

Jekka's Herb Farm
Rose Cottage
Shellards Lane
Alveston
Bristol BS12 2SY
Tel: 01454 418878
Owner: Jekka McVicar
One of the leading suppliers of mail-order organic herbs. Sold at selected branches of Crabtree & Evelyn

Marshford Organic Nursery
Churchill Way
Northam
Nr Bideford
North Devon EX39 1NS
Tel: 01237 477160
Organic herbs

National Herb Centre
Banbury Road
Warmington
Nr Banbury
Oxfordshire OX17 1DF
Tel: 01295 690999
Research, hillside gardens and bistro

Netherfield Herbs
Nether Street
Rougham
Nr Bury St Edmonds
Suffolk IP30 9LW
Tel: 01359 270452
Owner: Leslie Bremness

Poyntzfield Herb Nursery
Black Isle
By Dingwell
Ross & Cromarty
Scotland 1V7 8LX
Tel: 01381 610352
Specializes in herbs that are native to Scotland, and hardy herbs. Good alliums

Ryton Organic Gardens
Ryton-on-Dunsmore
Coventry CV8 3LG
Tel: 01203 303517
Organic gardening centre, with several herb gardens, restaurant. Sells herbs from Jekka's Herb Farm

Wye Valley Plants
The Nurtons
Tintern
Gwent NP6 7NX
Tel: 01291 689253
Pot-grown organic herbs

Yorkshire Garden World
Main Road
West Haddlesey
Nr Selby
North Yorkshire YO8 8QA
Tel: 01757 228279

SEED SUPPLIERS

Suffolk Herbs
Monks Farm
Pantlings Lane
Kelvedon
Essex CO5 9PG
Tel: 01376 572456
Mail order

ROSE SUPPLIERS

David Austin Roses Ltd
Bowling Green Lane
Albrighton
Wolverhampton WV7 3HB
Tel: 01902 376300

SPECIALIST SHOPS

Wing Yip
Chinese and Asian Foods

Branches at:

375 Nechells Park Road
Birmingham B7 5NT
Tel: 0121 327 6618

395 Edgware Road
London NW2 6LN
Tel: 0181 450 0422

Oldham Road
Manchester M4 5HU
Tel: 0161 832 3215

550 Purley Way
Croydon
Surrey CR0 4RF
Tel: 0181 688 4880

bibliography

Yaohan Oriental Shopping Centre
399 Edgware Road
London NW9 OJJ
Tel: 0181 200 0009
Japanese

Cool Chile Company
PO Box 5702
London W11 2GS
Tel: 0973 311714
Mail-order chillies and
dried herbs from Mexico
and South America

Tawana Oriental Supermarket
18–20 Chepstow Road
London W2
Tel: 0171 221 6316
Treasure palace of Thai,
and South-east Asian foods,
good for herbs including
pandanus, laksa leaves
and holy basil

HERB BODIES

The Herb Society
Banbury Road
Warmington
Nr Banbury
Oxfordshire OX17 1DF
Tel: 01295 692000
Contact: Nicky Westwood
Advice for herb-growing
gardeners

The British Herb Trade Association
164 Shaftsbury Avenue
London WC2H 8HL
Tel: 0171 331 7415

The Garlic Information Centre
Saberdene House
Church Road
Catsfield
Battle
East Sussex TN33 9DP
Tel: 01424 892440
Garlic and garlic products
by post

Stephanie Alexander, *The Cook's Companion*, Penguin Books (Australia), 1996
Liberty Hyde Bailey and Ethel Zoe Bailey, *Hortus Third*, Collier Macmillan Publishing, 1976
Monisha Bharadwaj, *The Indian Pantry*, Kyle Cathie, 1996
Vatcharin Bhumichitr, *Vatch's Thai Cookbook*, Pavilion Books, 1994
Lesley Bremness, *Herbs*, Eyewitness Handbooks, Dorling Kindersley, 1994
Lynda Brown, *The Shopper's Guide to Organic Food*, Fourth Estate, 1998
Giacomo Castelvetro (translated by Gillian Riley), *The Fruit, Herbs and Vegetables of Italy*, Viking (Penguin Group), 1989
Colin Clair, *Of Herbs and Spices*, Abelard-Schuman, 1961
Claire Clifton, *Edible Flowers*, The Bodley Head, 1983
Bruce Cost, *Foods from the Far East*, Century, 1990
Elizabeth Cullum, *A Cottage Herbal*, David & Charles, 1975
Nicholas Culpeper, *Culpeper's Complete Herbal*, W. Foulsham & Co Ltd
Elizabeth David, *Spices, Salt and Aromatics in the English Kitchen*, Penguin, 1970
Sarah Dyer, *A Pocket Book on Herbs*, Octopus, 1982
A. Gardiner, *Fifty Useful Herbs*, Selecta Books Ltd, 1996
Jane Grigson, *English Food*, Penguin Books, 1993
Geoffrey Grigson, *Gardenage or The Plants of Ninhursaga*, Routledge & Kegan Paul Ltd, 1952
Geoffrey Grigson, *The Englishman's Flora*, Helicon, 1996

Sophie Grigson, *Sophie Grigson's Meat Course*, Network Books, 1995
Sophie Grigson and William Black, *Fish*, Hodder Headline, 1997
Good Housekeeping Complete Book of Preserving, Ebury Press, 1991
Rosemary Hemphill, *Fragrance and Flavour*, Angus & Robertson, 1959
Herbs, Dorling Kindersley Pocket Encyclopaedia, 1990
Jason Hill, *Wild Foods of Britain*, A & C Black, 1939
Geraldine Holt, *Geraldine Holt's Complete Book of Herbs*, Conran Octopus, 1991
Madhur Jaffrey, *Madhur Jaffrey's Flavours of India*, BBC Books, 1995
Caroline Liddell and Robin Weir, *Ices*, Grub Street, 1995
Kasma Loho-Unchit, *It Rains Fishes*, Pomegranate Artbooks (California), 1994
Richard Mabey, *Flora Britannica*, Sinclair-Stevenson, 1996
Christine Mackie, *Trade Winds*, Absolute Press, 1987
Maya Kaimal MacMillan, *Family Recipes from South India*, Abbeville Press, 1996
Jill Norman, *The Classic Herb Cookbook*, Dorling Kindersley, 1997
Elizabeth Lambert Ortiz, *The Encyclopaedia of Herbs, Spices & Flavourings*, Dorling Kindersley, 1992
Sri Owen, *Indonesian Food and Cookery*, Prospect Books, 1986
Roger Philips, *Wild Food*, Pan Books, 1983
Roger Philips and Nicky Foy, *Herbs*, Pan Books, 1992
Julie Sahni, *Classic Indian Cookery*, Grub Street, 1997

Margaret Shaida, *The Legendary Cuisine of Persia*, Lieuse Publications, 1992
Charmaine Solomon, *The Complete Asian Cookbook*, Grub Street, 1993
Charmaine Solomon, *Charmaine Solomon's Encyclopedia of Asian Food*, William Heinemann (Australia), 1996
Constance Spry and Rosemary Hume, *The Constance Spry Cookery Book*, J. M. Dent & Sons Ltd, 1956
Tom Stobart, *The Cook's Encyclopaedia*, Papermac (Macmillan), 1982
Sue Style, *Fruits of the Forest*, Pavilion Books, 1995
Priya Wickramasinghe, *Leith's Indian & Sri Lankan Cookery*, Bloomsbury, 1997
Rev. John M. Wilson (ed.), *The Rural Encyclopedia*, A. Fullarton & Co, 1849
Marcus Woodward, *Leaves from Gerard's Herball*, Gerald Howe Ltd, 1931
Maria Dolores Torres Yzáball and Shelton Wiseman, *The Mexican Gourmet*, Thunder Bay Press (California), 1995

index

Contents

Introduction

Many bizarre and gruesome creatures roam the world of mythology. Their origins may be lost in the mists of history but they have preyed on people's superstitions and imaginations since ancient times. For thousands of years, people have lived in fear of the undead, evil beings that come back to life after death to terrorise the land of the living. The most famous are vampires, who are said to leave their burial places at night to feast on the blood of their victims. But vampires are only one form of the undead. Spine-chilling tales of zombies and mummies are also told around the world. Are you ready to go over to the dark side? It will send shivers down your spine...

④

Vampires

Flapping its black bat wings, a hideous bony creature prepares to feast on the blood of its unfortunate victim. This is the vampire of your nightmares!

A vampire is the soul of a dead person. It comes to life at night, leaving its grave or coffin to hunt for humans and animals. It needs to drink their blood in order to carry on its evil existence. It hunts in human form, or as a bat or other animal, and must return to its resting place before daybreak. The vampire has been known since ancient times, but most vampire folklore comes from 18th-century eastern Europe.

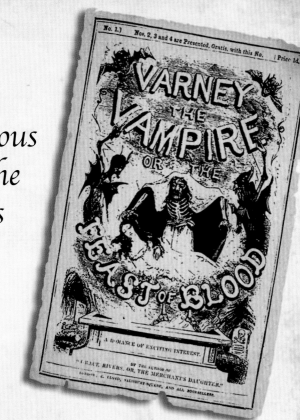

Varney the Vampire was a story serialised between 1845 and 1847 in pamphlets called penny dreadfuls. It was based on myths from eastern Europe.

Vampires are associated with places of the dead, such as graveyards (the spookier the better!), although vampires are said not to touch sacred ground.

Becoming a Vampire

So what makes a person turn into a blood-sucking vampire? The most common belief is that a person becomes a vampire because his or her soul is trapped on Earth after death.

A vampire's soul is said to be trapped for various reasons. Vampires are believed to have committed some wicked deed in life, to have died in a particularly violent way, or committed suicide. Anybody who has been bitten by a vampire is also thought to become a vampire, as are

The Vampire, painted in 1893 by Edvard Munch, appears to show a female vampire sucking the blood of a man.

witches, wizards and werewolves, and anyone who has eaten a sheep killed by a wolf. People who do not receive a proper burial can also become vampires. Assorted objects, including holy bread, cloves of garlic, lemon and poppy seeds placed on a coffin are said to prevent a person becoming a vampire. Nailing bodies into their coffins, and even putting a nail through the head, or decapitating it and placing the head between the legs before burial, can prevent the dead person from becoming a vampire.

The Premature Burial, by Antoine Wiertz. Some myths say that a person buried before he or she was really dead became a vampire. When the coffins of suspected vampires were dug up, scratch marks from fingernails were found on the insides.

Vampires are creatures of the night, and are said to be harmed or killed if struck by sunlight.

Vampire Features

The vampire image we are familiar with comes from the movie industry. Mythical vampires had similar features to these vampires, but lacked the luxurious velvet cape and sophisticated hairstyle.

A promotional photograph for the 1922 movie Nosferatu, based on the story of Dracula.

The typical vampire has a mesmerising face, with bright, clear eyes, eyebrows that meet in the middle and an open mouth revealing fangs (long, sharp, canine teeth). Sometimes blood drips from the corner of its mouth and from its nose. Vampires also have long fingernails and hair, apparently because their nails and hair keep growing after death.

Goths dress in black clothes and wear black make-up, inspired by Gothic literature, such as Dracula.

One way of recognising a vampire is to view it in a mirror – if there is no reflection, it is a vampire.

Vampires are said to shapeshift into bats, perhaps because of the real-life vampire bat. This creature bites animals with its sharp teeth and laps up blood that leaks from the wound.

The popular 'movie' vampire is very bony with deathly pale skin. In contrast, vampires of folklore were said to be red-faced and bloated, with red or purple skin, caused by taking a meal of fresh blood. Vampires were also shapeshifters, taking the form of bats, dogs and cats at will. They could even become clouds of mist and smoke.

A woman notices that her visitor has no shadow in the light of her fire – a sure sign that he is a vampire.

11

Vampire Lifestyle

The vampire is believed to be a creature of the night, when it emerges to carry out its terrible work. By day, it rests in its grave or coffin.

Vampires are dead, but still have to find a regular supply of blood to drink to maintain their 'life force'.

A vampire awakes as the sun sets, leaves its grave and ventures out in search of victims. It can shapeshift into a bat or dog to travel fast and unseen. Finding an unfortunate victim, it bites into the jugular vein in its neck, sucking out the blood. Its work done, the vampire returns to its grave – before sunrise, for a shaft of sunlight will destroy it.

A coffin in the crypt of a church in Poland – the typical resting place of a vampire!

Orava Castle in Slovakia, where the vampire movie Nosferatu was filmed. Many vampires of legend lived in castles like this.

A vampire descends the stairs of its gloomy home to greet a visitor – perhaps to make him a victim.

Warding off a Vampire

How can you defend yourself against a vampire? According to folklore, displaying or wearing various items, such as garlic, will keep it away. Killing a vampire is a little trickier.

Vampire-repelling items can be placed in and around a house to stop vampires getting in, or worn for protection when outside or asleep. Most popular are garlic, holy water, a crucifix, and objects made of iron or silver. Mustard seeds are also said to work, as is a branch from a wild rose bush or hawthorn tree. Vampires are unable to cross church grounds or running water, and can only enter a building when invited.

A vampire hunter's kit available in central Europe in the 1840s. Typical items in these kits included tubes of garlic powder and holy water, wooden stakes, a crucifix and prayer book, silver bullets and a revolver.

People have been known to sleep with cloves of garlic in their mouths to ward off vampires.

Although it is already dead, there are various grisly ways of killing a vampire. The most famous method is to drive a wooden stake (usually made of ash or aspen) through the vampire's heart. The corpses of suspected vampires have been dug up from their graves and a stake driven through them. Alternative treatments include beheading, cutting out the heart and then burning, shooting or drowning. The vampire's body will then turn instantly to dust.

A vampire hunter preparing to drive a stake into the heart of a vampire disturbed in its lair.

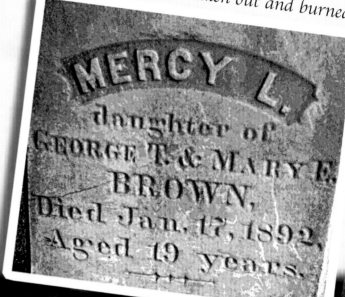

The gravestone of Mercy Brown, a resident of Exeter, Rhode Island, USA, whose body was dug up because she was suspected of being a vampire. Her heart was taken out and burned.

Vampires in Europe

The majority of vampire legends come from eastern Europe, particularly from Hungary, Romania, Greece and Albania. The myths were reinforced by some infamous cases of people who killed for blood.

In the 16th, 17th and 18th centuries there were many outbreaks of vampirism in eastern Europe. Things reached a peak in the 1730s, when there was mass hysteria, with many suspect corpses dug up.

The heart of the vampire myth is Transylvania, an area of mountains and dark forests in Romania. This is the 1550 coat of arms.

A strigoi rises from its grave. It is a vampire-like creature from Romanian mythology. In Romania, vampires were also called strigoi.

Perhaps Europe's most famous real-life 'vampire' was Elizabeth Bathory, a Hungarian countess, who lived in around 1600. She is thought to have tortured and murdered over 300 local women for their blood. She drank and bathed in the blood because she believed it would keep her young.

Another famous case concerns Serbian man Peter Plogojowitz. After his death, he was said to have killed his son and nine people in his village. His corpse was dug up and a stake put through its heart.

A portrait of Countess Elizabeth Bathory. She was tried for mass murder in 1611, and imprisoned for life, escaping death only because she was a royal.

The remains of Cachtice castle, Slovakia, the home of Elizabeth Bathory. She was imprisoned in the dungeon where she murdered her victims.

Count Dracula!

The most famous vampire of all, Count Dracula comes from the novel, Dracula, by Irish author, Bram Stoker. The creature described in the novel has become the popular image of a vampire.

In the book, a young English solicitor, Jonathan Harker, visits Count Dracula's castle in Transylvania to discuss Dracula's purchase of an estate in England. Harker discovers that Dracula rests in his coffin at night.

Bram Stoker set part of the Dracula story in Whitby, England. The churchyard by Whitby Abbey is the scene of one of Dracula's attacks.

Bram Stoker based his terrifying vampire on a cruel Romanian prince called Vlad Dracula, who was born around 1430.

A portrait of Vlad Dracula (which means Vlad Junior). He ruled part of Romania from 1456 to 1462.

Vlad Dracula executed thousands of people on spikes, and became known as Vlad the Impaler.

Dracula travels to England, taking his coffin with him, and killing all the crew on the ship he sails in. Harker joins forces with vampire expert Professor van Helsing, to try to kill Dracula. Eventually, they catch him in Transylvania and put a stake through his heart.

Dracula feeding on the blood of a victim. In the book, Dracula makes victims of both Jonathan Harker's fiancée, Lucy, and her friend.

Vampires Around the World

Although the classic vampire figure comes from European folklore, myths about vampires and vampire-like creatures also come from the ancient peoples and cultures of the Americas, Africa and Asia.

The chupacabra (meaning 'goatsucker') is a mythical vampire of Central America. It is said to suck animals dry of their blood, leaving two small holes in their skin. Sightings of this terrible creature have been reported in modern times – firstly in Puerto Rico, where several dead animals were discovered.

The Japanese nukekubi is a human whose head detaches at night and flies through the air searching for victims to bite.

A chupacabra attacking a sheep.
The creature is said to look like a reptile, with grey-green skin, spines along its back and large fangs.

In stories from Hindu mythology, the goddess Kali sucks the blood of her victims. She is known as the Dark Mother and is sometimes depicted as a violent figure.

The loogaroo is a vampire-like creature found on the island of Mauritius in the Indian Ocean and other islands in the Caribbean. It is said to be a woman who has a pact with the Devil to supply him with blood each night. The soucouyant of Trinidad is one of many similar creatures from the Caribbean.

A statue of Sekhmet, Egyptian goddess of war and destruction, who was created to kill men and drink their blood.

The Undead

In the middle of the night, the dead emerge from their graves to take revenge on the living. Vampires are joined by zombies, mummies and other undead creatures.

A bronze relief from Madrid shows the Dance of Death, in which an undead corpse leads the living to their graves.

For thousands of years humans from every part of the world have feared the dead coming back to life. The 'undead' as they are called, are reanimated corpses. They are created from people that are dead, but still act as though they are alive. Unlike ghosts, the undead are physical creatures that can be touched and can also harm the living …

The undead are a popular subject for horror fiction. The 'man who could not die' features in this 1950s comic.

Zombies

A human figure, stiff legged, with staring eyes and arms outstretched, blunders towards you. It is a zombie, or, at least, the popular idea of a zombie.

Voodoo is still followed in some places. Reverend Zombie's Voodoo Shop is in the French quarter of New Orleans, USA.

A zombie is the corpse of a dead person that is 'reanimated' – it is able to move even though it is dead. It is mindless, moving about as if under remote control. The idea of the zombie comes from Voodoo, a religion from the country of Haiti in the Caribbean, which has its roots in West Africa. In Voodoo, a zombie is a dead person revived by a person called a bokor, or sorcerer, to act as a slave.

Marie Laveau is famous for practising voodoo in New Orleans, USA. She died on 16 June 1881, but it is claimed she was seen a few days later.

The zombie is a favourite subject of popular entertainment, appearing in horror films, books and computer games. The popular image of the zombie is different to the original Voodoo idea. Hollywood has added the stumbling walk, the open wounds, the shredded clothing, the hunger for human flesh, and the idea that zombie-ism can be passed on by biting.

Zombies take centre stage in many popular movies today. The first walking dead people appeared in the famous 1968 film, Night of the Living Dead.

Going into a zombie-like trance has been linked to a neurotoxin (a poison that affects the nervous system) found in puffer fish.

25

Mummies

Wrapped in ragged bandages, a hideous creature staggers from its ancient Egyptian tomb. This is a mummy, returned to life to take revenge on the grave robbers who have disturbed its resting place. This living mummy is a modern invention – there are no ancient myths or legends about mummies coming to life.

Mummies became famous after the discovery in 1922 of the tomb of Tutankhamen by British archaeologist Howard Carter.

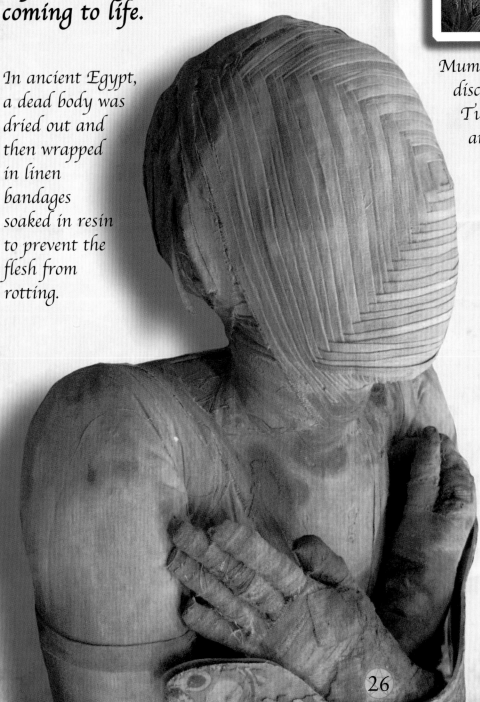

In ancient Egypt, a dead body was dried out and then wrapped in linen bandages soaked in resin to prevent the flesh from rotting.

A mummy is a human (or other animal's) body that has been preserved after death. Mummification was a common practice thousands of years ago in ancient Egypt, and is also found in a few other civilisations around the world, including the Incas. The ancient Egyptians believed that mummification allowed the spirit to live on after death. Mummies were entombed with objects that might be needed in the afterlife, such as food and drink, and sometimes even servants.

In the 1932 movie The Mummy, Boris Karloff plays Imhotep, an Egyptian prince. He comes back to life thousands of years after his death when an expedition of scientists discovers his tomb.

The mummies of ancient Egypt have come to life in many horror films to cause mayhem with their superhuman strength. Some Egyptian tombs contained curses that would affect grave robbers, and the mummy's curse is a common film theme.

The popular image of a mummy that comes to life.

More of the Undead

As well as zombies and mummies, there are many more examples of terrifying undead creatures from around the world. Read on to discover the grisly details of just a few of these spine-chilling beings.

Inuit folklore features the akkiyyini, a skeleton that drums by hitting its arm bone on its shoulder blade.

A vetala is a vampire-like creature from Hindu mythology, created when a spirit is caught between life and death and takes over the corpse of a dead person. In China, a Jiang Shi (which means 'stiff corpse') is a vampire-like zombie that sucks the life force from its victims. The creature appears half decomposed, with mould on its skin. It is blind, with pale skin and furry green hair.

In Norse mythology a draugr, seen here aboard a boat, was an undead creature that lived in the graves of dead warriors.

The Danse Macabre (or Dance of Death) shows that death comes to all people, who are led by the undead to their graves.

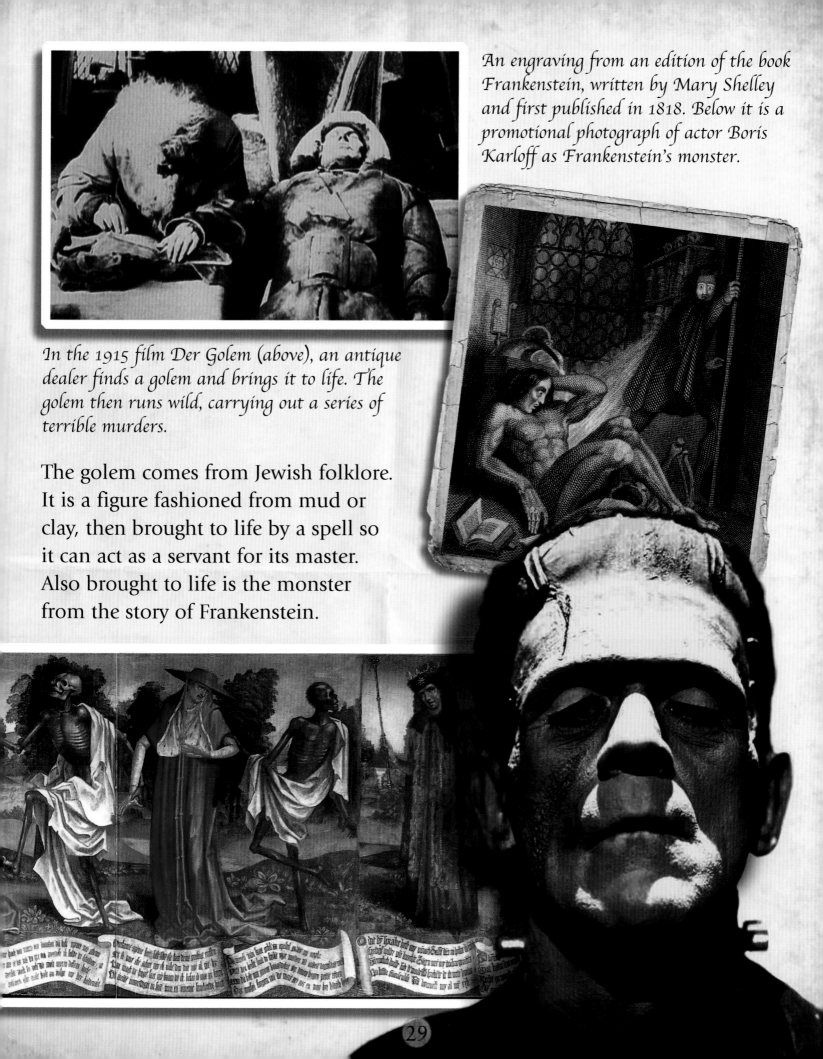

An engraving from an edition of the book *Frankenstein*, written by Mary Shelley and first published in 1818. Below it is a promotional photograph of actor Boris Karloff as Frankenstein's monster.

In the 1915 film *Der Golem* (above), an antique dealer finds a golem and brings it to life. The golem then runs wild, carrying out a series of terrible murders.

The golem comes from Jewish folklore. It is a figure fashioned from mud or clay, then brought to life by a spell so it can act as a servant for its master. Also brought to life is the monster from the story of Frankenstein.

Glossary

Crucifix A cross with a figure of Jesus Christ on it.

Curse Words or a spell used to bring harm to someone.

Decomposed Rotted away.

Executed Put to death.

Folklore Traditional stories and legends of a people or culture that sum up their beliefs and often describe events that happened in their past.

Hindu To do with the culture, the religion and language of many of the people of India.

Infamous Having a bad reputation; notorious.

Jugular vein A large vein in the neck.

Legends Traditional stories, often based on supposedly historical events.

Mass hysteria When a lot of people go into a frenzied emotional state.

Mesmerising Hypnotising or spell-binding to look at.

Mythology Traditional stories, not based in historical fact, but using supernatural characters to explain human behaviour and natural events.

Pact An agreement.

Promotional Material used to promote or advertise a film or book.

Reanimated Brought back to life, even though something is dead.

Reinforced Made stronger.

Shapeshift The power to change form from human to animal, animal to animal, or animal to human.

Stake A large stick of wood.

Trance A dream-like state, as if a person is asleep.

Vampirism The state of being a vampire.

Voodoo A religion practised in Haiti in the Caribbean.

Further Reading

Ganeri, Anita. *An Illustrated Guide to Mythical Creatures.*
Brighton: Book House, 2009.

Jenkins, Martin. *Vampires* (Informania). London: Walker
Books, 2000.

McCall, Gerrie. *Monsters and Villains of the Movies and
Literature.* London: Scholastic, 2008.

Oxlade, Chris. *Can Science Solve the Mystery of Vampires and
Werewolves?* Oxford: Heinemann Library, 2008.

Stoker, Bram and Calcutt, David.
Dracula (Oxford Playscripts).
Oxford: Oxford University Press, 2003.

*Are vampires based
on real-life bats?*